Connecting Teaching
and Learning

Connecting Teaching and Learning

History, Evolution, and Case Studies of Teacher Work Sample Methodology

Edited by
Hilda Rosselli, Mark Girod,
and Meredith Brodsky

ROWMAN & LITTLEFIELD PUBLISHERS, INC.
Lanham • Boulder • New York • Toronto • Plymouth, UK

Published by Rowman & Littlefield Publishers, Inc.
A wholly owned subsidiary of The Rowman & Littlefield Publishing Group, Inc.
4501 Forbes Boulevard, Suite 200, Lanham, Maryland 20706
http://www.rowmanlittlefield.com

Estover Road, Plymouth PL6 7PY, United Kingdom

British Library Cataloguing in Publication Information Available

Library of Congress Cataloging-in-Publication Data

Connecting teaching and learning : history, evolution, and case studies of teacher work sample methodology / edited by Hilda Rosselli, Mark Girod, and Meredith Brodsky.
p. cm.
Includes bibliographical references and index.
ISBN 978-1-4422-0458-4 (cloth : alk. paper) — ISBN 978-1-4422-0460-7 (electronic)
1. Student teachers—Training of—United States. 2. Student teachers—Rating of—United States. I. Rosselli, Hilda C. II. Brodsky, Meredith Morgan, 1947- III. Girod, Mark.
LB2157.U5C57 2010
370.71'1—dc22   2010034110

In memory of
H. Del Schalock

February 4, 1929–December 3, 2006

Contents

List of Figures

Foreword

David Imig and Scott Imig

Del Schalock headlined the Education Trust's National Conference in Washington, D.C., in November 2000. At the time, few lobbying groups in Washington were more influential than the Education Trust. Kati Haycock, president of the trust, had immediate access to the architects of what would become the No Child Left Behind (NCLB) Act of 2001. She was influential in pressing the so-called highly qualified teacher agenda. Haycock's national conference was the place where lobbyists and policy makers, school principals, and politicians gathered. Ms. Haycock could have invited almost anyone and they would have gladly accepted the invitation. This event heralded Del's ascendency to the top of the education profession and sent a clear message that his forty-year record of focusing on student learning was to become a signature piece for the Bush administration's education agenda. Del was celebrated for his insistence that "prospective teachers had to think systematically" about connecting their teaching to state learning standards and "to act systematically" to ensure that students progress toward those standards.

Throughout his career, Del Schalock insisted that student learning was the touchstone on which teachers and teacher educators should focus their efforts. Those who wrote NCLB were echoing Schalock's theme when they crafted language that would couple teacher accountability provisions with the learning of students. He insisted that teachers matter greatly in the achievement of students and that teacher education had much to contribute—but only if there was careful attention to student learning. Del Schalock and his colleagues at the Oregon College of Education (OCE, later the Western Oregon State College and now Western Oregon University) came to dominate the conversation when scholars and academics, policy makers, and practitioners gathered to consider the connections between teaching and learning. But it wasn't always that way.

Del was a scholar's scholar, in that his was a long and slow ascendency to national prominence built on the essential work of a collegiate professor. He and his OCE colleagues thoughtfully crafted a research agenda and embarked upon it in the early 1970s. They carefully gathered evidence on teacher performance and student learning, analyzed reams of data, and wrote scores of thoughtful pieces that appeared in dozens of refereed journals, handbooks, and monographs. In personal conversations and during professional presentations he insisted that university-situated teacher education would not survive unless it was more carefully coupled with student learning. Teacher Work Sample Methodology (TWSM), he asserted, was the means to that end.

Schalock's experiences at OCE in helping refashion teacher education led him to carefully consider the importance of teachers focusing on what students should learn over the course of a lesson, unit, or syllabus. Immersed in the effort to create performance-based teacher education, it was natural that he would focus on measures to be used to assess the attainments of teacher candidates. Oregon's subject-specific learning goals (later the core content standards) provided the framework for his work—with Schalock insisting that teacher education was about ways to help teacher candidates learn to appropriately "steer" a group of students to meet well-defined content standards over the course of a lesson or unit. Finding appropriate measures to assess student learning was essential. Schalock was doing this work at a time when psychometricians were seeking ways to assess student learning, ETS was creating the new PRAXIS series, academics and practitioners were developing national standards, and scholars were debating the merits of authentic testing, fairness issues, and matters of validity and reliability.

Shortly after Del Schalock died, Malcolm Gladwell's annals of education appeared in the December 15, 2008, issue of the *New Yorker*. Entitled "Most Likely To Succeed: How Do We Hire When We Can't Tell Who Will Succeed?" Gladwell described the challenge of predicting who will be successful in teaching and who will not. He compared efforts to find good teachers to those of finding good quarterbacks for the NFL and carefully documented the efforts of a football scout to identify the skills and abilities of potentially successful players. In the commentary, Gladwell embraced a literature dismissive of teacher education and argued that it is only in the classroom where one can predict teacher success. I thought of Del in reading that piece and wanted to say, "But we have a tool to help in making those determinations in teaching—and that tool is TWSM."

During a long and illustrious career, Del kept raising key questions about the effectiveness of teachers and their impact on student learning. Long before others caught up, he was insisting that the "input models" used to measure teacher-candidate proficiency lacked predictive validity. Schalock noted that teacher candidates who scored high on early administrations of the National Teacher's Examination weren't necessarily the ones who could successfully move a third-grade class to meet the learning standards for mathematics in Oregon. Never timid but always respectful, he challenged "luminaries" in the field with his persistent questions about their use of measures other than those associated with the attainment of students.

Del influenced the redesign of the teacher licensing system in Oregon and helped to enhance that system with a reliance on TWSM. He early recognized that the power of his ideas alone was insufficient to move big systems like teacher education and sought alliances and partnerships to advance the use of his methodology. Over the course of his fifty-year career in higher education, he served on national panels and association committees that advanced an agenda of high-quality teacher education. He was early associated with the Texas R&D Center for Teacher Education and culminated his career with guidance to the Renaissance Group on TWSM.

Long before "systems theory" prevailed in school reform, Schalock was raising concerns about the lack of alignment between teacher preparation and state learning standards, student assessments, and teacher's professional development. He always was seeking ways to shift the dialogue to focus on the effect of the teacher in the classroom. He argued that student learning was the only measure that mattered, and he was continuously searching for meaningful ways of connecting student learning to teacher work. He was an essential part of the remaking of teacher education in Oregon and helped to enable that state to lead the country in aligning Oregon's P–12 educational goals (later "standards") with teacher preparation in the state. Del demonstrated a deft hand at broadcasting his message of using the "external" to achieve "internal" change. He was a champion of the concept of "teacher warranties" (the idea that teacher preparation programs needed to "guarantee the effectiveness" of their graduates) and brought the concept of teacher productivity to the forefront. He wrote for both scholarly peer-reviewed journals and the specialized press. He used platforms at the Education Commission of the States summer meetings and the annual meetings of the National Association of State Directors of Teacher Certification to advance the cause for TWSM, and he used professional association meetings and other policy forums to raise questions of importance regarding the connection between teacher preparation, teacher practice, and student learning. He repeatedly challenged leaders in teacher education to think critically about the connections between good teaching and student learning. Others would capture the agenda and find new ways to measure student performance, but Schalock's was a persistent voice that ultimately prevailed.

What was remarkable then as it remains today was that Schalock and his Monmouth colleagues helped to move the conversation from norm-referenced tests (NTE, PRAXIS, NES) to new forms of assessment that focused on student attainment on teacher-developed assessments. He helped to more explicitly and carefully define professionalism to focus on teacher practices. He saw teacher education as equipping teacher candidates to carefully plan lessons and units of study, to be able to organize and deliver instruction, to be able to individualize or personalize teaching, and to be able to use content-driven assessments to measure student attainments. He saw teachers as capable of changing instruction when students failed to master standards. He championed the use of professional learning goals (and the alignment of local, state, and national learning standards). Schalock insisted that teacher education programs would foster unceasing attention to the learning of P–12 students and saw student teachers using pre- and post-testing to collect and analyze data for students in relation to a unit the student teacher designed and taught. This text highlights these contributions and gathers together an array of writing on ways of measuring teacher effectiveness. It includes writers who have benefitted from Schalock's contributions and who are extending his efforts to more carefully consider effective teaching.

Though thirty years apart, our first encounters with Del were in gatherings of teacher education leaders of the day from across the nation. Diminutive in stature and quiet in demeanor, Del was far too easy to overlook in an assembly of the academic "elite"—until he opened his mouth and quietly took control of the conversation. His scholarly demeanor and quiet intelligence, his grasp of the possible, and his insistence on the integrity of the process were just as evident in an early-1970s AACTE meeting on performance-based teacher education as they were in a 2004 meeting of the Teachers for a New Era research directors.

As we contemplate the reauthorization of the Elementary and Secondary Education Act of 1965, teacher accountability is the most important policy issue of the day. For nearly half a century, Schalock insisted that teacher education had to focus unceasingly on student learning; reframing teacher education to accomplish that end was his lifelong professional passion. He warned of the dire consequences of deviating from that goal. The field of teacher education is now better equipped to confront such challenges given the enormous talent, effort, and influence of Del Schalock.

Introduction

Hilda Rosselli

PART I: CONTEXT AND EVOLUTION

Although the term *Teacher Work Samples* (TWS) is familiar to many teacher educators, few realize that the work undergirding this popular form of pre-service teacher-performance assessment actually dates back forty years ago to a visionary researcher, Del Schalock. Part I is coauthored posthumously by Del and his son, Mark Schalock, and provides a rich contextual history of how Teacher Work Samples were first envisioned, tested, researched, and implemented. It is obvious that Del Schalock predicted with amazing clarity and clairvoyance the need for change in teacher preparation to fully align with standards-based education models. He worked quietly and unassumingly to further an agenda whose time is just now fully blossoming.

PART II: PRACTICE

Case studies are featured in this part focusing on key developments surrounding the implementation of Teacher Work Samples by individual institutions and consortiums of teacher preparation programs. In chapter 2, Buckner and Smith illustrate how the convergence of several national agendas that focused on student achievement, accountability, and teacher education reform set the stage for change in teacher preparation programs. By trying to determine how programs knew their teacher candidates could teach, faculty in teacher preparation programs began to shift their focus beyond building more knowledgeable and skillful teachers, often interpreted as more courses and more content, to developing more "effective" teachers and using evidence of student learning as the most pure measure of that effectiveness. Ironically, this subtle shift in language is still being debated in Washington, D.C. policy discussions as the ineffectiveness of federal requirements around highly qualified teachers (HQT) begins to morph toward "highly effective teachers."

The case study highlighting Coastal Carolina University (CCU) traces a typical implementation of practices focused on Teacher Work Samples that parallels the journey of many other teacher preparation programs nationwide. And Buckner and Smith are honest in their evaluation of how many institutions have missed the mark by viewing the Teacher Work Sample as only an assessment tool rather than a methodology, which is a reminder of how even a good idea can devolve over time. Their description of ways in which CCU's program curriculum changed as a result of TWS implementation is one mirror that reflects what happens when institutions embrace TWS as a "methodology to help candidates learn to think about how their teaching influences the learning of their students."

Pankratz's chapter on the development of the Renaissance Teacher Work Sample Model adds a valuable extension to the historical context provided by Schalock and Schalock in section I. The case study illustrates how a solid idea can be enhanced through collaborative efforts and how critical external funds can lead to the development of credible performance assessments and data management systems that extend beyond an individual institution. Funded by the Title II Teacher Quality Enhancement grants, sadly no longer available, the Renaissance Project played a key role in positioning Teacher Work Samples on the radar screens of institutions and funding agencies nationwide.

With eleven universities (*and* the involvement of eleven university presidents), the Renaissance Project raised the bar around powerful discussions regarding the potential of TWS to address teacher preparation's accountability for P–12 student learning. Similar to Beghetto and Samek (chapter 7), Pankratz demonstrates the power of shared and focused objectives that support cross-institutional faculty research efforts and program improvement. Lacking today's more common manifestations of performance assessments and data systems called for by NCATE Standard 2 (see Elliot, chapter 13), the partners were treading in new territory. Within a year, the partners quickly ramped up and began implementing a Renaissance Teacher Work Sample, which though fraught by the challenges of any new assessment protocol, survived and ultimately prospered. Pankratz is right in noting the role of synergy that kept the project moving forward. The opportunity for site coordinators from different institutions to interact and share successes with each other bolstered the project. Lessons were learned and shared at a level and rate that probably is seldom possible within one institution.

Biannual meetings with dedicated face-to-face time also appear to have contributed to the success of the project and the case serves as a testimony to the valuable need for precious resources of time and funding.

With the power of data from 4,700 work samples representing 117,000 P–12 students, TWS became part of the state credentialing rules in Kentucky, Kansas, and Oklahoma. No doubt the eleven participating institutions also made notable headway in meeting other emerging demands of regional accrediting agencies around student learning outcomes and use of assessment data for program improvement as a result of the project. The funding supported the development and dissemination of valuable resources that continue to be available online (http://edtech.wku.edu/rtwsc/index.htm). Numerous research studies, presentations, and publications stemmed from this project, and as the third-party evaluation showed, TWS were found to be of professional interest, not too expensive to implement, and able to improve service delivery. And, as noted in Pankratz's final reflection, Teacher Work Samples "exceeded everyone's expectations."

The case study provided by Robinson in chapter 4 offers a glimpse into the application of TWS to the preparation of school administrators. Bringing her extensive experiences from the use of Teacher Work Samples in preservice teacher preparation to bear on her involvement in University of Northern Iowa's principal preparation program, Robinson effectively emphasizes the recursive nature of student learning and how it should be driving all of our actions.

Just as student learning has become the key focus of teacher preparation, it has also emerged as the key focus of administrator preparation highlighted in the chart provided by Robinson. As instructional leaders, principals must be able to promote a school culture that promotes learning. Whether coaching newly hired teachers, analyzing student data, or evaluating teachers, the insights gained by the principals in this case study point to the value of using TWS or other performance assessment tools focused on student learning in the preparation of school leaders operating in a standards-based environment.

Wetherill and Calhoun's case study in chapter 5 addresses the often missing partner: K–12 schools and their role in determining the impact of teaching on student learning using Teacher Work Samples. Although the rich history of partnerships between the university and local school districts no doubt enabled this work to accelerate at the rate it did, we must remember, as these authors point out, "schools and schools of education are equally obligated to focus on student learning." The enhancements that the Watson School of Education was able to add to the use of Teacher Work Samples are valuable contributions to this volume and to any teacher preparation program seeking to collaboratively focus on P–12 student learning. Collective inquiry structured through regular site meetings and professional development opportunities enhances the merging of roles and territories involving teacher preparation, faculty members, and school practitioners. The use of a coaching cycle and structured scaffolding further maximizes the instructional decision-making processes embedded in the Teacher Work Sample process, or as these authors aptly label it, the cognitive engagement of interns, partnership teachers, and supervisors in the higher-order instructional dispositions. With NCATE's move to more clinically based preparation of teachers, this work is timely indeed.

In chapter 6, Girod and Girod offer an innovative view of yet another use of Teacher Work Samples that has not yet garnered the full attention warranted. As teacher preparation programs continue to explore commonalities with the medical or legal professions, it is timely to consider the benefits of simulations in teacher preparation. These authors have afforded preservice candidates a safe context within which they can practice the complex myriad of instructional decisions made almost subconsciously by teachers every day in America's classrooms.

The results of their study of Cook School District simulation users showed positive results from self-reported data and, even more importantly, from performance-based data. Blind ratings of Teacher Work Samples, reflective writings, and classroom observations produced significant differences favoring those who had used the simulation. The power of controlled classroom contexts and classroom demographics bode particularly well for programs that may lack access to more diverse types of classroom settings for live field experiences. With the advent of avatars, can this form of simulated instructional preparation be far behind in revolutionizing our field?

Beghetto and Samek's case study involving the Oregon Collaborative Research Initiative (OCRI) may pale in comparison to the Renaissance Project, but the story outlined in chapter 7 provides a rich example of how strategic research partnerships can use "problems of practice" as a useful focus for research and increase the capacity for teacher education research. With additional examples now provided by states like California, Massachusetts, New York, and Ohio, there now exist powerful models that show how public and private institutions, ranging from large Research I universities to small four-year colleges, can work together to resolve some of the many challenges facing our profession.

The use of a state chapter of the American Association of Colleges for Teacher Education (AACTE) is notable in this case as is the minimal funding that was used to implement OCRI. The ability to tell an adequate story about teacher preparation and its benefits for P–12 student learning in ways that policy makers and the public understand most likely requires more than most individual institutions have to offer. Truly collaborative partnerships, including those with K–12 schools, must continue to become the marker for how we do business.

PART III: RESEARCH

The nation's current interest in scaling up research-based practices is a timely reminder of the importance of creating solid and credible evidence to support practices in teacher preparation. For at least a decade, researchers have lamented the lack of empirical evidence in teacher preparation (Cochran-Smith & Fries, 2001; Wilson, Floden, & Ferrini-Mundy, 2001). The case studies selected respond to this call and honor early efforts to establish a rigorous and defensible research base around TWS drawing upon data from nearly one thousand teachers and ten thousand K–12 students further described in section I by Schalock and Schalock.

In chapter 8, Norman, Evans, and Pankratz and their colleagues at Western Kentucky University describe their continuing diligent efforts to design and conduct relevant studies examining the efficacy of Teacher Work Samples as a valid and reliable tool for teacher preparation. Stemming from collaborative research supported through the Renaissance Partnership (chapter 3), Norman, Evans, and Pankratz have examined the consistency and reliability of TWS scoring by faculty and provide helpful discussion of their process and results. Their ability to discern differences within and across programs, and across TWS components, validates the methodology as empirically defensible.

Further studies outlined by Norman and his colleagues to analyze the actual impact on student learning hold much promise for other teacher preparation institutions, as do their reminders to practitioners who score the TWSs, both in higher education and K–12 schools, of the importance of debate and consensus on established standards for components within the TWS.

In chapter 9, Denner, Newsome, and Newsome's case similarly tackles a thorny and critical issue involving the generalizability of TWS scores across raters and of candidates' TWS scores across different occasions. Their study is a valuable next piece in the research literature supporting authentic performance assessments as credible tools for addressing elements of NCATE Standard 1 and also for establishing the necessary thresholds for fair, accurate, and consistent assessment protocols called for in NCATE Standard 2.

Both of these cases illustrate how policies and accreditation changes (see chapter 13) have created powerful contexts within which individual institutions are able to amass significant amounts of data on one common assessment, allowing for more rigorous statistical analyses frequently absent within the parochial nature of teacher preparation.

In the case developed by Fredman, McKean, and Dahlem (chapter 10), the authors illustrate Oklahoma's early solution to the national call for long-term data on teacher candidates and impact on student learning. They assess the impact of teacher preparation on student learning with first- and second-year teachers who were examined using Teacher Work Samples, portfolios, and Pathwise Induction Program observations based on Daniel-son's Framework for Teaching. Unlike French, Skolits, and Malo (chapter 14), Fredman and her colleagues set out to specifically answer a research question often addressed inadequately through new teacher follow-up and employer satisfaction surveys: the impact of teacher performance on student learning. Conducted prior to current studies underway in Tennessee, Louisiana, and Florida linking teacher identifier and preparation programs to student performance on state standardized tests, this study attempted to determine if observations conducted during the induction phases of a new teacher's career combined with a modified Teacher Work Sample and other elements within a portfolio could provide a valid and reliable measure of the effectiveness of teacher preparation.

Notable for the continuing study of TWS is their finding of distinct constructs measured by the Teacher Work Sample and Pathwise observation scale, indicating that different aspects of teaching were assessed by the two instruments, with student gains containing moderate loadings from both instruments. Although initial findings indicated that TWS had greater predictive value of student achievement over the Pathwise observation data, these findings were reversed in a subsequent replication study, still leaving unanswered questions that warrant further replication. Similar to French and colleagues, Fredman, McKean, and Dahlem's work substantiates the use of TWS with an observation tool as a means of helping teachers improve practice. However, without further analyses linking candidates back to their respective teacher preparation programs, it may be premature to use these findings to establish the usefulness of this approach at the in-service level of improving teacher preparation programs.

In chapter 11, Buchanan and Johnson describe a research study conducted around the need for content-specific Teacher Work Samples to analyze candidates' ability to demonstrate discipline-specific competence. They review other similar work in the areas of science, mathematics, and special education that support a growing practice in institutions to enhance TWS scoring rubrics to better address content-specific pedagogy and SPA standards.

Their case provides a step-by-step accounting of the use of an existing generic scoring rubric to study the competence of early childhood candidates at their institution. Findings from their study, corroborated by candidate survey results, were used to refine TWS guidelines, candidate expectations, and ultimately course content and delivery. One is left to wonder if the survey results of graduates alone would have stimulated changes in course content to include more focus on collaboration with families and communities and early childhood environments.

Henning and Kohler further uncover the power of establishing a line of research using Teacher Work Samples for the purpose of program improvement in chapter 12. They argue for the added value of programmatic research approaches that result in the "sustained examination of a research agenda that unfolds over time." Their case study highlights the benefits accrued when faculty establish agreement around one common tool of analysis which, in the case of the University of Northern Iowa, provided a seven-year course of research.

Starting with descriptions of pilot studies, followed by implementation studies, impact studies, and specific analysis studies, the authors lay out a plausible path that other institutions adopting TWS might anticipate for long-term research agendas. What remains less clear in this case study is how these research results actually impacted programmatic improvements and, ultimately, P–12 student learning, topics that are more adequately addressed in Henning, Kohler, and Robinson's book entitled *Improving Teacher Quality: Using the Teacher Work Sample to Make Evidence-Based Decisions*.

PART IV: POLICY

Legendary graphic designer and filmmaker Saul Bass once quipped, "Have you ever thought that radical ideas threaten institutions, then become institutions, and in turn reject radical ideas which threaten institutions?" In section IV, we examine how Teacher Work Samples have become established and in turn have influenced institutional, state, and national policy, perhaps even becoming threatened by new radical ideas.

In chapter 13, Emerson Elliott provides a historical context for NCATE's decisions and processes of moving toward performance- and outcome-based accreditation processes over the past twenty years in ways that shifted the focus toward P–12 student learning. Elliot's unique contribution in this case comes from his decades of involvement with NCATE in various capacities and his ability to identify pivotal issues, individuals, and agencies (NBPTS, INTASC, CCSSO, and the SPAs) to influence decisions made by the nation's largest accrediting agency of teacher preparation programs. He offers insights as to how the language of "impact on student learning" crept into NCATE's lexicon and standards. (We should have all guessed that the focus on students emanated from a discussion among members of the *elementary* standards drafting committee!)

Elliott also credits a 1988 article by Del Schalock, the researcher, and David Myton, the policy maker, along with Oregon's early changes in teacher preparation at the state level as fundamental in influencing early iterations of NCATE's revised standards. While Schalock and Myton's collaboration in Oregon resulted in Teacher Work Sample Methodology becoming a key assessment of candidates' ability to have a positive influence on student learning, Elliott takes us back to NCATE's broader philosophical intentions, absent a specific assessment tool or preferred approach. He acknowledges how NCATE's focus on student learning, which he dubs a "power" feature, led the way to increased emphasis on assessment literacy for candidates, an agenda that some view as still in its infancy stage.

Although not prominent in Elliott's discussion of key contextual factors, Del Schalock previously attributed much of his own focus on student learning as a national response to the emerging standards-based education movement and the need to prepare professionals to work in standards-based environments. As educators more clearly defined and reached common agreements on what students should know and should be able to do at various points in their development, the world of teaching moved from isolated, behind-closed-doors work to a more public focus with increased emphasis on accountability. The standards-based movement made it apparent that the work of teaching and learning was more demanding than was expected in norm-referenced models of education as illustrated in chapter 1 by Schalock and Schalock.

Elliott's case study holds value when you consider that the change made by NCATE directly affects approximately two-thirds of all new teacher graduates nationally (NCATE, 2006). In addition, a majority of states have adopted or adapted NCATE's standards for all institutions in their state, so even nonaccredited institutions are being judged by similar standards to those used at accredited institutions, as noted by Rosselli (2008) in NCATE's publication entitled *It's All About Student Learning: Assessing Teacher Candidates' Ability to Impact P–12 Students*.

No doubt policy will continue to be influenced by a changing cast of players, research studies, and contextual factors, but it's very possible that Elliott would argue that attention to student learning will never go away. The most recent evidence of this is found in AACTE's recent call for a National Performance Assessment that includes attention to impact on student learning and NCATE's new accreditation option focused on university's collaborative transformative changes around P–12 student learning.

In chapter 14, authors French, Skolits, and Malo recount a process by which the state of Louisiana adopted the use of a streamlined Teacher Work Sample as part of a portfolio process used to recommend newly employed teachers for certification or continuation in a state assistance and assessment program. In the case of Louisiana, the addition of Teacher Work Samples within the Louisiana Teacher Assistance and Assessment Program (LaTAAP) grew out of a need to replace a structured interview process with an efficient technology-based assessment that could be evaluated by two reviewers. LaTAAP acknowledged the necessary separate nature of mentoring and evaluation while still operating both processes from a common set of state standards defining effective teaching. French and his colleagues show how the "crosswalk" of TWS components align with the state's competencies for effective teaching, a process mirrored in other states at the preservice level to align performance assessments used in teacher preparation with state-adopted professional teaching standards.

Unlike many states where TWS was integral in the preparation of teachers, Louisiana's use of TWS preceded its acceptance within teacher preparation programs. With all teacher preparation programs now required to become NCATE-accredited, attention to student learning within teacher preparation programs is certainly implied, and many programs within Louisiana have since adopted TWS. From a system perspective, the lack of a continuum spanning preservice and in-service stages of teacher development can contribute to silos and unnecessary disconnects as educators progress through the various stages of their professional careers. More and more policy makers are calling for alignment across all levels of a teacher's professional development (White, Makkonen, & Stewart, 2010). French and his colleagues outline the potential for alignment around Teacher Work Samples used at both levels. However, they note that time and geographic logistics precluded the continuation of required involvement of higher-education faculty as assessors in the LaTAAP process, and ultimately many unspoken benefits of shared conversations were lost across providers of preservice and in-service education.

French, Skolits, and Malo's case provides state policy–based support for Teacher Work Samples as valid and reliable evaluation tools used in high-stakes decisions, given that all measures of fairness, reliability, and validity are addressed. The TWS components of Louisiana's LaTAAP portfolios could provide a rich source for analysis of new teachers' thinking, decision making, and professional development embedded in authentic classroom contexts. However, Louisiana also adopted Teacher and Student Advancement (TAP), a nationally recognized accountability system for teachers tied to student performance now implemented in forty-one Louisiana schools that, according to Lowell Milken, founder of the Milken Foundation, improves student learning by providing teachers with powerful opportunities for career advancement, professional growth, fair accountability, and competitive compensation (Milken, 2010). Unlike the original premise of LaTAAP that combined observations with TWS classroom-based evidence of student learning, the third component of TAP, Instructionally Focused Accountability, minimizes the rich contextual sum of the integrated parts.

In TAP, each teacher has six classroom observations/evaluations a year conducted by trained and certified evaluators using the TAP Teaching Skills, Knowledge and Responsibility Standards, and each teacher is also evaluated based on how much learning growth the students in his or her individual classroom have achieved during the school year. More than likely, the richness of the contextual variables embedded within the instructional decision

making by teachers using the LaTAAP portfolio is lost in the latter evaluation, which singles out student performance on a state standardized instrument separate from teaching and learning self-contained within the classroom setting. Similarly, the addition of a Value Added Teacher Preparation
Program Assessment Model piloted in 2004–2005 now publically reports
the effectiveness of teacher preparation programs in preparing new teachers
based solely on students' demonstrated academic growth on standardized
tests. With the implementation of linkages between classroom teachers' impact on P–12 student performance in states like Louisiana and Tennessee,
the volume of quantitative data available for public review has accelerated
the call for policy to link these data back to teacher preparation programs.
And, to date, the policy discussions have largely ignored the possible use of
student performance data resulting from preservice Teacher Work Samples,
although the latter is more legitimate and appropriate as evidence of the
impact of a teacher preparation program's ability to prepare teachers who
can influence student learning. However, the work unfolding in California
promises to create a new chapter in preservice performance assessments as
discussed in chapter 15 by Ray Pecheone and Ruth Chung Wei.

A long-time colleague of Del Schalock, Pecheone recognizes the parallels between the Performance Assessment for California Teachers (PACT)
and Teacher Work Samples, and he underscores the "power of assessment
to drive reform in teacher education and to improve teacher quality."
Pecheone's earlier work with the Interstate New Teacher Assessment and
Support Consortium (INTASC), Connecticut's Beginning Educator Support
and Training Program, and the National Board for Professional Teaching
Standards (NBPTS) were all valuable precursors for what may be considered the most ambitious state educator assessment system to date. His case
illustrates how large-scale reform can start from plans of well-intentioned
legislators and state commissioners to "overhaul" teacher credentialing,
and California's reform of teacher preparation certainly provides a fascinating read for those intrigued with the interaction between public opinion
and public policy.

The development of a Teacher Performance Assessment Consortium
focused on testing and refining a multifaceted assessment system that features candidate performance reflective of core instructional approaches in
specific content areas is a much-needed next step as noted by Buchanan
(chapter 11). Similarly, the Planning, Instruction, Assessment, Reflection
and Academic Language (PIAR-L) model parallels many of the elements of
TWS but adds a valuable focus on academic language.

As noted by Pankratz (chapter 3) and Beghetto and Samek (chapter 7),
Pecheone and his colleagues emphasize the valuable engagement between
program learning, faculty learning, and candidate learning that is already
resulting from PACT's initial implementation. The case study also high-

lights the ability of higher-education institutions that are willing to collaborate and achieve sample sizes large enough and research designs empirically strong enough to garner the support of state legislators. Similar efforts have occurred in very few states to date, and no doubt the results in California will be carefully monitored. Clearly, a subsequent case study is currently evolving as the American Association of Colleges for Teacher Education, the Council of Chief State School Officers (CCSSO), and Stanford University move forward in partnership to develop a national Teacher Performance Assessment (TPA) based on PACT. With leadership from Linda Darling Hammond, collaboration with the CCSSO, funding from the Ford Foundation, and participation from twenty states, PACT may well provide the needed national attention from Congress that was never available to push TWS into the mainstream of public awareness.

PART V: REFLECTIONS

This is the work that Del Schalock never finished, his magnum opus and a call to his colleagues. As a fitting last chapter for the volume, chapter 16 lays out in detail his plan for developing the needed empirical framework for linking teacher preparation to student learning. Although he had attracted the attention of interested colleagues before he died, the work never was officially started.

It is expected that the reauthorization of the Elementary and Secondary Education Act will require a more quantifiable linkage between individual student performance, the teacher of record, and the preparation program of record. The development of unique teacher identifiers has already occurred in several states. However, the causal relationships between what happens in a teacher preparation program to prepare candidates with the essential skills of an effective teacher-to-student performance are far from being well established in the research, and without this essential framework, one wonders how relevant the available data will be.

REFERENCES

Cochran-Smith, M., & Fries, K. (2001). Studying teacher education: Foreground and background. In M. Cochran-Smith & K. Zeichner (Eds.), *Report of the AERA panel on research and teacher education*. Washington, DC: American Educational Research Association.

Milken, L. (2010). *A message from chairman and founder, Lowell Milken*. Retrieved from www.tapsystem.org/about/about.taf?page =message_lm.

Rosselli, H. (2009). Assessments that connect teaching and learning in teacher preparation: Origins, challenges, and future directions. In A. Wise, Pamela Ehrenberg,

& Jane Leibbrand (Eds.), *It's all about student learning: Assessing teachers candidates' ability to impact P–12 students*. Washington, DC: NCATE.

National Council for Accreditation of Teacher Education. (2006). *NCATE's mission*. Retrieved from www.ncate.org/documents/NCATEMission.pdf.

White, M. E., Makkonen, R., & Stewart, K. B. (2010). *Updated multistate review of professional teaching standards* (REL Technical Brief, REL 2010, no. 014). Washington, DC: U.S. Department of Education, Institute of Education Sciences, National Center for Education Evaluation and Regional Assistance, Regional Educational Laboratory West. Retrieved from http://ies.ed.gov/ncee/edlabs.

Wilson, S., Floden, R., & Ferrini-Mundy, J. (2001). *Teacher preparation research: Current knowledge, gaps, and recommendation*. Washington, DC: Center for the Study of Teaching and Policy.

I

CONTEXT AND EVOLUTION

1

Teacher Work Sample Methodology at Western Oregon University

Del Schalock and Mark Schalock

This chapter was originally to be written by my father, Del Schalock.[1] He was able to complete the first part of the chapter before his untimely death in December 2006. I was asked, and ultimately agreed, to complete the work he started. I have used, nearly verbatim, his writing for the first twelve pages or so, and as a result I consider myself simply a coauthor.

Many people at Western Oregon University (WOU) contributed greatly to the development of Teacher Work Sample Methodology (TWSM) over the four-plus decades of work in this area. In the end, though, this chapter is dedicated to the forty years of work by my father based on the power of one idea—keeping student learning front and center in the discussion of teacher preparation, licensure, and ultimately teacher effectiveness.

INTRODUCTION

This chapter provides a brief summary of the forty-year history of work at WOU surrounding Teacher Work Sample Methodology. This history is unique in many ways, with its genesis in a research and development agenda, a long-standing and mutually beneficial relationship between a "soft-money" organization (the Teaching Research Institute, TRI) and a teacher preparation program, a university president willing to provide financial backing to a fledgling effort to connect teaching and learning, and one individual who relentlessly pursued an agenda to connect teacher work to K–12 student learning.

This chapter will trace the precursors of TWSM at WOU, the research and policy initiatives that resulted in Oregon adopting TWSM as part of an "outcomes-based" approach to teacher preparation in 1986, early implementation and research efforts around TWSM, and finally the intensive development and refinement efforts of the last half of the 1990s that set the foundation for TWSM being adopted around the country and further refined to where it is today.

THE EMERGENCE OF AN IDEA

Teacher Work Sampling had humble beginnings and a long period of gestation. Shortly after a Center for the Study of Teaching was established at the Oregon College of Education in 1960 (now called the Teaching Research Institute at Western Oregon University), Del Schalock was asked to join its faculty and establish a program of research around teaching and teacher effectiveness.

The 1960s

After pursuing this line of inquiry through several projects, Del Schalock became involved in the creation of the Northwest Regional Education Research Laboratory in Portland—the first round of "the labs" established by the U.S. Department of Education (USDE). Faculty from TRI were asked by the laboratory to take the lead in preparing a three-state proposal (Washington, Oregon, Idaho) for one of the eight Elementary Teacher Education Models projects subsequently funded by the USDE. The proposal was funded, and WOU/TRI was asked to take the lead in developing and testing what came to be called the ComField (Competency-Based and Field Centered) model. It was from this model-building work in the late 1960s and early 1970s that the language of competency-based teacher education emerged. The concepts of "evidence-based" teacher education, "quality assurance" in teacher preparation and licensing, and "teacher education programs as contexts for research" also had their genesis in this model-building work, but they were too far ahead of their time and too sparsely developed within the context of the models to be widely discussed or pursued.

The work within this model-building context led Del Schalock and others at WOU/TRI to realize early on (1970) that attending only to what teachers knew or were able to do, which was the focus of all eight models at the time, was inordinately limiting from the perspective of assuring the quality of teachers as facilitators of learning. Connecting teaching, teacher preparation, and K–12 learning was not the focus of conversation at that point in our history, but as project staff pursued model-building and testing work at WOU, those connections assumed increasing prominence. Del's first writing on these connections found its way into conference proceedings: "The Focus of Performance-based Certification: Knowledge, Teaching Behavior, or the Products That Derive from a Teacher's Behavior" (proceedings of the Conference on Performance-Based Certification, May 1970, Miami Beach, Florida).

The 1970s

After four years of further exploring the concept and its implications within the Elementary Teacher Education Program at OCE a follow-up paper titled "The Impact of Competency Definition on Teacher Preparation Institutions" was finally published (H. Schalock, 1974). This clearly was the line of thinking that led to the evolution of Teacher Work Sample Methodology at WOU in the late 1970s and early 1980s.

A great deal happened between these early "breakthrough in thinking" years and developing a methodology that would reasonably and defensibly connect a teacher's work to the learning of his or her students. The elementary-teacher education program at WOU, which was designed around the ComField Model, received the national American Association of Colleges for Teacher Education (AACTE) Outstanding Teacher Preparation Program award in 1976. At approximately the same time the AACTE award was received, faculty who had pushed the model's emphasis on knowledge and skill mastery as the focus of teacher licensure to near perfection were asking, "So what?" By pursuing this focus, they had no information about student-teacher effectiveness as facilitators of learning in those they teach. The key questions that faculty asked included, what are we supposed to prepare them to do, and what are they employed to do, to carry their moral and ethical obligations as teachers? How can we obtain such information within the time and resources available to teacher candidates and faculty that is reasonable in cost, manageable to use, and defensible in both licensure-related decisions *and* as a dependent variable in teacher education–related research?

This sense of "so what?" led to the decision within the teacher preparation program to begin a program of research and development, in conjunction with the Teaching Research Institute, to create a methodology that would meet these demands. As a consequence of this decision, and the work that followed from it, the methodology of Teacher Work Sampling emerged in primitive form by the early 1980s.

The rationale for including evidence of a prospective teacher's ability to foster learning gains in P–12 students as a condition of licensure, which is a primary aim of TWSM, was first articulated in a 1979 publication on teacher selection (H. Schalock, 1979). In attempting to bring order to the widely varying literature around this issue at the time, faculty took the stance of teacher selection being essentially a matter of *predicting the effectiveness of a teacher's job performance*, with job performance defined primarily in terms of helping students progress in their learning. Using the concept of the fidelity of predictors to this definition of effectiveness, available research was organized around seven broad categories of "predictors" that had been investigated:

1. Work samples, for example, the teaching of lessons or a unit of study, with attention given to student learning
2. The ability to engage students in learning activities
3. The ability to perform the functions required of teachers
4. Skills related to teaching
5. Knowledge related to teaching
6. Experience with children and youth
7. Intelligence and academic ability

The hypothesis guiding this frame of reference was that the higher the fidelity of a measure, the better it would be as a predictor of teacher effectiveness measured by P–12 student learning gains.

Not surprisingly, there simply was not enough research available by the late 1970s on the relationship between such variables and defensible measures of a teacher's effectiveness as a facilitator of learning to fairly test the hypothesis underlying the review. Some evidence indicated that the first three categories were in fact better predictors than the next four, but predictive relationships within any category were consistently small or inconsistent. The overall conclusion drawn from the research available at the time was that "research on teacher effectiveness had little to contribute to the decision about who should enter the teaching profession" (H. Schalock, 1979, pp. 407–408).

The relatively weak support for the hypothesis framing this literature review did not deter pursuing the hypothesis further. In fact, it provided a new impetus to an overarching rationale for its continued pursuit. It seemed inconceivable that after more than twenty years of concentrated research on teaching (1955–1978), educators could know so little about the connections between teaching and learning. Essentially nothing was known at the time about the connections between teacher preparation and either the classroom performance of teachers or the learning of K–12 students.

The 1980s

In the 1980s as this line of work commenced, a number of other developments within Oregon occurred that interacted powerfully with the research and development task that WOU faculty had set for themselves. Oregon's adoption of a "goal-based" (a precursor to today's "standards-based") approach to schooling forced attention by Oregon educators to the outcomes expected from schooling and their assessment and played a significant role, both directly and indirectly, in the evolution of TWSM.

Additionally, in light of this move toward outcomes and measures for K–12 students, pressure came from the state boards of education and higher education for evidence from follow-up studies on the effectiveness of graduates from the state's various teacher preparation programs in helping K–12 student progress in their learning. In 1986, Oregon's teacher licensing agency, the Teacher Standards and Practices Commission (TSPC), voted to move from a course, credit, and GPA counting approach in teacher licensure to an outcome-driven, evidence-based approach (H. Schalock & Myton, 1988).

SUPPORT ENLARGED

These various policy decisions triggered a flurry of statewide discussions to functionally connect teaching, teacher preparation, and K–12 learning. These included the development of joint state boards of education and higher education and TSPC work groups attempting to establish programs and procedures that responded sensibly to these new policy directions.

One of the reasons for the continued pursuit of the hypothesis was that researchers at TRI and faculty at WOU were well along by that time in developing and refining Teacher Work Sample Methodology. The developers had shifted their attention to *units of instruction*, rather than individual lessons, and this shift provided a more promising means of overcoming the many weaknesses inherent in trying to link teacher effects on student progress to the standardized achievement tests in use by both school districts and state education agencies at the time. Most of these tests were linked so loosely to the curriculum structure guiding teaching and learning in most schools that any hope of meaningfully and defensibly connecting the two was not possible without the kind of "value-added" methodologies finally developed in the late 1990s by Bill Sanders and his colleagues in Tennessee or by Bill Webster and his colleagues in the Dallas, Texas, schools. During the late 1970s through 1986, however, the logic, relative simplicity, and low-cost/low-tech nature of TWSM to make these connections appeared to offer an attractive and promising alternative.

There were, however, limitations inherent in such an approach to connecting teaching and learning. For example, using nonstandardized units of instruction and teacher-developed measures of the student learning outcomes made any comparisons across student teachers difficult. However, the promise of the methodology for both teacher-candidate instruction and assessment purposes, as well as a measure of teacher effectiveness that could be used in related research, led to proceeding with its development and research around its application.

From 1979 until 1986, WOU explored an outcome-based approach to teacher preparation and licensure, which included Teacher Work Sample requirements. A rich and continuous cross-fertilization of research and development activities in the K–12 schools and in the teacher preparation programs at WOU was used to focus on connecting teaching, teacher preparation, and K–12 learning. This was done through the Valley Education Consortium, a three-county, twenty-plus school district consortium created and managed to help small districts within the mid-Willamette Valley deal with the barrage of new state and federal demands coming at them, including the state's shift toward a wholly different way of thinking about schooling, the new and startling demands of Public Law 94-142 for the public schools, and the many-sided fallout from the *Nation at Risk* report, as a self-supporting R & D and service–technical assistance agency. Del Schalock organized the consortium and served as its executive director throughout its nearly twenty-year history during these historic times. It was within this period of great uncertainty and flux (the late 1970s and early 1980s) that the methodology of Teacher Work Sampling took shape and the label was assigned.

Because of the centrality of these connections to the education-policy community at the time, the Oregon K–12 and teacher preparation educators met, shared, and discussed findings from R & D efforts. K–12 curriculum and assessment groups were developing, implementing, and assessing the effects of K–12 goal-based instructional programs in all the major K–12 subject areas, including developmentally sequenced goals for learning and tests of goal attainment on a grade-by-grade basis. Representatives of WOU's teacher education faculty participated in all aspects of this work, informed their colleagues about it, and helped reshape the focus and content of their preparation programs accordingly.

Throughout these formative years Oregon's K–12 instructional programs and WOU's teacher preparation programs also functioned as contexts for research on the connections among teaching, teacher preparation, and K–12 learning. Data collected through the consortium's goal-based grade-level tests provided the dependent variable in studies of teacher and program effects in the schools, and data collected on K–12 learning through Teacher Work Samples provided the dependent variable for research on both teaching and teacher preparation effects. Since both arenas for research involved partially to fully operational data-collections systems during this time, studies were able to be refined and replicated from one year to the next. Because of the developmental nature of both sets of data, however, and because the primary purpose that each was to serve was either the refinement of instructional programs or the refinement of data collection, analysis, and reporting methodologies, only a few of these early research findings were published, though they were frequently reported nationally as well as within state conferences and meetings.

What did get published on the research side during these years was a series of papers and chapters dealing with the rationale for and issues encountered in research connecting teaching teacher preparation and K–12 learning, and in the design and operation of teacher preparation programs as contexts for research (H. Schalock, 1980, 1983, 1987, 1988; M. Schalock, 1987). Little changed in the realm of teacher education research from these efforts, however, for by 1986 the conclusion was reached that:

> The sad truth seems to be that while the literature reviewed in the *Third Handbook of Research on Teaching* (Wittrock, 1986) has increased in both quality and volume, we are (still) without any reliable predictors of who will or will not be good teachers. (H. Schalock, 1988, p. 8)

It is ironic that Del's last major publication (H. Schalock, M. Schalock, & Ayres, 2006) should return to these early roots in a call for "Scaling-up Research in Teacher Education: New Demands on Theory, Measurement and Design."

Another sad truth during this time was that the teacher education community was not yet ready to engage in such research, and the many issues it would raise as to theory, methodology, and design. A paper submitted to the *Journal of Teacher Education* in 1983 reporting our early findings that connected teaching and teacher preparation to K–12 learning was rejected as being "too researchy."

Of particular importance to this history, the philosophy and design of Teacher Work Sampling took shape within this many-sided milieu, and as such was structured from the beginning to reflect and accommodate the demands of a standards (goal-based) orientation to schooling. This cross-fertilization and interchange resulted in the formalization of Teacher Work Sample Methodology within the context of WOU's teacher preparation programs, and its subsequent inclusion in the 1986 standards redesign for teacher preparation and licensing in Oregon.

Translation into Policy

Both the methodology (in general terms) and label were formalized in the dramatically revised 1986 standards for teacher licensure in Oregon which moved the state not only to an outcomes-based licensing system but one that acknowledged K–12 learning as the ultimate outcome of interest (H. Schalock & Myton, 1988). The Oregon Licensure Commission has maintained this orientation and its commitment to the role of Teacher Work Sampling in the preparation and licensing process since that time forward.

FROM POLICY TO PRACTICE: THE LATE 1980s AND 1990s

Following the incorporation of Teacher Work Sampling into state preparation and licensing policy in 1986, WOU faculty began a new phase of related program design and research as they revised courses to accommodate the methodology. And the methodology itself continued to be refined. Faculty, based on data collected through TSWM, increased specifications about the types and level of learning outcomes, and they increased attention to contextual variables that influenced both teacher performance in a classroom and the learning gains made by the pupils taught. For example, teacher candidates were encouraged to go beyond simple recognition and recall types/levels of outcomes in the work samples to more complex outcomes requiring comprehension, application, and reflection. Similarly, prospective teachers were asked to document and reflect on the students in their classroom and the specific demands they placed upon them as a teacher, such as differentiation of curriculum and instruction. Faculty continued to refine the methodology by reviewing data from student teachers and based on their experiences working with student teachers on campus and in K–12 classrooms.

TWSM at WOU

Work Sample Methodology (WSM) at WOU was developed as both a teaching device and a measurement tool. As a vehicle for teaching, it was intended to give prospective teachers experience in designating learning outcomes to be accomplished through a two-to-five-week unit of instruction, developing plans for instruction and assessment that are aligned with the outcomes desired, and then collecting, interpreting, and reflecting upon evidence of student progress toward outcome attainment. This learning experience was enhanced through ongoing feedback from faculty during development and implementation of the initial Teacher Work Sample (TWS). When used as a vehicle for learning, TWSM was designed to force prospective teachers to think about the following issues and bring them into alignment:

- What is the instructional context for my teaching?
- What are the learning outcomes I want my students to accomplish?
- What activities and instructional methodologies are appropriate/necessary for these students to achieve these outcomes?

- What resources, and how much time, do I need to implement these activities/methodologies?
- What assessment activities/methodologies are appropriate for these students, and these outcomes, when using these instructional methodologies?
- How successful was I at helping my students achieve the outcomes desired (organizing, interpreting, reflecting on assessment information)?
- What went right? What went wrong? Why? What are the logical next steps? What would I do differently next time?

At WOU, Teacher Work Sample Methodology and the instruction and ongoing support provided by the teacher education programs to student teachers during the development of the initial work sample placed a heavy emphasis on issues of *alignment* (outcomes to instruction, instruction to assessment, assessment to outcomes); it provided for the consideration of the specific *context* within which the instruction occurred; and it recognized and required that a *diversity* of instructional and assessment strategies be employed (this diversity was often directly related to the contextual factors present in the student teacher's setting). Courses focused on these issues and student teachers were provided feedback as to how they were addressing these issues, both through observation and work sample development.

Steps Involved in the Methodology: Questions, Tasks, Criteria, and Resulting Documentation

At WOU, the work sample had nine distinct steps that made up the performance task related to these questions. Each step had specific criteria that student teachers had to meet and then develop documentation that became the work sample. The connections between the underlying questions, steps, criteria, and products—which could be assessed—are presented in table 1.1.

The actual product created in documenting the underlying performance task is the Teacher Work Sample that student teachers prepare and present at the conclusion of their instructional unit. As a vehicle for measurement, TWSM was designed to allow prospective teachers to document their work and the learning of their students within the context of the two-to-five-week unit of instruction. It was designed to let teachers accompany the information they provided about pupil learning with information about the context in which teaching and learning occurred, and to interpret information on learning in light of information on context. In this contextually grounded portrayal of teaching, data on learning gains by pupils tend to be viewed by prospective teachers as meaningful and a reasonable indictor of their effectiveness.

Table 1.1. Questions, steps, criteria, and documentation

Questions underlying TWSM process	Steps involved in addressing questions	Criteria	Products documenting processes
What are the learning outcomes I want my students to accomplish?	1. Define the sample of teaching and learning to be described. 2. Identify the learning outcomes to be accomplished with the work to be sampled.	A set of 2 to 3 integrated goals and their corresponding objectives, some of which are higher order covering multiple subject matter, usually from more than one domain	Description of and rationale for teaching/learning outcomes to be accomplished
What activities and instructional methodologies are appropriate/necessary for *these* students to achieve *these* outcomes?	3. Assess the status of students prior to instruction with respect to the postinstruction outcomes to be accomplished. 4. Describe the *context* in which teaching and learning are to occur.	Assessments of student learning judged in terms of: alignment with outcomes, clarity/understanding, reliability, feasibility, variety, and developmental appropriateness Context rated in terms of levels of demand and support	Pre-assessment developed and used to measure student progress Pre-instruction data Description of the teaching/learning context
What resources and how much time do I need to implement these activities/ methodologies?	5. Align instruction and assessment, through development of instructional and assessment plans, with learning outcomes to be accomplished. 6. Adapt outcomes desired and related plans for instruction and assessment to accommodate the demands of the teaching-learning context.	Instructional plans rated in terms of their appropriateness, usefulness/quality, and feasibility	Instructional plans
As I proceed through this unit, what changes do I need to make to ensure success for all students?	7. Implement planned instruction and make adaptations as needed.	Teacher Standards and Practices (TSPC) Competencies	Completed competency ratings

Questions underlying TWSM process	Steps involved in addressing questions	Criteria	Products documenting processes
What assessment activities/methodologies are appropriate for these students and these outcomes when using these instructional methodologies?	8. Assess the accomplishments of learners, and calculate on a student-by-student basis the growth in learning achieved.	Assessments of student learning judged in terms of: alignment with outcomes, clarity/understanding, reliability, feasibility, variety, and developmental appropriateness	Post-assessment developed and used to measure student progress

Post-instruction data

Evidence of student learning |
| How successful was I at helping my students achieve the learning outcomes desired?

What went right? What went wrong? Why? | 9. Summarize, interpret, and reflect on student growth in learning. | Reflective product (essay) rated on analysis of data, interpretation of data, use of data, and professional growth | Interpretation and reflection on the success of the teaching-learning unit, oriented toward what this means for future practice and professional development |

This basic structure, with an underlying performance task tied to a set of focusing questions, has remained fairly intact at WOU until today.

Ongoing Research, Development, and Refinement

Research continued on the connections between teaching, teacher preparation, and K–12 learning made possible by the methodology, and made increasingly promising through improvements in the methodology. Annual replications of studies continued to be run, and by the close of the 1980s, it was clear that the various measures provided through the methodology (teacher work and practice, classroom context, quality of measurement, and complexity of outcomes) could account for as much as 50 percent of the variance in K–12 student learning gain scores accomplished through the unit of study (McConney, Schalock, & Schalock, 1998).

It also was during this time period that publications began to appear on the nature and role of work sampling in Oregon's design for teacher preparation and licensure (H. Schalock, 1989a, 1989b; H. Schalock & M. Schalock, 1993; H. Schalock, M. Schalock, Cowart, & Myton, 1993; H. Schalock, M. Schalock, Myton, & Girod, 1993; M. Schalock, Cowart, & Staebler, 1993; M. Schalock, H. Schalock, & Edwards, 1993). In 1991, Oregon adopted a new "Design for 21st Century Schools," which included redesign of teacher preparation and licensure. With funding through the Oregon state system of higher education, TRI and WOU joined with the Teacher Standards and Practices Commission to undertake a two-year study of all implications in this regard. Studies completed about TWSM provided guidance for the revision work which was completed in 1996, with legislative adoption in 1997. While major changes occurred in the 1986-defined preparation and licensing process within Oregon as a consequence of the 1996 revision, TWSM was had an even more significant role in performance assessment with its extension to a second-stage license.

While much of the early work around the methodology centered on its design and implementation across teacher preparation programs in Oregon in response to the 1986 changes in licensure laws in Oregon, from a research standpoint, work focused on the student learning and contextual data being generated through its use. A group of WOU faculty and administrators designed and tested measures, formulated questions of interest to the faculty, and designed studies to answer these questions.

During this time from the late 1980s through 1995, data from nearly one thousand student teachers and ten thousand K–12 students were collected, analyzed, and reported back to the College of Education faculty. Data from TWS generated student learning outcomes, observational data from school and college supervisors, and detailed information about classroom contexts in which student teachers were teaching were summarized and presented to faculty several times a year to support reflection on program design and adequacy.

A significant amount of work went into developing a method to compare K–12 student learning results across student teachers. The long-standing and seemingly intractable issue at hand was the lack of a defensible outcome measure in conducting research on teacher preparation. A major challenge within this issue was creating a "level playing field" by which to make sense of the differences in learning outcomes observed. WOU approached this challenge from three directions. First, faculty attended to context. Faculty had long been aware that some student teaching contexts were so easy that student teachers could not fail, and, conversely, some contexts were so difficult that student teachers struggled to survive. Systematic collection of data on teaching contexts was instituted early in this time period with frequent feedback to and from faculty to continue discussions and refinement of contextual measures.

Second, faculty were becoming concerned about the "low-level" learning outcomes being addressed in TWSM. To address this concern, three actions were taken. Student teachers thought that "easy" tests leading to better post-assessment scores would reflect positively on grading the work sample. A conscious decision was made to require student teachers to address higher-order outcomes, faculty provided instruction in courses on developing and assessing higher-order outcomes, and finally an assessment/outcome taxonomy was derived to provide a basis to assess the complexity of the outcomes assessed within a TWS and provide comparative ratings across student teachers. The purpose of these efforts was to move student teachers beyond simple low-level recognition and recall types of assessments to higher-level assessments addressing the kinds of student outcomes being demanded in K–12 schools at the time.

Finally, faculty and researchers had to find a means for creating a common metric to capture student learning gains across the array of assessments used by student teachers. To bring some level of standardization to the scores derived across these diverse assessments, a simple metric developed by Dr. Jason Millman at Cornell University (Millman, 1981) was adopted for use in analyzing student learning outcomes within the research. This metric was termed the Index of Pupil Growth (IPG). The index compared the actual change in scores from pre-post to the potential change or 100 percent. This resulted in a ratio score that could range from –1 to +1. Practically speaking, however, scores ranged from 0 to +1, since post-assessment scores were rarely, if ever, lower than pre-assessment scores.

By 1994, after analyzing these data from over one thousand student teachers and ten thousand K–12 students, the methodology and the student learning data were at a point where it seemed appropriate to have an external review conducted. In October 1994, a national invitational conference was held to expose the methodology and resulting learning gains as a means for connecting teaching and learning for licensure and research purposes to a thorough, objective external evaluation. Over thirty leading scholars in the areas of evaluation, research, teacher preparation, measurement, and policy spent three days reviewing the methodology and findings up to that date (see appendix A for a list of major contributors to the review of the methodology). A full summary of this conference can be found in *Proceedings of a Conference* (H. Schalock & M. Schalock, 1995). The overall reaction from conference participants was that while the work to date was commendable and the findings promising, further work was needed to more fully develop and validate the methodology. Participants also strongly indicated that external funding to support such work was critical.

One other significant outcome from the conference was a joint commitment from a number of participants to move this and similar work forward in the form of a book to be edited by Jason Millman. There was strong interest in exploring the use of student learning data for teacher and school evaluation, and making public many such efforts underway across the country. Three well-established systems (the Dallas, Texas Value-Added Accountability System; the Tennessee Value-Added Assessment System; and the Kentucky Instructional Results Information System) along with Western's Teacher Work Sample Methodology were highlighted in the book (Millman, 1997).

THE TEACHER EFFECTIVENESS PROJECT (TEP)

As a result of the October 1994 conference, three years of funding was obtained from the Atlantic Philanthropies to carry the work forward as recommended by conference participants. This work, titled the Teacher Effectiveness Project, was funded to achieve four broad outcomes:

1. Refine and validate Teacher Work Sample Methodology (TWSM) for teacher preparation and licensure. By the end of the project, staff were to have a fully developed, validated, and reliable Teacher Work Sample Methodology that provided a conceptual framework with which teachers and teacher development programs (preservice and in-service) could think about, learn about, practice, and demonstrate their proficiencies along a number of dimensions related to functioning effectively in standards-based schools, including fostering K–12 student learning.
2. Develop a state, regional, and national network around connecting teaching and learning. By the end of the project, staff were to have established a state, regional, and national network that focused the

initial preparation and continued professional development of teachers on connecting K–12 student learning to teacher work, within the context of a standards-based design for schooling.
3. Develop materials and procedures needed to replicate TWSM. By the end of the project, staff were to have a fully developed set of internally consistent materials and procedures needed to replicate TWSM within teacher preparation programs outside of Oregon, and started efforts to replicate TWSM in other programs.
4. Make a significant contribution to the national debate on the effectiveness and productivity of teachers and schools through an aggressive writing and presentation agenda. This goal was to include theory, measurement, knowledge, and practice pertaining to the use of K–12 student learning in determining the effectiveness of teacher preparation programs, teachers, and teacher-continued professional development programs and schools, and to the implication of a standards-based design for schooling in making such a determination.

To help guide and review this work, a National Advisory Panel was formed, lead originally, until his death, by Jason Millman of Cornell University. Dan Stufflebeam of Western Michigan University chaired the panel after Dr. Millman's death. Other panelists included Ray Pecheone, Connecticut Department of Education; Peter Airasian, Boston College; Herb Walberg, University of Illinois, Chicago Circle; Russell French, University of Tennessee; David Mandel, National Board for Professional Teaching Standards; Robert Mendro, Dallas, Texas, Independent School District; and Ruth Mitchell, The Education Trust.

Refinement and Validation of TWSM

The work of TEP centered on researching and developing the conditions necessary for generation and use of the valid and reliable TWSM scores on both K–12 student learning and teacher performance in high-stakes initial licensure decisions. To facilitate this work, additional project staff were hired, and teaching faculty were "bought out" quarter-time to ensure that a broad representation of skills and perspectives were brought to bear on the task at hand. During these three-plus years of the project, faculty from education and the TRI worked to meet the TEP outcomes.

Building the Foundation: Reacting to the 1994 National Review of TWSM

In response to a 1994 national panel of external reviewers, TEP staff summarized a list of questions around TWSM that the panel had considered important and yet to be addressed (H. Schalock & M. Schalock, 1995).

The working group of TEP staff and WOU education faculty convened to address these questions and propose TWSM guidelines, components, definitions, and criteria for use in assessing work sample quality. Together these would comprise and formalize the College of Education's policies regarding TWSM and its use in making licensure decisions.

Over the course of 1995–1996, a working group of TRI and WOU faculty developed draft responses to questions and underlying rationales. These answers were reviewed and refinements suggested through a series of seminars for the entire College of Education teacher preparation faculty over the course of the year. The seminars provided the mechanism to gain individual, divisional, and cross-divisional faculty input and consensus.

The working group developed and published a manual capturing the faculty agreements around TWSM (Ayres, Ling, Girod, McConney, Schalock, & Wright, 1996). The agreements were incorporated into changes in the Student Teacher Handbook, thus giving students developing work samples a clearer picture of faculty expectations and policies.

Once agreements were reached by faculty around TWSM, the project turned its focus toward developing valid and reliable measures of student teacher work that could be assessed through a work sample. It was at this point that faculty began to raise the issue of the consequences for the instructional power of TWSM by focusing solely on the assessment potential of TWSM. Faculty had begun to see the instructional effects of using TWSM and had concerns that this power might be diminished if assessment began to drive design. This began a long balancing act of compromise between developing the methodology to best meet *both* instructional and assessment uses. To a large degree these compromises were addressed by first focusing on the underlying performance task asked of student teachers and then aligning the documentation of that task (the Teacher Work Sample) and the assessment of that documentation. Ensuring that the underlying performance task was authentic and meaningful for teachers provided a strong basis for tying the steps of the performance task to program instruction and feedback, as well as the development and use of valid and reliable assessment instruments.

Redevelopment of TWSM measures was conducted to reflect the newly agreed-upon guidelines, definitions, components, and criteria, as well as to address the lack of variability found in the scores generated from existing measures. The working group conducted extensive research on the measurement and spent roughly a year developing drafts of a new set of measures more in line with agreed-upon processes, definitions, components, and criteria associated with TWSM. For example, measures were developed to assess the components of the Teacher Work Sample related to instructional planning, assessment, implementation, context, reflection, and student learning.

WOU faculty tested the revised TWSM measures using several student-teacher-developed work samples (McConney, Schalock, & Ayres, 1996). This allowed project staff to identify potential areas where disagreement would be likely by faculty raters, and to estimate the time cost associated with the use of much more detailed measures of work sample quality. TEP staff began development of a training-and-review session for education faculty.

Concurrently, the working group developed a manual addressing both institutional and external audiences. The manual included the underlying rationale, definitions, components, criteria, processes, revised measures, and multiple uses for TWSM (Ayres, Girod, McConney, M. Schalock, H. Schalock, & Wright, 1996).

Through a series of seminars over the course of the year, the entire faculty used an early draft of the revised measures to assess a number of work samples. This provided faculty the opportunity to review and refine the new set of TWSM measures and resulted in individual, divisional, and cross-divisional input and consensus.

TEP staff, overseen by the working group, refined the revised TWSM measures to reflect faculty input. The working group convened and conducted three focus-group sessions with early career teachers who were recent graduates from WOU teacher preparation programs (elementary, secondary, and special education). The focus groups were designed to elicit in-depth feedback around graduates' in-program experiences with TWSM and, importantly, TWSM's subsequent impact on their teaching practice. While practicing teachers did not maintain the level of detailed planning, assessment, and reflection called for in a TWSM, the underlying processes required by a TWS were maintained (Ayres, McConney, Schalock, Cuthbertson, & Bartelheim, 1997). An additional significant finding from these focus groups was the sense of personal and professional accountability for K–12 student learning that had been instilled through the TWSM process (M. Schalock, 1998).

Redesign of the School of Education Programs

In 1997, the working group engaged in a comprehensive review of literature on teacher preparation, programs, and teacher roles and functions to guide the redesign effort. They conducted an initial cross-match between the emerging elements of the redesigned teacher preparation program and the recently agreed-to TWSM definitions, components, criteria, and measures.

TEP staff provided the School of Education faculty direct assistance and general oversight in developing an overall assessment framework for mapping the progress of preservice teachers at specified benchmarks as they progressed through the redesigned "proficiency-based" preparation program. A critical aspect of this effort was mapping the multiple potential sources of evidence for assessing prospective teachers' progress through the program, including TWSM at the third and fourth benchmarks in the program, which at that time represented practica setting during pre–student teaching and the full-time student teaching experience.

TEP staff worked closely with the Oregon Association of Colleges of Teacher Education (OACTE) to develop a common frame of reference for TWSM across the public and private teacher preparation programs in Oregon. An important basis for this effort was the work already completed at WOU, reflecting agreements reached across the faculty on the newly revised TWSM measures and the new proficiency-based, program-level assessment system that recognized TWSM as an integral and central source of evidence for assuring the quality of WOU's graduates.

TEP staff provided ongoing support for the implementation of the new School of Education program, including the refinement and use of the program's assessment framework. TEP staff also provided the College of Education with assistance in completing successful National Council for Accreditation of Teacher Education (NCATE) and TSPC reaccreditation efforts. Two significant parts of this assistance were: (1) analyses on the work sample database that demonstrated the program's commitment to continuous improvement and quality assurance through systematic, ongoing evaluation, and (2) a compilation of the scholarship that had resulted from the faculty's engagement in TWSM development, and TEP generally.

Dissemination and Networking

Efforts to develop and maintain a national network of people, projects, and programs focusing on the connections between teaching and learning centered on three related strategies guided by Del Schalock. First and foremost was to continue work with the National Advisory Panel.

Second was to organize two national symposia focusing on teaching and learning. This strategy was not as successful as hoped, in that the focus became one on standards-based schooling generally rather than connecting teaching and learning specifically. As a result, networking was largely at the state level, and around specific state and school district policies and practices. Teacher Work Sample Methodology and connecting teaching and learning was not the central focus.

A third strategy was the aggressive pursuit of formal relationships with Education Trust, AACTE, and NCATE. This strategy proved most successful and allowed staff and faculty to refocus their energies on refining and validating Teacher Work Sample Methodology as a means to prepare, license, and evaluate beginning and experienced teachers.

These three efforts resulted in an active network of educators across the country who implemented and further developed application, research, and policy related to TWSM in a variety of educational settings. Textbox 1.1 provides a summary of the states and organizations that were active in the network.

TEXTBOX 1.1. STATES AND ORGANIZATIONS IN THE TEACHER EFFECTIVENESS PROJECT NATIONAL NETWORK

STATES

- Colorado
- Connecticut
- Kentucky
- Louisiana
- Oregon
- Tennessee
- Texas
- Washington

ORGANIZATIONS

- The Education Trust
- American Association of Colleges for Teacher Education
- The Renaissance Group
- The Evaluation Center, Western Michigan University
- Tennessee Value-Added Research and Assessment Center
- Council of Basic Education Holly Jones
- Council of Chief State School Officers, State Leadership Office
- National Council for the Accreditation of Teacher Education
- National Governor's Association, Education Policies Unit

As work evolved and was disseminated, the national debate on the effectiveness and productivity of schools and teachers was heating up considerably. While a portion of our impact on the national debate went on through discussions with policy makers and practitioners, our major contribution was through an aggressive agenda of writing and presentations at the local, state, and national level.

Over the course of the three and a half years of the TEP, a total of twelve book chapters and journal articles were published; five full-length monographs were produced and widely disseminated; six products were developed and are in use; twenty-five papers or workshops were delivered at regional, national, and international conferences; and eighteen technical reports/papers were prepared for the National Advisory Panel, Western's School of Education, Oregon's Teacher Standards and Practices Commission, and NCATE.

These efforts were often collaborative in nature, resulting in a total of thirty-six different authors, presenters, and workshop instructors being listed in the references for this chapter. These individuals represented faculty and staff from the Teacher Effectiveness Project, Western's School of Education, the Oregon Department of Education, Oregon school districts, the Proficiency-based Admission Standards System (PASS) Projects, Oregon's Teacher Standards and Practices Commission, the Confederation of Oregon School Administrators, Michigan State University, and the University of Tennessee, Knoxville.

Development of Replication Materials

Our first work in developing replication materials was focused on producing "A Guide to Teacher Work Sample Methodology," which was developed for our presentation at the annual meeting of the American Association of School Personnel Administrators held in Portland, Oregon, in October 1996. This guide was updated several times to reflect our evolving measures and was disseminated across the country.

Starting in early 1997, work began on developing "Teacher Work Sample Methodology: A Handbook for the Preparation and Licensing of Teachers." This Handbook later took on a different title and was published by AACTE (Girod, 2002). The handbook was organized around five sections and appendixes. Section 1 describes TWSM and why it is important. Section 2 presents ideas and examples on how to teach the concepts and skills needed to develop a Teacher Work Sample. Section 3 describes student-teacher supervisory strategies and functions to implement and use TWSM. Section 4 presents the policy, programmatic, and logistic requirements for implementing TWSM within a teacher preparation program. Section 5 presents case studies of the use of TWSM in preparing and licensing elementary, secondary, and special education teachers.

Summary

In the fall of 1998 as the work of TEP came to an end, the National Advisory Panel was asked to make a judgment as to whether TWSM, as used at WOU, could validly and legally be used as part of a high-stakes teacher licensure decision. Their conclusion was that yes, it could, but they agreed with our conclusion that there were five conditions both necessary and sufficient for this to occur. First, the performance tasks that student teachers were being asked to carry out within the work sample must be valid. Second, the program must be structured to provide student teachers with the knowledge and skills necessary not only to carry out the underlying performance task, but also to document that performance in ways amenable to valid and reliable scoring. Third, the program must be structured to allow practice and feedback on these sets of knowledge and skills prior to a final independent effort. Fourth, scoring rubrics must be developed that, when used as designed, produce valid scores on the domains of the teaching task being assessed. Finally, a training program must be developed and implemented to ensure scores are reliable enough to use within a high-stakes licensure decision context. The principles underlying these conditions are summarized in table 1.2.

In the end, the National Advisory Panel deemed the methodology as sufficiently robust, valid, and reliable to be included as one measure that could be used to justify a high-stakes decision around licensure, if all the conditions were met. They were clear, however, that in and of itself, it could not be used to make licensure decisions, but that it could and should play a prominent role in a multiple-measure approach to licensure decision.

A GOOD IDEA TAKES OFF (1999–2010)

The networks of states and organizations developed through the Teacher Effectiveness Project provided the launching pad for TWSM's emergence nationally. This was amplified by the convergence of several political/policy initiatives, notably Title II of the 1998 Higher Education Act and the NCATE 2000 standards. TWSM was viewed as a viable response to both the Title II demands for information around quality assurance standards and measures employed at the state level in preparing and licensing teachers and to NCATE"s requirement for clear linkage to state standards for learning and evidence on the success of program graduates in helping their students progress toward those standards. As states faced these hard realities and teacher licensing agencies became aware of the potential contributions of Teacher Work Sample Methodology to the enhancement of their teaching workforce, a number of states moved to include its use in their teacher preparation and licensing process. Colorado was the first state outside of Oregon to mandate its use (in 2000), with Louisiana following suit shortly thereafter (in 2002), and Kansas, Kentucky, and Oklahoma followed. A final catalyst was the American Association of Colleges for Teacher Education endorsing the methodology as a useful and defensible vehicle for connecting teaching, teacher preparation, and K–12 learning. This support was concretized by the publication of the first handbook detailing its philosophy and use (Girod, 2002).

Table 1.2.   Principles of design for teacher preparation programs that wish to incorporate with integrity the core elements of teacher work sampling

Principle 1.   An instructional program needs to be aligned with and supportive of what candidates are asked to do, including the documentation and reporting that is required in completing a work sample.

Principle 2.   School contexts that model and are supportive of what candidates are asked to do need to be available for practicum and student teaching placements.

Principle 3.   A supervision, evaluation, and feedback system needs to be in place that provides guided practice in applying and carrying out the tasks Teacher Work Sampling demands of candidates.

Principle 4.   Judgments about a candidate's effectiveness as a teacher need to take into account the gains in learning made by every student taught.

Principle 5.   Documentation of a candidate's effectiveness as a teacher needs to be accompanied by observations of practice and descriptions of context, as well as evidence of learning gains by students.

Principle 6.   Multiple lines of evidence need to be considered in reaching a recommendation for licensure, only some of which come through Teacher Work Sampling.

Principle 7.   Multiple reviewers of evidence need to be involved in preparing a recommendation for a license to teach, only some of whom represent a teacher education faculty.

Principle 8.   Evidence needs to be assembled and reported by a teacher education faculty on the confidence that can be placed in all lines of evidence collected through Teacher Work Sampling that inform a licensing decision (the reliability and validity of information used).

Principle 9.   A conceptual, as well as a contextual (school, district, state, national) map needs to inform and give meaning to an intending teacher of principles 1 through 8.

Central, however, to the extended use and policy adoptions around the methodology has been the work of the Renaissance Partnership for Improving Teacher Quality, under the leadership of Roger Pankratz at Western Kentucky University. This group of eleven institutions worked collaboratively for a period of five years on refining and testing the robustness of the methodology under widely varying institutional conditions. This history and resulting case studies are well represented in the chapters that follow.

One of the great endearing characteristics of TWSM is its inherent flexibility. While the methodology as used at WOU had certain nonnegotiable principles and design requirements, others who picked up the basic methodology were quick to see how it could be modified and improved to meet their own contexts and needs. This inherent flexibility and the utility of TWSM are evident in the many and continuing presentations at the AACTE annual meetings over the past decade as well as the National Teacher Work Sample Conferences held in Oregon in 2004, 2006, and 2009. That good idea—keeping student learning front and center in the discussion of teacher preparation, licensure, and ultimately teacher effectiveness—has indeed taken off.

REFERENCES

Ayres, R., Girod, G., McConney, A., Schalock, M. D, Schalock, H. D., & Wright, D. (1996). *A Guide to Teacher Work Sample Methodology* (A. McConney, Ed.). Monmouth, OR: Teacher Effectiveness Project, Teaching Research Division, Western Oregon University.

Ayres, R., Ling, M., Girod, G., McConney, A., Schalock, M. D., & Wright, D. (1996). *Work Sample Methodology*. Monmouth, OR: Teacher Effectiveness Project, Teaching Research Division, Western Oregon University.

Ayres, R., McConney, A., Schalock, M. D., Cuthbertson, L., and Bartelheim, F. (1997). *Preliminary findings from three focus group sessions with recent Western Oregon University teacher education graduates*. Monmouth, OR: Teacher Effectiveness Project, Teaching Research Division, Western Oregon University.

Girod, G. R. (Ed.) (2002). *Connecting teaching and learning: A handbook for teacher educators on Teacher Work Sample Methodology*. Washington, DC: AACTE Publications.

McConney, A., Schalock, M. D., & Ayres, R. (1996, November). *An overview of measures used in Western Oregon's Teacher Work Sample Methodology*. Paper for the 1st national symposium on Reaching World-Class Standards through Standards-Based Teaching and Learning, Portland, OR.

McConney, A., Schalock, M. D., & Schalock, H. D. (1998). Focusing improvement and quality assurance: Work samples as authentic performance measures of prospective teachers' effectiveness. *Journal of Personnel Evaluation in Education, 11*(4), 343–363.

Millman, J. (Ed.). 1981. *Handbook of teacher evaluation*. Chicago: Rand McNally.

Millman, J. (Ed.). 1997. *Grading teachers, grading schools: Is student achievement a valid evaluation measure?* Thousand Oaks, CA: Corwin Press.

Schalock, H. D. (1970, May). The focus of performance-based certification: Knowledge, teaching behavior, or the products that derive from a teacher's behavior. *Proceedings of the Conference on Performance-Based Certification*, Miami Beach, FL.

Schalock, H. D. (1974, January). The impact of competency definition on teacher preparation institutions. *Educational Leadership*, pp. 318–321.

Schalock, H. D. (1979). Research on teacher selection. In D. C. Berliner (Ed.), *Annual review of research in education* (pp. 364–417). Washington, DC: American Educational Research Association.

Schalock, H. D. (1980). Eating humble pie: Notes on methodology in teacher education research. In G. E. Hall, S. M. Hord, & G. Brown, (Eds.), *Exploring issues in teacher education: Questions for future research* (pp. 519–536). Austin: Research and Development Center for Teacher Education, University of Texas at Austin.

Schalock, H. D. (1983). Methodological considerations in future research and development in teacher education. In K. Howey & W. Gardner (Eds.), *The education of teachers: A look ahead* (pp. 38–73). New York: Longman.

Schalock, H. D. (1987). The central issue in teacher warranties: Quality assurance for what? *Journal of Teacher Education, 38*(5), 52–58.

Schalock, H. D. (1988). Teacher selection: A problem of admission criteria, certification criteria or prediction of job performance? In W. J. Gephart & J. B. Ayers (Eds.), *Teacher Education Evaluation* (pp. 1–22). Boston: Kluwer Academic Publishers.

Schalock, H. D. (1989a). Student learning: The professional touchstone for teachers and teacher educators. *Proceedings of the 1988 Far West Meeting of the Holmes Group* (pp. 165–178). Boulder, CO.

Schalock, H. D. (1989b). A new paradigm for teacher licensure: Oregon's demand for evidence of success in fostering learning. *Journal of Teacher Education, 29*(6), 8–16.

Schalock, H. D. & Myton, D. V. (1988). A new paradigm for teacher licensure: Oregon's demand for evidence of success in fostering learning. *Journal of Teacher Education, 39*(6), 8–16.

Schalock, H. D., & Schalock, M. D. (1995). *Proceedings of a Conference: Advances in Theory and Research on Teacher Effectiveness.* Monmouth, OR: Teacher Effectiveness Project, Teaching Research Division, Western Oregon University.

Schalock, H. D., Schalock, M. D., & Ayres, R. A. (2006). Scaling-up research in teacher education: New demands on theory, measurement and design. *Journal of Teacher Education, 57*(2), 102–119.

Schalock, H. D., Schalock, M. D., Cowart, B., and Myton, D. V. (1993). Extending teacher assessment beyond knowledge and skills: An emerging focus on teacher accomplishments. *Journal of Personnel Evaluation in Education, 7*(2), 105–134.

Schalock, H. D., Schalock, M. D., & Girod, G. (1997). Teacher work sample methodology as used at Western Oregon State College. In J. Millman (Ed.), *Grading teachers, Grading schools: Is student achievement a valid evaluation measure?* (pp. 15–45). Thousand Oaks, CA: Corwin Press.

Schalock, H. D., Schalock, M. D., Myton, D. V., and Girod, J. (1993). Focusing on learning gains by students taught: A central feature of Oregon's outcome based approach to the initial preparation and licensure of teachers. *Journal of Personnel Evaluation in Education, 7*(2), 135–158.

Schalock, M. D. (1987). Teacher productivity: What is it? How might it be measured? Can it be warranted? *Journal of Teacher Education, 38*(5), 59–62.

Schalock, M. D. (1998). Accountability, student learning, and the preparation and licensure of teachers: Oregon's Teacher Work Sample Methodology. *Journal of Personnel Evaluation in Education, 12*(3), 269–286.

Schalock, M. D., Cowart, B., & Staebler, B. (1993). Teacher productivity revisited: Definition, theory, measurement and application. *Journal of Personnel Evaluation in Education, 7*(2), 179–196.

Schalock, M. D., Schalock, H. D., & Edwards, J. (1993). Extending teacher assessment and professional development beyond knowledge and skills: Applying student learning gains to a faculty incentive-reward program. *Journal of Personnel Evaluation in Education, 7*(2), 159–178.

Wittrock, M. C. (Ed.). (1986). *Handbook of research on teaching* (3rd ed.). New York: Macmillan.

II

PRACTICE

2

Answering the Call

How Do We Know They Can Teach?

Barbara Chesler Buckner and Douglas W. Smith

DOCUMENTING EFFECTS ON STUDENT LEARNING: CHANGE TAKES TIME

In 1996 the National Commission on Teaching and America's Future (NCTAF) published the report *What Matters Most: Teaching for America's Future*, and proposed that "by the year 2006, America will provide all students in the country with what should be their educational birthright—access to competent, caring, and qualified teachers" (p. 10). That year has come and gone and in some fortunate classrooms this has been achieved, but in many it has not. Change takes time. This is the story about how one institution, Coastal Carolina University (CCU), in Conway, South Carolina, is responding to the call to produce competent, caring, and qualified teachers who are worthy to work with America's students. In part, this is accomplished at CCU through collection and thoughtful analysis of the pre- and post-instructional accomplishments of public school students using the Teacher Work Sample Methodology (TWSM) in order to measure and ensure candidates' instructional effectiveness and impact on student learning.

HOW WE GOT HERE

The NCTAF was jointly formed and funded in 1994 by the Rockefeller Foundation and Carnegie Corporation of New York. Its goal was to create a national agenda focusing on raising student achievement by building a more knowledgeable and skillful teacher workforce that is committed to meeting the needs of all students. The problem with this goal was the assumption that "knowledgeable and skillful" meant the same as "effective," and that teachers' knowledge and skill would automatically translate into their ability to apply their knowledge and skills to foster the learning of all students. Del Schalock and David Myton (2002) recognized the error of this assumption in their writing about TWSM. While they recognized that knowledge and skills are important, they focused on the imperative evidence for student learning as the true measure of teacher effectiveness.

> It is the fundamental difference in focus between *what teachers know and are able to do* and *what children learn*, that sets TWSM apart from other efforts to ensure the quality of teachers and teaching in our schools. Teacher work sampling also attends to what teachers know and do, but it is a methodology that emphasizes the *alignment* of these dimensions of teacher work with specific learning outcomes to be accomplished by pupils and the contextual demands of the classroom in which teaching and learning occur. Teacher work sampling represents an applied performance approach to teacher assessment that is close to a teacher's work, in that it reflects the realities of a teacher's work with meaningful indicators of its consequences. (pp. 23–24)

As is described elsewhere in this volume, the National Council for the Accreditation of Teacher Education (NCATE) standards initiated a new era of accountability in teacher preparation (2002). The new standards answered the call to create a teacher workforce that was knowledgeable, competent, and caring, but even though not stated, they included the criteria of effective as well. The new standards pushed institutions to go one step further in meeting the needs of all children; they required that candidates be able to apply knowledge and skills to assist in student learning. Elements 4 and 7 in NCATE Standard 1 aligned with Schalock's and Myton's missing pieces of the NCTAF. Element 4, "Professional and Pedagogical Knowledge and Skills for Teacher Candidates," required institutions to provide evidence that their candidates could apply their knowledge and skills to facilitate learning. Element 7, "Student Learning for Teacher Candidates," required evidence that teacher candidates could assess and analyze student learning, use assessment in instruction, and develop meaningful learning experiences. The new NCATE standards closed the gap between the intention of the NCTAF and the educational birthright of American students; that is, a teacher that is knowledgeable in the subject they teach, a teacher committed in meeting the needs of all students, a teacher that cares and has the disposition that all students are able to succeed, and a teacher that can plan effective instruction based on assessment of student learning.

The No Child Left Behind Act (NCLB) of 2001 also served to clarify some of the intentions of the aforementioned teacher education reformation efforts, including the work of the NCTAF, coining and then defining the term "highly qualified." In their 2003 report, "No Dreams Denied," the NCTAF defined highly qualified teachers as those who:

- possess a deep understanding of the subjects they teach;
- evidence a firm understanding of how students learn;
- demonstrate the teaching skills necessary to help all students achieve high standards;
- create a positive learning environment;
- use a variety of assessment strategies to diagnose and respond to individual learning needs;
- demonstrate and integrate modern technology into the school curriculum;
- support student learning;
- collaborate with colleagues, parents, and community members, and other educators to improve student learning;
- reflect on their practice to improve future teaching and student achievement;
- pursue professional growth in both content and pedagogy; and
- instill a passion for learning in their students. (pp. 6–7)

Through these criteria the NCTAF better defined teacher quality and set the bar for effective and highly qualified teacher practitioners.

A FRAMEWORK FOR TEACHER PREPARATION

Because research has confirmed that teachers are central to student achievement, scholarly work has been done to determine the best ways to prepare preservice teachers for effective classroom practice. To give direction, studies have narrowly focused on various aspects of teacher preparation and teacher quality from investigating qualifications of teachers, to the context of teaching, to the importance of developing assessment literacy (Ferguson, 1991; Sanders and Horn, 1994; Sanders and Rivers, 1996; Stiggens, 1991, 1995; Wright, Horn, and Sanders, 1997). From this research, Darling-Hammond and Bransford (2005, p. 3) suggest that one goal of teacher preparation programs should be to provide preservice teachers with a framework for teaching, thereby enabling preservice and beginning teachers to simultaneously reflect upon and improve their own practice and foster student learning.

The TWSM provides the kind of framework necessary for developing competent, caring, effective, and highly qualified teachers who reflect upon their own work. It provides a framework that focuses on student learning and assists novice teachers in putting together best classroom practices, such as

- thinking about the contextual aspects that affect student learning,
- establishing student learning outcomes that are performance-based and provide information on what we want students to know at the end of a teaching and learning engagement,
- using assessment to guide and support instruction,
- analyzing student learning to determine if learning outcomes have been met, and
- engaging in reflective practice to determine how an individual's teaching can improve (Girod, 2002).

When provided with a framework, teacher candidates can better develop the capacities and dispositions needed to be successful in the classroom and in the teaching profession.

THE IMPACT OF ACCREDITATION ON TEACHER WORK SAMPLE METHODOLOGY

With the advent of NCATE 2000 and the call for new teacher-preparation accountability assessment systems, colleges of education began scrambling to gather evidence to support their claims about the effectiveness of their candidates and programs relative to NCATE Standard 1, specifically element 7, "Student Learning for Teacher Candidates," and faculty across the nation began to seek out how to provide evidence demonstrating that their candidates impact the students they teach; assess, analyze, and monitor student learning; and adjust instruction to meet the needs of all students.

In 2000, the Renaissance Group was born when eleven institutions received a Title II grant that was a five-year initiative to advance the quality of their graduates and the teachers in their respective partner schools by focusing attention on P–12 student learning. Even though it was not the intention of the grant, two of the goals fell perfectly in line with NCATE Standard 1, element 7:

- become accountable for the impact of teacher candidate on P–12 student learning, and
- improve teacher performance in key areas and show an increase in candidate's ability to facilitate learning of all students.

The institutions involved in the grant adopted and modified TWSM from Western Oregon University. The consortium identified seven processes and tasks that would be their focus, and by 2002 they had created a rubric that would be used for scoring candidates' work and collecting data. The website with all documents created during the five-year grant can be found at http://www.uni.edu/itq. As the consortium continued to conduct research and disseminate their accomplishments, more and more institutions were beginning to take notice because they saw TWSM as *something* their candidates could do to produce data for accreditation.

The timing of the new NCATE 2000 accreditation standards and the TWSM collaboration work of the Renaissance Group occurred separately but simultaneously. The NCATE standards were released, and institutions were asked to begin reporting outputs of their candidates rather than inputs of the faculty. Faculty began searching for assessment tools, and for many TWSM was the answer, but the *methodology* became lost in the shuffle and instead became a *project* at most institutions known simply as Teacher Work Sample. This loss is due to the fact that the theory and concepts that supported the methodology were not the reason for the adoption and were not researched by many. Instead, faculty adopting it for accreditation saw it as an assessment tool and not as a methodology to help candidates learn to think about how their teaching influences the learning of their students. Without this initial understanding that TWSM focused on the results and effectiveness of teaching, some institutions only gather the surface results and not the rich gains made by the pupil-by-pupil analysis that is called for in every Teacher Work Sample produced. Thus, for many institutions the rich data that could be included in analysis are not gathered and ultimately are also lost.

TWS IMPLEMENTATION AT COASTAL CAROLINA UNIVERSITY

As the TWSM movement was generating attention, Coastal Carolina University (CCU) was preparing for NCATE accreditation. Like many institutions, they were searching for a way to meet element 7 of Standard 1. And, like many institutions, the M was removed, and Teacher Work Sample arrived at its shores.

As was true with most teacher education units, CCU had neither adequate data nor a collection scheme in place to produce the data demanded by NCATE 2000. In short, if the teacher education unit at CCU was to remain vital, it would have to abandon many of the old accreditation habits and embrace a data-driven methodology for the preparation of candidates. It was for this purpose that faculty and administration at CCU became keenly aware of the TWSM.

Like many other teacher education units, CCU found the TWSM to be very attractive because it provided a structure within which to address the question that was being put to all teacher education units by NCATE, specifically, "How do you know that your candidates are effective in their classrooms?" In fact, of the eleven characteristics of highly qualified teachers, as specified earlier (NCTAF, 2003) ten are either directly or indirectly supported through TWSM. Table 2.1 shows the correlations between tenets of the NCTAF's definition of a "highly qualified" teacher and the sections of the TWS process that support them.

While there is no such thing as a panacea for teacher training, the TWSM appeared to be the next best thing. With high hopes, CCU became fully committed to the implementation of TWSM across all teacher education programs at both the undergraduate and graduate levels. However, instead of a methodology, it was seen as a project that would provide data for accountability purposes.

At CCU, the Teacher Work Sample (TWS) project was viewed as a collection of exhibits of teaching performances that provide direct evidence of a candidate's ability to design and implement standards-based instruction, assess student learning, impact P–12 student learning, and reflect on learning and teaching processes. The project is infused in all teacher certification programs. Although implementation differs somewhat between programs, the bulk of the practice is essentially the same. The remainder

Table 2.1.   Correlations of TWS processes and "highly qualified" (as defined by the National Commission on Teaching and America's Future)

Teacher Work Sample Process	Correlated Tenet of "No Dream Denied"
Contextual Factors	• Create a positive learning environment. • Support student learning.
Goals for Instruction	• Possess a deep understanding of the subjects they teach.
Assessment Plan	• Demonstrate teaching skills resulting in high levels of achievement. • Use a variety of assessment strategies to diagnose and respond to individual learning needs.
Design for Instruction	• Evidence a firm understanding of how students learn. • Demonstrate teaching skills resulting in high levels of achievement. • Create a positive learning environment. • Use a variety of assessment strategies to diagnose and respond to individual learning needs. • Demonstrate and integrate modern technology into the school curriculum.
Instructional Decision Making	• Instill a passion for learning in their students.
Analysis of Student Learning	• Use a variety of assessment strategies to diagnose and respond to individual learning needs.
Reflection and Self-Analysis	• Reflect on their practice to improve future teaching and student achievement. • Pursue professional growth in both content and pedagogy.

of this discussion will focus on the implementation of TWS in the elementary education teacher certification program and on how the data are gathered and the results used for program accreditation and continuous program improvement.

HOW TWS WAS ADOPTED IN
THE ELEMENTARY EDUCATION PROGRAM

Elementary education candidates are required to complete two TWS projects during their studies. The first is completed the semester immediately prior to internship, and the second is completed during the internship. During the semester prior to internship, candidates are involved in a course that has been constructed to reflect the seven processes of TWS. Through guided instruction during the initial weeks of the semester, candidates focus on the first three processes involved in the TWS; that is, contextual factors, learning goals, and design of an assessment plan. In addition, candidates engage in a ninety-hour clinical experience during which they are required to pre- and post-assess pupils, designing and carrying out instruction while data-gathering. Upon completion of the clinical experience, candidates return to campus and receive instruction on interpreting data gathered during and following instruction, and determining pedagogical implications of their data. By guiding TWS in this manner, candidates develop an understanding of the processes and challenges associated with developing standards-based instruction that is driven by assessment results, and they begin their personal journey on becoming assessment literate.

After completing the first TWS project, candidates are better prepared to work more independently during their internship semester. The results of the TWS project gathered prior to internship are used for the purposes of constructive feedback to candidates, for final review of the complete act of teaching, and as a portion of a course grade. That is, during the first semester, all data gathered about candidate performance are used as a formative assessment, and all data gathered about candidate performance during the internship are used as a summative assessment.

Pre- and post-data collected by candidates from these two experiences reveal that overall quality of teaching (as measured by student achievement) improves from preinternship to internship. Because we collect data of the pre-post testing by our candidates and because we assist them in an analysis of pupil gain scores, along with the practice of carefully aligning content to specific goals for instruction, the TWS data collected is considered a snapshot of teaching effectiveness. As such, these data are regularly used to monitor candidate progress and improve program and candidate effectiveness. Improvement in overall quality of the TWS projects from first to second submission is an indicator that candidates begin to develop habits of mind characterized by greater focus on teaching and reflectivity. Another benefit to the candidates of programmatic use of TWS is that assessment becomes easier, and analysis of student learning becomes more thoughtful. We view this as evidence that our candidates are becoming what Stiggens (1995) refers to as "craftsmen in assessment practices."

BECOMING CRAFTSMEN IN ASSESSMENT

One of the most challenging aspects of becoming an effective teacher is to become literate in assessment (Stiggens, 1995). In order to maximize student learning, teachers must not only think about the results of their students' learning outcomes, but they must also begin a unit of study with an understanding of students' prior knowledge and end with an understanding of their own instructional effectiveness and student achievement. Good assessment leads to these results. Because assessment is interwoven throughout the framework of TWS, candidates develop the necessary concepts needed to become knowledgeable in assessment practices and to use assessment effectively with instruction.

A key assessment skill candidates learn by completing the TWS at CCU is pre- and post-assessment of students' content knowledge. By identifying the goals for instruction and then pre-assessing their students relative to their intended critical learning, candidates learn to identify areas of content that require increased instructional intensity. By post-assessing, candidates also learn how well their students succeeded in meeting learning outcomes and how well they as teachers planned for effective instruction.

MOVING FROM TWS TO TWSM:
GOING THROUGH THE BACK DOOR

The initial implementation of the TWS project at our institution was clearly for the purpose of meeting the needs of accreditation. However, as we engaged in TWS for the past three years, faculty of the elementary education program have reached a much deeper understanding of the methodology that the TWS "project" embraced. Analyzing the accomplishments of their candidates has led to a climate change within the faculty characterized by increased focus on data-driven instruction and program changes, heightened awareness of the importance of including assessment within and throughout the curriculum, and more importantly an emphasis on making visible the complexity of documenting candidate effectiveness on student learning.

The elementary faculty has since developed and redesigned curriculum based on program needs discovered through the use of TWS. For instance, in order to better prepare candidates in understanding assessment, an assessment course is now offered earlier in the program and tied with a field-based student learning assignment. Program syllabi better reflect the theories that underlie effective teaching and learning. Increased field experiences prior to internship have evolved, providing candidates with more opportunities to practice planning, assessing, analyzing, and reflecting on how best to improve the learning gains of children under their care. It was by analyzing the data collected by TWS that faculty began to understand the importance of embracing Teacher Work Sample *Methodology* within their program and with how they reflect on their own teaching practices.

TWSM was brought to our campus as a vehicle to gather data to show that our candidates are competent, caring, qualified, and effective in the classroom. Initially brought for accreditation purposes, we used the data collected to meet a number of national standards for elementary teachers and to show that our candidates can apply professional and pedagogical knowledge and skills to facilitate learning. It was by way of using a "project" that we tied our curriculum tighter to the current research base, and we, as faculty, learned that having our candidates focus on how they impact the students they teach provides us with a better understanding of how well our candidates meet our programmatic candidate learning outcomes. It is because of the influence of this project on our program that our methods have changed and we are moving toward embracing TWSM. We acknowledge the importance of teaching our candidates to engage in analyzing children's learning and to focus not only on how well they design and teach their lessons but on how well their pupils learn from their teaching.

REFERENCES

Darling-Hammond, L., & Bransford, J. (Ed.). (2005). *Preparing teachers for a changing world*. San Francisco, CA: Jossey-Bass.

Girod, G. (Ed.). (2002). *Connecting teaching and learning: A handbook for teacher educators on Teacher Work Sample Methodology*. Washington, DC: AACTE Publications.

National Commission on Teaching and America's Future. (1996). *What matters most: Teaching for America's future*. New York: Author.

National Commission on Teaching and America's Future. (2003). *No dream denied: A pledge to America's children*. Washington, D.C.: Author.

National Council for Accreditation of Teacher Educators. (2002). *Professional standards for the accreditation of schools, colleges, and departments of education.* Washington, D.C.: NCATE.

Schalock, H. D., & Myton, D. (2002). Connecting teaching and learning: An introduction to Teacher Work Sample Methodology. In G. Girod (Ed.), *Connecting teaching and learning: A handbook for teacher educators on Teacher Work Sample Methodology* (pp. 23–24). Washington, DC: AACTE Publications.

3

The Development, Implementation, and Institutionalization of the Renaissance Teacher Work Sample Model

Roger Pankratz

ABOUT THE RENAISSANCE PARTNERSHIP FOR IMPROVING TEACHER QUALITY

The eleven universities that formed the Renaissance Partnership for Improving Teacher Quality were members of the "Renaissance Group," a larger consortium of about thirty teacher preparation colleges and universities across the country that together produce nearly one of every nine classroom teachers in America. The presidents, provosts, deans, and teacher education directors of Renaissance Group institutions have been meeting semiannually since 1987 to share and encourage productive university strategies that produce quality teachers. Representatives of the eleven institutions that comprise the Renaissance Partnership had been meeting for about two years before Title II funding to design plans to become more accountable for the impact of teacher graduates on P–12 students' learning. Thus, the focus and communication structures among these eleven institutions began more than two years before the beginning of the five-year-funded Title II Teacher Quality Enhancement grant.

The "Renaissance Partnership" consisted of eleven universities and their partner schools directly involved in a five-year Title II Teacher Quality Enhancement Project which began in October 1999 and was completed in October 2005. The partner schools included the following:

1. California State University, Fresno
2. Eastern Michigan University
3. Emporia State University

4. Idaho State University
5. Kentucky State University
6. Longwood University, Virginia
7. Middle Tennessee State University
8. Millersville University, Pennsylvania
9. Southeast Missouri State University
10. University of Northern Iowa
11. Western Kentucky University

HOW IT ALL BEGAN

Beginning in 1999, the Title II Teacher Quality Enhancement Partnership Program provided a unique opportunity for eleven Renaissance Group institutions to advance their quest "to become accountable for the impact of their teacher graduates on P–12 student learning." However, the seeds for this focused effort were planted two years earlier in 1997 when deans, provosts, and presidents from about twenty Renaissance Group universities met in San Antonio for their tenth annual fall meeting. The theme of the conference was accountability as university administrators from mainstream teacher preparation institutions met to discuss how they might address new demands by accrediting agencies and state government to account for the performance of their teacher graduates.

By the late 1990s, public schools across the nation were feeling the pressures of accountability for student achievement and were making new demands on colleges and universities that prepared their teachers regarding the graduates they were sending to classrooms in their schools. At the same time, the National Council for the Accreditation of Teacher Education (NCATE) was drafting new standards that would begin in the year 2000. These new expectations would require accredited members to show how they were preparing new teachers to impact student learning, and to provide evidence that their graduates were able to facilitate the learning of all students.

At a meeting of education deans, one of the members questioned the purpose of the meeting and asked, "Why are we here?" After considerable silence, a newcomer and teacher education faculty member said that, being an interloper, he really had no idea about the purpose of their meeting, but if the deans were looking for a new challenge, he had a timely suggestion to offer: "Collect, analyze, and report data on the impact of teacher graduates on P–12 student learning, and people will begin to turn their heads at Renaissance Group institutions." The suggestion was received about as well as navy admirals would take to the suggestion that we should boil the oceans to expel all enemy submarines. However, becoming accountable for the impact of graduates on the students they teach sounded very noble. And university presidents especially liked it as a sound bite they might use to promote their institution.

In spite of the immediate shock of such an impossible task, discussion about the idea continued, and two initiatives were agreed to at the San Antonio meeting: (1) assessment experts from interested institutions would begin working at subsequent semiannual Renaissance Group meetings to frame a strategy for linking the performance of graduates to P–12 student learning, and (2) a study was commissioned to investigate the potential in member institutions to collect achievement data on P–12 students taught by teachers they prepared. In both the 1998 spring and 1998 fall meetings of the Renaissance Group, representative faculty with expertise in assessment met to consider ideas and strategies for better ways to assess teacher candidate performance, especially with respect to evidence that graduates can facilitate learning of all students. Del Schalock from Western Oregon University (WOU) was one of the invited speakers to share the potential of Teacher Work Samples, a concept he had been developing over the past decade. Also, during the 1998 year, a ten-institution study was conducted that revealed two startling facts: (1) the Renaissance Group's best teacher preparation institutions used instructional time teaching methods compared to assessment of student learning at a ratio of about 7 to 1, and (2) none of the ten institutions had a performance assessment and data management system that included the quality components specified by the new NCATE 2000 standards.

All assessment representatives from the ten Renaissance Group institutions that met over the next two years agreed that a lot more should be done to develop performance assessment and data management systems, but funding for any development at the local level simply did not exist. When the assessment group met in Las Vegas in 1998, the participants reached consensus that obtaining financial support for development programs would be absolutely essential if programs of accountability were to become a reality.

By the spring of 1999, two actions were initiated that became the foundation for a five-year development effort toward performance accountability. *First,* a concept paper entitled "Becoming Accountable for the Impact of Graduates on Students and Schools: Making Operational the Shift from Teaching to Learning" was presented at the annual meeting of the American Association of Colleges for Teacher Education in February of 1999 (Pankratz, 1999). This discussion document expanded on proposals by (Barr & Tagg, 1995) that we change our focus from teaching to producing student learning. While teaching was important, it had to produce learning and had to relate to results. This basic concept was applied to teacher preparation. Also, the concept paper presented new strategies that might be considered to focus teacher preparation programs on P–12 learning. Among innovations suggested was the use of Teacher Work Samples that had been developed at Western Oregon University (Schalock, Schalock, & Girod, 1997). Another strategy that was proposed by the author was the development of accountability systems to collect, measure, analyze, and report teacher performance and achievement data on P–12 students taught.

The *second* important initiative taken by the Renaissance Group in the spring of 1999 was the development of a proposal submitted to the Title II Teacher Quality Enhancement Partnership Program. The request for proposals of the partnership program aligned with the goals of the Renaissance Group's quest for accountability for P–12 student learning. The partnership program required partnering with arts and science faculties and school practitioners with the end results being enhanced teacher quality and improved student learning. From its inception, the Renaissance Group consortium supported strong collaboration with the arts and sciences and with public schools to develop quality teacher preparation programs. The Title II Partnership Program offered an increased opportunity for them to support strategies of collaboration between teacher educators, arts and science faculty, and school practitioners with a focus on improving P–12 student learning. Title II also provided support for teacher preparation institutions to demonstrate accountability for the performance of their teacher graduates.

A preliminary proposal was submitted to the Title II Teacher Quality Enhancement Partnership Program in March 1999. The proposed concepts were accepted, and a full proposal was submitted in June of that year. The Renaissance Grant proposal involved ten universities and their partner schools and presented a five-year plan to (1) become accountable for the impact of teacher candidates and graduates on P–12 student learning and (2) improve teacher performance in key areas and show an increase in teachers' ability to facilitate learning of all students. The proposal also presented a work plan for six project objectives that all institutions would address:

1. Develop an accountability system that regularly collects and reports data on the impact of their graduates on student learning.
2. Use Teacher Work Samples in their teacher education programs as a means of improving teaching skills and increasing the teacher's impact on student learning.
3. Implement a team mentoring model consisting of school practitioners, arts and science faculty, and teacher educators that facilitates the ability of teachers to impact student learning in partner schools.
4. Establish dynamic partnerships with businesses that provide learning opportunities for teacher candidates and/or students in partner schools.

5. Build an electronic network among all Renaissance institutions and partner schools to share information, materials, ideas, and data related to improvement of teacher quality and student learning.
6. Design and conduct research programs that link teacher performance to P–12 student learning.

The Renaissance Group proposal was approved, and a U.S. Department of Education grant of $5,730,011 supplemented with $3,573,921 of nonfederal funds was awarded in September 1999. Western Kentucky University was the grantee, with subcontracts to nine partnership universities.

Thus, on October 1, 1999, the Renaissance Partnership for Improving Teacher Quality officially began as a five-year development effort. Idaho State University, the eleventh institution, was added to the partnership in the third year of the project.

BUILDING A PARTNERSHIP TO ACHIEVE PROJECT GOALS AND DEVELOP INSTITUTIONAL PROGRAMS

Forming a partnership of individual entities assumes that a collaborative endeavor and a collective effort can achieve more than operating independently. This certainly was the position of the Title II Partnership Program with respect to colleges of education, colleges of arts and sciences, and partner elementary/secondary schools. While this three-way collaboration effort was a focus of the Renaissance Partnership, it was multiplied by ten across universities preparing about eight thousand teachers each year in ten states. Building a dynamic and functional program of teacher preparation reform among many different entities with different basic purposes spread across the country was a most important but difficult challenge. This diversity of entities separated by distances also became a real strength of innovative synergy responsible for project successes.

Early Struggles to Get a Focus

While the six project objectives together framed a clear project vision to the developers of the proposal, they were little more than professional platitudes to teacher educators, arts and science faculty, and school practitioners across eleven project sites that were expected to implement the project work plan. Getting "buy in" to a project vision and activities by different groups in different geographical areas, each with their own agenda, was a real challenge. In this project, commitment to accountability systems, use of Teacher Work Samples, and team mentoring was especially difficult because there were few operating models to examine and emulate.

Even though all Renaissance partner institutions were accredited by NCATE, none had systems of performance assessment, data management, and program evaluation that operationally met the new NCATE standards. And, what was even more discouraging, a search for operational models at NCATE institutions across the country that truly met Standard 2, "Program Evaluation," came up empty.

A similar scenario was experienced with Teacher Work Samples. Although Western Oregon University had developed and used Teacher Work Samples for the greater part of a decade, the processes and materials used locally among faculty at this institution were not directly transportable to Renaissance partners, especially for universities such as California State–Fresno and Eastern Michigan, which each prepared nearly two thousand teachers per year.

The same challenge emerged when project leaders began to explore the potential of team mentoring of teacher candidates that involved teacher educators, arts and science faculty, and school practitioners. While the professional literature is abundant with descriptions of mentoring programs, processes, and models, involving three different professional role groups in a collaborative enterprise was an innovative concept that had to be developed from ground zero in the project.

Year one of the project started off with great enthusiasm. However, a lot of time was spent groping around for understanding of what we were all about, the direction in which we needed to move, and, most importantly, a clear vision of project objectives.

The proposal spelled out three activity leadership groups with project representatives from each of the eleven sites: assessment coordinators, Teacher Work Sample coordinators, and mentoring coordinators. The chief liaison at each site was a designated institution coordinator responsible for all operations and budgets connected with the Title II project at each of the eleven universities.

Most of the activities of the first year were directed at Teacher Work Samples. Several Western Oregon University faculty were employed as consultants to share their ideas and experiences. Site representatives traveled to Western Oregon to review Teacher Work Sample materials and talk to teacher candidates about their perceptions. Most importantly, Renaissance Project leaders were able to question Western Oregon faculty about processes and practices of using work samples as exhibits of performance assessment tools for developing critical processes that facilitate student learning. Renaissance Partnership faculty wanted to learn about the potential of Teacher Work Samples to provide evidence that candidates and graduates can produce learning in the students they teach.

Based on these initial interactions with Western Oregon faculty, task-force groups began to develop their own Renaissance Partnership processes for Teacher Work Samples, including candidate performance tasks (prompts) and scoring guides (rubrics) that best met the needs of Renaissance partner project sites. While Western Oregon had provided the basic theory and conceptual framework for Teacher Work Samples, Renaissance Partnership members needed to develop standards of performance for teaching processes they believed were most important and instrumentation (Teacher Work Sample prompts and rubrics) they "collectively owned" and understood.

The first year of the project produced some rocky beginnings. Assessment Coordinators met in St. Louis to set parameters of measurement and key indicators of performances for Teacher Work Sample prompts and rubrics. At times the debate over issues such as what constitutes evidence of P–12 learning, what teacher performances were most important, and the format of instrumentation became quite heated. While a visitor to the discussions might have perceived chaos, reflecting back on those early meetings it was clear they were the essential interactions between project representatives from eleven sites that were needed to build a strong partnership.

In the spring of 2000, a project task force met with consultants who had worked on performance assessments for the National Board of Professional Teaching Standards to develop the initial draft of a "Renaissance Partnership Teacher Work Sample." The first prompts and rubrics were completed by May, and training of Teacher Work Sample coordinators and mentoring coordinators from the eleven project sites was conducted in the summer of 2000. Fall of 2000 became the maiden voyage for the Renaissance Teacher Work Sample Model. The waters were treacherous at most project sites, and on a number of occasions the ship ran aground. Only the strong leadership and persistence of a site coordinator and the mutual support of partnership colleagues prevented those first drafts of teacher samples from becoming permanently beached. In early drafts, the directions to teacher candidates in the work sample prompts were unclear, the terminology used in the prompt and rubric were ambiguous and inconsistent, and the expectations of teacher candidates with respect to what comprised the work sample exhibit they submitted needed some structure. The fall 2000 year ended with a number of site coordinators having real doubts about the potential of Teacher Work Samples, wondering if a really good candidate exhibit existed, and, most of all, questioning whether their decision to become a participant in the Renaissance Partnership had been ill advised.

St. Louis 2001: Gateway to Partnership Progress

Assessment coordinators, Teacher Work Sample coordinators, and mentoring coordinators convened in St. Louis in January 2001 for a three-

and-a-half-day work session. Sites that had piloted the first draft of the Renaissance Teacher Work Sample Model brought teacher candidate exhibits to score. Most also brought war stories of teacher candidate frustration with the work sample task and back-home faculty resistance to the idea of work samples. But several coordinators came to St. Louis with stories of real successes and exhibits of outstanding candidate performances. The published purpose of the January work session was to review progress, revise the work sample prompt and rubric, and plan for the second semester of Teacher Work Sample implementation in spring of 2001. Stephanie Salzman and Peter Denner from Idaho State University who had developed and piloted their own model of Teacher Work Samples at their institution were employed as facilitators for the St. Louis session.

The work session exemplified the concept of synergy. The right people were in the right place at the right time, and partners from eleven institutions accomplished far more collectively than any delegation from each of the individual project sites could have done separately. The failures and successes from the fall semester of 2000 were used as learning experiences. Standards for the seven teaching processes of the Teacher Work Sample were agreed to and clarified. The original teaching tasks, candidate prompts, and scoring rubric were reworked, reformatted, and revised. Teacher educators, arts and science faculty, and school practitioners from different project sites worked as professional colleagues in teams. Arts and science faculty brought a clearer content focus to K–12 learning, and school practitioners provided a reality base that was needed. Everyone pushed toward a single goal: the creation of a user-friendly set of Teacher Work Sample performance tasks and a scoring rubric that could provide credible evidence of a teacher candidate's ability to plan, teach, and report the learning results of a standards-based instructional unit.

The teacher educators, arts and science faculty, and school practitioners who came to St. Louis in January 2001 worked long and hard for more than three days and most said they left feeling professionally rewarded and that progress had been made. All left with a set of Teacher Work Sample materials they had helped to develop, which were much improved and more likely to produce results with teacher candidates. Their understanding of standards-based teaching and learning had grown, professional ownership in Teacher Work Samples had increased, and confidence in the power of the partnership process was established.

Project site leaders who were part of the January 2001 experience look back and see this event as a significant turning point in the Renaissance Partnership toward real progress and synergistic productivity. That high level of energy, camaraderie, and professionalism continued throughout the project.

SEMIANNUAL PARTNERSHIP WORK SESSIONS: A DRIVING FORCE TO IMPLEMENTATION OF KEY PROJECT INITIATIVES

The January 2001 work session by project teacher educators, arts and science faculty, and school practitioners from the eleven partner sites established the structure and work standard for the remaining four years of the Title II project. After that first 2001 event, sixty to seventy coordinators, faculty, and school practitioners from partner sites in ten states convened in St. Louis twice each year for three days of program development, sharing experiences, networking, and production of training and support materials. These intense three-day work sessions held on a Wednesday, Thursday, and Friday of mid-January and June were the driving force of partnership support that enabled the project to exceed its original goals and achieve the results that will be described later in this chapter. Key issues and concerns about project initiatives were brought to the semiannual meetings and were addressed as a partnership effort.

These semiannual group events in the year 2001 focused on the development and refinement of the Renaissance Teacher Work Sample model. In the year 2002, work sessions were used to establish validity and scorer reliability of Teacher Work Samples and to share successful practices from each of the eleven project sites. In 2003 and 2004, efforts were directed toward training and support materials contained in three manuals that include (1) "how-to" processes for designing performance assessments and establishing credibility of assessment instruments, (2) assessment tools for teachers and teacher candidates in the design and teaching of standards-based units, and (3) mentoring processes and practices that have been found to work and produce high performance in teacher candidates.

In the sixth and final year of the Title II grant, support performance assessment and accountability systems were developed, Teacher Work Samples were introduced to focus everyone's attention on P–12 student learning, mentoring processes were designed to significantly improve teacher candidate performance, and courses were tested and experiences that prepare teachers at eleven universities were redesigned and in some cases recreated. In our final project year, we implemented strategies to institutionalize the innovations and initiatives we had introduced and developed.

In looking back at the project strategies that have enabled the partnership to achieve its goals and objectives, most project leaders would rank the value of our St. Louis work sessions high. First, the partnership work sessions served as our primary vehicle for communicating expectations of the project work plan. Every work session began with an update of progress relative to the project goal and seven objectives, as well as the activities designed to achieve the objectives. Every three-day session ended with back-home planning to see what was developed or learned at each local project site. Second, the St. Louis events were a catalyst for communication and networking. There were times where professionals made connections to other people, ideas, and resources that could be followed up electronically back home. In addition, work sessions were occasions where both successes and concerns about project implementation were shared and discussed. The synergy of these events gave key project representatives a broader perspective that they were a valued part of teacher preparation and quality reform across the nation and that they were not alone in their quest to impact teaching and learning. A third recognized benefit of the St. Louis work sessions was the opportunity to assemble the best minds and talents of professionals from eleven universities and partner schools at one location for three days to design and develop reform strategies. The successes of the "Renaissance Teacher Work Sample Standards, Prompt, and Scoring Rubric" document is a prime example of where sixty-six heads were better than six and the whole was more than the sum of its parts. Coordinators from the eleven project sites have often commented about the role that St. Louis work sessions have played in the development of the Renaissance Partnership.

The Renaissance Teacher Work Sample

The Renaissance Teacher Work Sample package consists of performance outcomes, teaching tasks, and prompts and scoring rubrics for seven teaching processes that partner institutions believed were critical to a teacher candidate's ability to produce P–12 student learning. These are as follows:

1. use of student and classroom context to design instruction;
2. development of instructional unit goals aligned with local and state content standards;
3. development of a unit assessment plan that includes pre-, post-, and formative evaluation with adaptations for special-needs students;
4. development of instructional strategies that are aligned with the teaching context, unit goals, and assessments;
5. use of formative assessments to guide instructional decision making;
6. analysis and presentation learning results for a unit of instruction; and
7. reflection and evaluation of teaching and learning.

The teaching exhibits produced by candidates that addressed the seven processes were to be no more than twenty pages plus charts and graphs. See appendix B for the Renaissance Teacher Work Sample. While several universities developed modifications to meet their program needs, the seven teaching processes were generally common among Renaissance partners.

Supplemental to the "basic" Renaissance Teacher Work Sample package, the partnership developed the following documents as well:

1. Renaissance Teacher Work Sample Scoring Guide
2. Manual for Mentors: Coaching Candidates through Teacher Work Samples
3. Manual for Teacher Candidates: Tips for Preparing Teacher Work Samples
4. "How-To" Manual for Teacher Educators Who Want to Collect, Use, and Report Valid and Reliable Data on Teacher Candidates with a Link to P–12 Learning

WHAT THE RENAISSANCE PARTNERSHIP ACCOMPLISHED OVER FIVE YEARS WITH THE TITLE II PROJECT SUPPORT

The Implementation Institutionalization and Dissemination of Teacher Work Sample Methodology

By the end of year two of the project (fall 2001), all eleven institutions were pilot testing the use of Teacher Work Samples. Only about 740 work samples were produced by student teachers during the 2001–2002 academic school year. However, in the 2003–2004 school year, the number of work samples produced had grown to more than 2,300. During the final year of the project (fall 2004-spring 2005), the eleven partner universities reported that more than 4,700 work samples had been produced by student teachers—directly impacting the learning of 117,000 P–12 students. Also, by the close of the project, ten of the eleven universities were requiring Teacher Work Samples of all student teachers.

Based on leadership from the Renaissance Partnership Project, state standards boards of Kentucky, Kansas, and Oklahoma now require all new teachers in their respective states to produce Teacher Work Samples and demonstrate their ability to impact student learning as a requirement for initial certification. Also, over the six years of the Partnership Project, more than twenty-five separate research studies were conducted; more than one hundred workshops and presentations were provided by project personnel; more than seventy professional presentations were made at state, regional, and national meetings; and more than fifteen newsletters and professional journal articles were published resulting from project initiatives.

Mentoring of Teacher Candidates

A second objective of the Partnership Project was to develop mentoring programs that would assist candidates in achieving high levels of performance
on Teacher Work Samples. As mentioned earlier, two mentoring manuals
were developed for both student teachers and mentors that provided exemplars of "good" performance, suggestions for designing instruction and
analyses, and protocols for mentor-candidate coaching and instruction.
Over the six years of the project, 224 arts and science faculty, 560 teacher
educators, and 3,580 school practitioners were trained to mentor teacher
candidates in developing work sample teaching exhibits.

Program Revision and Improvement

As a product of introducing and using Teacher Work Samples, a number of
key concepts essential for addressing the seven teaching processes needed
to be incorporated and/or strengthened in preparation programs. Examples
include use of context to design instruction, high-quality classroom assessments, and strategies to analyze and report student learning to a variety
of audiences. By the close of the project in 2005, faculty from the eleven
universities collectively reported that 191 teacher preparation courses had
been significantly revised to better address one or more of the seven teaching processes of Renaissance work samples.

Institution Performance Accountability Systems

In preparation for the Renaissance Partnership Project, it was found that
none of the eleven universities had developed a comprehensive performance
data management and accountability system. Thus, comprehensive institution data management systems to enable teacher preparation programs to
analyze candidate performance, report performance results, and provide
useful information for program improvement was also a major objective of
the Renaissance Partnership. Early in the project, five critical elements of a
comprehensive performance data management system were identified that
were to be operational by the end of the project. These were

1. unit-wide commitment to performance accountability,
2. employment of an accountability system coordinator;
3. an ongoing effort to develop and operate performance assessment
   systems for all programs,
4. a functional electronic data management system, and
5. a process for systematically using performance data for program improvement.

At the beginning of the project, the eleven partner institutions were only at the "beginning" or "developing" level for the above five critical elements. By the end of the project, all eleven institutions were at the "meets standard" level for university-wide commitment to performance accountability, an ongoing performance assessment system, and a process for program improvement. None of the eleven universities had employed an accountability coordinator or had operational data management systems.

Networking

Support for Teacher Work Samples, an accountability system, and mentoring development, as well as for program redesign, was facilitated by two key networking structures: the project website http://www.uni.edu.itq and seven semiannual three-day work sessions over the life of the project.

The project website provided information specific to project operations and information specific to each project initiative, as well as training resources for downloading. Essential program materials and training manuals that were developed remained on the website for anyone to use after the project closed.

The semiannual work sessions for fifty to seventy project site representatives became the primary vehicle for program development and sharing of ideas across the institutions. Over the life of the project, more than two thousand professional person days were utilized for networking, professional development, and program improvement by key faculty and school practitioner representatives from each of the eleven project sites.

New Support Website

Financial support for maintenance of the above website ended in 2005 at the close of the Renaissance Partnership Project. In 2008, former members of the partnership decided to form a new support system for continued development and networking called the Renaissance Teacher Work Sample Consortium (RTWSC). Western Kentucky agreed to take over the maintenance of a new website http://edtech.wku.edu/rtwc. All Renaissance Teacher Work Sample protocols, training materials, TWS exemplars, and publications were transferred from the old to the new website with plans to greatly expand the contents and invite new members to join the consortium.

RESULTS OF A THIRD-PARTY EVALUATION RELATIVE TO RENAISSANCE PARTNERSHIP IMPLEMENTATION AND INSTITUTIONALIZATION OF TEACHER WORK SAMPLES

Implementation and Institutionalization of Teacher Work Samples

In the fall of 2002, the Renaissance Partnership contracted with AEL of Charleston, West Virginia to conduct an independent evaluation of the eleven-site Title II Project. AEL conducted the evaluation over a one-year period from August 2001 to August 2002. A multimethod research approach suggested by Brewer and Hunter (1989) was employed to corroborate data from different stakeholders to address evaluation questions. Data sources included in-depth interviews with presidents, provosts, and deans of the eleven universities as well as completed surveys from institution coordinators, assessment coordinators, Teacher Work Sample coordinators, institution faculty, project school practitioners, and student teachers who completed Teacher Work Samples.

At the end of the third year of the project, AEL reported the following findings:

1. The Teacher Work Sample project objective was "clearly the most advanced and the mentoring objective was met to a high degree." To some extent, the project objectives for accountability systems, course revisions, and networking have been achieved showing marked differences across institutions.
2. "Across program objectives there is a strong leadership component, faculty commitment, and buy-in and collaboration both within and across institutions." For Teacher Work Samples, respondents note that it is of professional interest, it is not too expensive to implement, and it improves service delivery. As a result, faculty are more interested and willing to complete activities pertaining to this objective (Cowley, Finch, & Meehan, 2003, p. 58).

Key recommendations for greater effectiveness and project productivity based on the findings of AEL included the following: (1) full implementation of Teacher Work Samples, (2) expand mentoring programs for higher performance, (3) initiate and conduct more research studies that link teacher performance to student achievement, (4) accelerate progress on data management systems, (5) fully integrate project initiatives into each university's culture, and (6) seek continued funding for key initiatives and research (Cowley et al., 2003, pp. 62–68).

In 2004, the Renaissance Partnership again contracted with AEL of Charleston, West Virginia, to conduct a second independent evaluation.

In this study, researchers were to determine the extent to which Teacher Work Sample Methodology was being institutionalized in teacher preparation programs and what factors and/or activities had most contributed to the adoption of work samples as a tool for performance assessment and instruction. Four project sites in Virginia, Kentucky, Kansas, and Iowa were selected for a qualitative in-depth study. AEL staff conducted four two-day visits to each site. Each visit included semistructured interviews with multiple project role groups having involvement with Teacher Work Samples. Group interview sessions included eighteen university administrators and project coordinators, seventy-nine university faculty, eighty-five teacher candidates and recent graduates, and twenty-seven cooperating K–12 teachers.

With respect to the progress of Teacher Work Sample Methodology at the four universities, researchers concluded the following:

> The concept of teacher work samples as both a process and a product has become firmly embedded in the culture of each of the four universities. At present, all students in the teacher education programs at three of the universities are required to complete at least one teacher work sample; at the fourth university, work samples will become mandatory for all student teachers by fall 2005, though most student teachers are already inserting this requirement. Further, all four universities have added a condensed or modified teacher work sample requirement as a precursor to the full-blown TWS activity during student teaching. In addition, one university mentioned incorporating the TWS into several graduate programs. Underlying these developments are the successes of each university in reshaping curriculum, laying a solid foundation to support TWS in the future, and obtaining a "critical mass" of faculty willing to be trained to include TWS in their courses. The concept of TWS seems to have been fully integrated into the unique environment of each university. (Cowley, Voelkel, & Finch, 2005, p. vi.)

With respect to factors contributing most to Teacher Work Sample development, researchers from AEL (Cowley et al., 2005) concluded that:

1. In all four project sites, a strong commitment by university leadership backed the effort of involved individuals (p. vi).
2. The "right individuals were identified to form a stable core for shaping and shepherding the burgeoning effort. This nuclear group was firmly committed, enthusiastic, respected, and able to bring others 'on board'" (p. vi).
3. There was a provision of awareness and training opportunities for various stakeholders at all four universities (p. vii).
4. At two institutions, university-wide faculty councils were instrumental in making TWS mandatory for all student teachers (p. vii).

5. The contribution of Teacher Work Samples to other initiatives and mandates (e.g., NCATE, state teacher standards) supported work sample development at all four universities (p. vii).

THE CONTRIBUTION OF THE RENAISSANCE PARTNERSHIP AND TEACHER WORK SAMPLES FROM THE PERSPECTIVE OF DEANS AND PROJECT SITE COORDINATORS

At the Fall 2004 Renaissance Group Conference, a panel of education deans and site coordinators from five project universities gave their views about the Renaissance Partnership and Teacher Work Samples to an audience of seventy-five presidents, provosts, and deans by responding to three questions. The deans' and coordinators' comments are summarized below:

Most Significant Reforms and Improvements

1. The full implementation of a valid and reliable assessment system to evaluate candidate performance and program effectiveness
2. Teacher Work Samples as a major assessment to document candidate performance
3. Involvement of teacher educators, arts and science faculty, and school practitioners in the development of a teacher performance assessment that focuses on P–12 learning
4. The grassroots, "bottom-up" development of Teacher Work Samples

Most Helpful Project Activities

1. Faculty in-depth discourse about the seven teaching processes of Teacher Work Samples
2. Formal and informal opportunities to share successes and consensus in an honest way to solve problems with partner universities
3. Collaboration between teacher educators, school practitioners, and administrators in defining a common base and essential skills for teachers
4. The fertilization of research, innovation, change, and group problem solving that occurs during the collaborative effort of a partnership
5. The semiannual Renaissance Partnership work sessions
6. Faculty forum events where Teacher Work Samples were displayed and discussed
7. Communication between assessment personnel and faculty with regard to Teacher Work Sample data

What Was Learned

1. Bringing together colleagues with different areas of expertise and perspectives but who share a common mission of preparing teachers can positively impact P–12 learning.
2. Diversity is strength: each university added to the whole with respect to materials, time, and ideas.
3. Pooling of talent and mutual support has strengthened institutional accountability and capacity for leadership to impact P–12 learning.
4. Meeting in a "neutral" place away from campuses resulted in relationship building that contributes to the success to meeting project goals.
5. The scale of what can be accomplished is exponentially increased through a partnership (e.g., development of programs, materials, presentations, credibility studies).

An Analysis, Reflection, and Conclusion by the Renaissance Project Director

As a thirty-five-year veteran of writing proposals for federally funded projects and directing development programs in teacher preparation, I have always tended to promise more than I could deliver and expect more than can reasonably be achieved over the life of a project. However, I can truthfully say that with the Renaissance Partnership for Improving Teacher Quality, we came nearer achieving, and in some cases exceeding, the objectives of any project I have directed. I attribute the higher level of success in this project to five key factors.

Use of Sound Concepts and Strategies

The relentless focus on P–12 student learning of content, the seven teaching processes that comprise the Teacher Work Sample, focused mentoring for higher performance, partnering between teacher educators, arts and science faculty, and school practitioners, and accountability for performance all represent concepts and processes that have a strong conceptual base and are supported by standards-based teaching and learning across the nation. In other words, the project was designed to advance teacher quality initiatives that had a high probability of working. In the case of Teacher Work Samples, the strategy has certainly exceeded everyone's expectations.

Development of User-friendly Materials

The development, revision, and wide distribution of the "Renaissance Teacher Work Sample Standards, Prompt, and Rubric" document and the "Renaissance Teacher Work Sample Scoring Guide" has been key to communicating the seven teaching processes to teacher candidates, teacher educators, arts and science faculty, and school practitioners. All were on the project website for anyone to download along with about thirty candidate-produced Teacher Work Samples. This effort was purposeful based on previous research on adoption of educational initiatives and I believe a primary factor in the growing, widespread use of Teacher Work Samples (Hall & Hord, 1987).

Availability of Outstanding Professional Talent

The teacher educators, arts and science faculty, and school practitioners who were leaders at each of the eleven project sites, and especially those sent to the work sessions in St. Louis, were the most talented, hardworking, and professional group I have had the privilege of working with in my educational career. They truly were the top performers from each project site, and working together became a powerful force for development and implementation of project initiatives.

A History of Collaboration among Renaissance Group Institutions

The ten years of collaboration, communication, and interaction between presidents, provosts, and deans prior to the startup of this project gave the Renaissance Partnership for Improving Teacher Quality a real advantage over any other partnership that formed only in 1999. Also, the fact that I, as director, had worked with most of the deans and some of the provosts of the eleven institutions prior to the Title II project was a plus.

Learning from Past Experiences

The common saying "You learn from past experience" was very much the case in the Renaissance Partnership. Since the late 1960s, I have had the opportunity to direct Head Start training projects, Teacher Corps projects, Career Ladder projects, school reform projects, and research. Consequently, I have had the opportunity to make a lot of mistakes and to learn from mistakes and successes. My professional contribution to this project as its director had a lot to do with the rich set of experiences that have come my way and the competent mentors I was privileged to interact with over the past thirty-five years.

A CONCLUDING COMMENT

Over the past four years, I have been privileged to be part of a community of learners that I believe is making a difference in how teachers are prepared and mentored. Also, it has been my good fortune to have had the support of the U.S. Department of Education and eleven universities and their partner schools to pursue a passion to improve learning for all children. The documented accomplishments of this project and reports from hundreds of professionals who are using ideas and resources developed by the Renaissance Partnership are gratifying. However, achievement of the primary goal of the Renaissance Partnership—to show accountability for the impact of teacher graduates on the students they teach—is just beginning to surface. While we have some evidence that teacher graduates have the skills and abilities to produce learning, years of teaching and learning coupled with data collection and analysis will be required to fully realize the fruits of our efforts in this project. Toward this goal, we must remain diligent.

REFERENCES

Barr, R. B., & Tagg, J. (1995, November/December). From teaching to learning: A new paradigm for undergraduate education. *Change, 26*(7), 13–25.

Brewer, J., & Hunter, A. (1989). *Multimethod research: A synthesis of styles.* Newbury Park, CA: Sage Publications.

Cowley, K. S., Finch, N .L., & Meehan, M. L. (2003). *Formative evaluation of the Title II Renaissance Partnership for Improving Teacher Quality Project.* Charleston, WV: Appalachia Educational Laboratory.

Cowley, K. S., Voelkel, S., & Finch, N. L. (2005, May). *Teacher Work Samples and accountability systems: An in-depth study of successful implementation at four universities participating in the Title II Renaissance Partnership for Improving Teacher Quality Project.* Charleston, WV: Appalachia Education Laboratory.

Hall, G. E., & Hord, S. M. (1987). *Change in schools: Facilitating the process.* New York: State University of New York Press.

Pankratz, R. S. (1999*). Improving teacher quality through partnerships that connect teacher performance to student learning.* Unpublished manuscript, Western Kentucky University.

Schalock, H. D., Schalock, M., & Girod, G. (1997). Teacher Work Sample Methodology as used at Western Oregon State College. In J. McMillan (Ed.), *Grading teachers, grading schools: Is student achievement a valid evaluation measure?* (pp. 15–45). Thousand Oaks, CA: Corwin Press.

4

Preparing Principals to Use the Teacher Work Sample in Their Schools

Victoria L. Robinson

After thirty-eight years as a high school teacher, principal, teacher educator, and associate professor of educational leadership, I have come to understand what Elbert Hubbard meant when he said, "A teacher is one who makes two ideas grow where only one grew before." Over the past ten years, the idea of using a Teacher Work Sample (TWS) as a summative assessment for teacher candidates grew into a reality at many teacher preparation institutions.

The TWS is a performance-based narrative written by teacher candidates that provides documentation of their ability to increase student learning. Directed by guidelines and informed by standards-based rubrics, teacher candidates describe the teaching and learning process for a three-to-four-week unit of instruction. Teacher candidates describe, analyze, and reflect on seven teaching processes: contextual factors, learning goals, assessment plan, design for instruction, instructional decision making, analysis of student learning, and self-evaluation.

The success of the TWS idea led me to wonder if a second idea, using the TWS as a learning tool in a principal preparation program, would enhance the original idea. In addition, it would contribute to a deeper understanding of curriculum, instruction, and assessment for future principals. This chapter will describe how the TWS is now part of the curriculum and learning opportunities for principal candidates at the University of Northern Iowa. The rationale for using the TWS, the instructional design incorporating the TWS, and candidate learning and reactions will be reported.

Walking many miles in the shoes of a teacher, principal, teacher educator, and associate professor of educational leadership has shaped my understanding of the similarities and differences in the preparation and roles of teachers and principals. As displayed in table 4.1, principals are prepared to do what teachers do but on a much larger scale that impacts multiple generations. Principals need a deep understanding of the teaching and learning process that connects curriculum, instruction, and assessment in order to ensure that this connection is made in all classrooms.

As my idea to use the TWS as a learning tool in the principal program developed, I realized that principals and future principals may be unaware of how teacher preparation programs prepare teachers to connect curriculum, instruction, and assessment. How might principals learn about how the TWS has benefited our teacher graduates if I neglect to introduce the TWS to them? How will they know to ask to review a teacher candidate's TWS during an interview if they don't even know such a document exists?

Thus, my early stage of using the TWS in the principal preparation program was an attempt to inform principals about new expectations of teacher graduates. I wanted to close a communication gap between P–12 schools and higher education. However, this early stage which was focused on communication about the TWS eventually moved beyond an introduction to actual TWS engagement by principal candidates. There are four major reasons why I believed principal candidates needed to be engaged with the TWS process.

RATIONALE FOR USING THE TEACHER
WORK SAMPLE IN PRINCIPAL PREPARATION

Seamless Transition from University to P–12 School

Teacher preparation is under much scrutiny and is criticized for a disconnect between what is taught at the university and what is needed at the P–12 level. A better connection and articulation between teacher preparation and P–12 schools needs to be developed. One instrument that serves this purpose is the TWS. If principals learn more about the TWS, then they can obtain some insights into what teacher candidates and novice teachers know and are able to do. If university faculty read TWS, then they can better understand how to revise the curriculum to fit the needs of the P–12 schools. The great divide between the ivory tower and the real world of P–12 schools can be narrowed with this exchange of insights revealed in the TWS.

As more teacher candidates from teacher preparations institutions are required to successfully complete a TWS, principals need to understand the product and the habit of mind and practice the process develops. If the

Table 4.1. Comparison between teacher preparation and principal preparation

Teacher Preparation	Principal Preparation
Standards-based	Standards-based
Focused on leading learning in classroom	Focused on leading learning in building
Elementary or secondary content specific	P–12
Pedagogy emphasis	Leadership emphasis
Management of classroom	Management of building
Supervision and evaluation of students	Supervision and evaluation of students and adults
Data-driven instructional decisions	Data-driven program decisions
Establish a learning community in classroom	Establish a learning community throughout the building
Apply age-appropriate instruction and feedback in classroom	Apply adult learning theory in professional development, mentoring and coaching

habit of mind and practice developed in writing a TWS is not reinforced or validated by the principal, a novice teacher might conclude that linking the seven teaching processes is unimportant. Much of what is learned through writing the TWS needs to be recognized by principals and used as a base in coaching a novice teacher. Just like a science or math curriculum needs to be articulated from grades PK to 12, likewise, teacher preparation curriculum and experiences needs to be articulated from teacher preparation to the first years of teaching experience. The role of principal is instrumental in assisting novice teachers to make a smooth and connected transition from university preparation to the classroom.

Principal as Instructional Leader

A second rationale for incorporating the TWS into the principal preparation program focuses on the role of principal as instructional leader. All principals in our state are evaluated according to the Iowa Standards for School Leaders. The second of these six standards identifies the principal's responsibilities in promoting the culture of learning. Several of this standard's criteria specifically address teaching and learning. These criteria specify that a principal do the following:

- Provide leadership, encouragement, opportunities, and structure for staff to continually design more effective teaching and learning experiences for all students.
- Monitor and evaluate the effectiveness of curriculum, instruction, and assessment.

- Evaluate staff and provide ongoing coaching for improvement.
- Ensure staff members have professional development that directly enhances their performance and improves student learning.

Our program is committed to incorporating authentic and relevant experiences that develop principals who will meet the standards. The TWS documents include the authentic voice of future teachers as they describe, analyze, and reflect on curriculum, instruction, and assessment. When scorers read a TWS, they begin to see the need for clarification, realignment, or reinforcement in the work of the novice teacher. This provides rich, authentic material that should be used by principal candidates to practice the development of coaching questions and enhance the professional development design for teachers of any grade or subject area.

Principals in Iowa earn a P–12 license. A former elementary teacher might become a middle school principal, or a former high school teacher might become an elementary principal. Therefore, principal candidates must have exposure to all levels of teaching and learning. The TWS is written by future teachers from all grade levels and subject areas. Scorers of the TWS have reported that reading the TWS from multiple subject areas and grade levels increases their understanding of P–12 curriculum, instruction, assessment, and unique challenges. Reading and analyzing the TWS offers principals the same opportunity to gain insights into all P–12 levels of teaching and learning.

Teacher Evaluation

The third rationale for incorporating the TWS in the principalship program includes the principal's role in teacher evaluation. Teachers in Iowa undergo comprehensive evaluations completed by their building principals. The evaluations are framed by the Iowa Teaching Standards. The Iowa Teaching Standards and the teaching processes included in the TWS coincide in purpose and scope. Both the Iowa Teaching Standards and the TWS processes require teachers to implement standards, demonstrate content knowledge, differentiate instruction, use multiple assessments, demonstrate competence in planning instruction, and engage in professional growth.

As principal candidates begin the transition from a teacher who was evaluated to a principal who evaluates, they must acquire a deep understanding of standards-based assessment of teacher performance. Principals must clearly communicate to their teachers what constitutes the differences between not meeting standards, progressing, proficient, or exemplary. Standards-based teacher evaluation has moved beyond one annual classroom observation. Multiple formal and informal teacher observations now accompany pre- and post–conferences, along with an extensive review of multiple sources and artifacts.

Multiple sources and artifacts include samples of student work and assessments, documented standards-based instruction, evidence of differentiated learning, response to community and the school's unique environment, analysis of achievement data, reflective dialogue, and a professional development plan. According to Reeves (2004), exemplary school leaders regularly engage in professional practices. Such practices include evaluating student work through collaborative scoring sessions in which the percentage agreement by the faculty is measured and posted or by reviewing faculty-created assessments as part of each teacher's evaluation and coaching meeting (p. 50). Exemplary practices also include an awareness of what teachers ask their students to do. Principals must expect the required student activities to be connected with goals, instructional design, assessment, and individual student needs.

The TWS provides a mechanism for principal candidates to become more familiar with standards-based assessment as they read these authentic documents. The rubrics describe performances that define and reflect the levels of reaching the standards. Likewise, the TWS paints a specific picture of what students are doing and includes artifacts of their work and assessments. Principal candidates can gain insights on how well student activity connects with curriculum, instruction, and assessment outcomes. This aids principals in crucial conversations with teachers, allowing teachers to develop and grow through guided reflection.

Reflective Practice

The final rationale for incorporating the TWS in the principal program addresses the transformation from superficial teacher feedback and conversation to an emphasis on deep reflection by teachers, colleagues, and administrators. Many novice teachers need assistance in developing their disposition to reflect and question their practice focused on student learning. Principals as instructional leaders must coach novice teachers to stretch their thinking about teaching and learning.

Our principal program did not provide candidates with authentic experiences that allowed them insights into how novice teachers think about teaching and learning. Principals do develop these insights through years of experience; however, while principals gain experience, the potential to help develop reflective practice is delayed. Principals must hit the ground running! The last section of the TWS includes reflection and self-evaluation. These samples offer principal candidates case after case of how novices reflect, and they offer future principals opportunities to consider how they will coach and how they will identify the questions they need to ask.

INSTRUCTIONAL DESIGN INCORPORATING
THE TEACHER WORK SAMPLE

The idea to engage principal candidates in the TWS emerged during TWS scoring sessions at our university. Each semester, over 250 Teacher Work Samples are scored on campus by faculty and supervising teachers. Supervising teachers often commented to me during parking lot or hallway conversations on how much teaching and learning insight they gained from reading and scoring the TWS. They praised the authentic nature of the TWS, its focus on student learning and data, and its use of a common language, rubrics, and reflections.

Supervising teachers also identified how necessary it was for all seven processes to be connected. One principal candidate who had served as a supervising teacher said to me, "Finally we have a picture of what is being taught, how it is taught, why it is being taught and how it is assessed." That statement remained with me for several semesters and framed the revision of a required three-hour course for principal candidates: Curriculum, Instruction, and Assessment.

Revising Curriculum, Instruction, and Assessment

The first step in the redesign of this course was to add the missing piece to the original course: assessment. Traditionally, the course had been listed in the course catalog as Curriculum and Instruction. In taking this issue to my department colleagues, they quickly agreed that assessment should be added to this course. Interestingly, they credited their involvement in TWS scoring as instrumental in their decision. By reading the TWS, they realized how important it is to have curriculum, instruction, and assessment connected. After completing a curriculum map, we also discovered that our principal preparation program included very little work in assessment. With my colleagues' blessing and feedback, I worked with our university's instructional designer to develop this all Web-based course.

All of our principal preparation courses are delivered through Web support and face to face either on campus or through interactive television, Iowa's Communication Network. Because of some unique scheduling issues for the first semester's delivery of this revised course, we needed to make it an all Web-based course. This seemed very foreign to me, and I was skeptical about the potential effectiveness of this venue. To my surprise, an all-Web delivery was extremely effective as evidenced by principal candidate feedback and the quality of work submitted. We have delivered this course five semesters as all Web-based to 116 principal candidates.

Coursework Description

The course is divided into five learning modules and is framed around what we teach, how we teach it, why we teach it, and how we know students have learned. The TWS prompt, rubrics, and mentor manual, plus actual Teacher Work Samples, serve as content resources for module 4. Similar to the first three modules, module 4 requires a culminating project, posted answers to instructor's questions, and dialogue with cohort class members. The time frame for module 4 is about four weeks during the semester and ten days during a summer session. The following presents the directions and expectations for principal candidates as they begin their TWS journey.

Module Overview

The title of this module, "Synthesis: Integration of What We've Learned," indicates to principal candidates that this module will link the previous modules by connecting curriculum, instruction, and assessment. The essential TWS teaching processes—contextual factors, learning goals, assessments, design of instruction, instructional decision making, analysis of student learning, and reflection—can only be effective when curriculum, instruction, and assessment are closely aligned.

In order for principal candidates to fully grasp the importance of this alignment, they read the prompt and mentor manual and become familiar with the rubrics. In addition, they read three TWSs found at www.uni.edu/coe/stdteach/. Combined with their individual reading, principal candidates post responses to focus questions, engage in Web discussions, and complete a project. My pledge to the principal candidates is that I will be online at least twice a day to answer their questions or comment on their responses. The module's three focus questions help prepare the students for their module 4 project.

Module 4, Question 1

Question 1 provides an introduction to the TWS prompt, rubric, and mentor manual. After students read these documents, they are directed to think about the description of the seven teaching processes, standards and indicators, how the rubric aligns with the prompt, and the scoring process. The TWS is standards-based and scored according to standard met (= 3), standard partially met (= 2), or standard not met (= 1). The analytical scoring rubric is used to provide feedback to teacher candidates. The overall TWS receives a 3, 2, or 1; each of the seven processes receives an overall score of 3, 2, or 1; and each indicator within the seven processes receives a 3, 2, or 1.

The scores for each indicator, or the seven processes, are not averaged to determine the overall score of the TWS. Scorer training includes benchmarking. Trainees holistically read Teacher Work Samples to determine what a 3 looks like, what a 2 looks like, and what a 1 looks like. This benchmarking and use of rubrics combined with professional judgment helps answer the essential question: Is this teacher candidate ready to become a novice teacher?

After reading and developing an understanding of the TWS prompt and rubrics, principal candidates read the mentor manual. The mentor manual helps principal candidates develop important coaching and mentoring skills. "Most new principals have little or no experience as supervisors or evaluators. It is an emotional leap to become comfortable establishing clear expectations of staff and then following through on them" (Bloom, Castagna, Moir, & Warren, 2005, p. 18). The TWS provides a foundation for principal candidates to begin their experience as instructional leader, supervisor, coach, and evaluator.

The following focus questions are intended to assist the principal candidates in thinking through their important role in the teaching and learning process. Each question asks students to respond to the questions in the "Discussions" page and respond to two of their cohort members' postings.

Module 4, Focus Question 1

(1) What is the purpose of the TWS? (2) Is it a product or a process? (3) How might writing a TWS help a teacher candidate, novice, or veteran teacher? (4) How might reading Teacher Work Samples help teacher educators, mentors, principals, or professional development consultants develop effective teachers?

Module 4, Focus Question 2

Principal candidates are directed to select and read a TWS available on the website. Elementary specialists are encouraged to read a secondary-level TWS, and secondary specialists an elementary-level TWS. As principal candidates read their selected TWS, they refer to the prompt and rubric with particular attention to how well the seven teaching processes of the TWS are connected.

> Did the author of the TWS link/connect the seven processes? If yes, briefly identify how the author connected the seven processes. If no, briefly identify how you knew the seven processes were not connected.

Module 4, Focus Question 3

Principal candidates may select from the website a TWS from any level or content area to read and score. They are reminded to also refer to the mentor manual. After they have scored a TWS, they are to imagine themselves sitting with the author of the TWS during a feedback and coaching session. Principal candidates are then to create a script on what they would say to the author about his or her TWS. They also develop questions to help the TWS writer to think more deeply and grow from this TWS experience.

Module 4 Project (Begin with the End in Mind)

The final project for module 4 asks principal candidates to score a TWS found on the website, justify the scores, and develop insights on what was learned about how teachers connect the seven processes. A scored rubric and a twelve-to-fifteen-paragraph paper organized as described below constitute the completed project.

Introduction: Provide the subject and grade level of the TWS and a brief overview of the contextual factors. Indicate the overall score awarded to the TWS (1, 2, or 3) and indicate any areas of special strength or concern noted while scoring the TWS.

Area 1: Reread the implications for instruction found in the last part of the "Contextual Factors" section. Describe evidence of how the writer connected the contextual factors to planning, implementing, assessing, decision making, and reflection. If little or no connection exists, suggest ways the writer could have made connections.

Area 2: How connected were the seven teaching processes? For example, were the goals actually measured in the assessments, was the instructional design in line with the goals, or were instructional decisions made based on the contextual factors? Specific examples should be given. If connections are weak, develop some coaching comments that would assist the writer's growth in this area.

Area 3: Focusing on the last two sections of the TWS, "Analysis of Student Learning" and "Reflection," analyze the writer's conclusions about student learning and reflection. Were the conclusions about student learning sound and based on reliable and valid data? What is the depth of reflection? Develop questions that would assist the writer in thinking more deeply.

Area 4: The final section asks principal candidates to identify their thoughts on the TWS as a product and a process. What are the benefits of the TWS? What are limits of the TWS? How might the use of the TWS be revised or expanded? How might principals get a glimpse into how teachers think and implement their lessons by reading a TWS? Might there be any use of the TWS with in-service teachers?

Conclusion: In the final paragraph, principal candidates are asked to address this last question. What do you now know and understand about linking the seven teaching processes, and how will this help you, the principal and instructional leader, as you work in the areas of curriculum, instruction, and assessment?

PRINCIPAL CANDIDATE LEARNING AND REACTIONS TO TWS

Principal candidates' responses to the three discussion questions and the final project have been very similar during the five semesters of the TWS inclusion in this course. The purpose of the three discussion questions was to introduce the TWS to the principal candidates and provide a discussion forum for their reactions. Often cohort members would express appreciation to other cohort members for posting insights they had not considered. The all-Web-based format allowed candidates a written record of thoughtful exchanges throughout the course. The final projects revealed the influence of this exchange and the benefit of the written record of discussions. The following offers a snapshot of the discussion quality and the voice of the principal candidates as they responded to the focus questions.

Examples of Principal Candidates' Discussion Postings

The examples of discussion postings listed below reflect how much the principal candidates appreciated their new learning about the TWS, their interpretation of the purpose of the TWS, and their thoughts on possible applications of the TWS beyond student teaching. These selected comments from hundreds of discussion postings during five semesters by 116 principal candidates reflect a consistent theme: the TWS is a valuable tool for educators.

- "My first impulse to this assignment was, 'Looks like another series of hoops.' Now I am thinking, 'Where has this been?' The TWS is a tool and guide for novice and experienced teachers to grow."
- "The TWS is an assessment and feedback tool that keeps educators focused on student learning."
- "The TWS allows teachers to articulate how they connect the seven learning processes and gives readers of the TWS insight into the teachers' thoughts and actions."
- "It serves two purposes: an evaluation product and a reflection process."
- "Many of us (in the postings) are advocating using the TWS for all teachers. The TWS could and should be a major part of every teacher's portfolio."
- "The TWS is a tool for implementing standards-based instruction, assessing and analyzing student learning, and eliciting teacher reflection and accountability."

- "Teachers and principals will benefit from using the TWS because it is a framework of what effective teachers do every day to impact student achievement."
- "Successful teachers make their decisions based on student learning and not their own desire. The TWS helps teachers stay student centered."
- "I think the TWS has many different purposes and can be used in many ways by teachers, mentors, teams, and principals."

Sharing thoughts and ideas about the TWS led principal candidates to develop applications of how they might use the TWS as a principal. The existence of one idea, using the TWS with student teachers, grew into multiple ideas as evidenced in the culminating project.

Application of Using TWS beyond Student Teaching

Final projects revealed what principal candidates learned about teaching and learning through their experiences with TWS as a product and a process. They addressed how teacher candidates struggled with connecting contextual factors to implications for instruction and often failed to identify strategies to overcome barriers to learning. Principal candidates saw firsthand the impact on learning when the seven teaching processes were not directly connected. The validity of the analysis of student learning and depth of reflection were also addressed by the principal candidates.

Principal candidates developed effective coaching questions they would ask teacher candidates. Most importantly, they began to think like principals who will be responsible for monitoring and evaluating teachers and ensuring the enhancement of teacher performance. Their thinking included using the TWS in various forms and for multiple purposes to fulfill these responsibilities. The following statements were selected from forty-six principal candidates' TWS projects. The TWS project included the assessment of a TWS, justification for the assessment scores, and an analysis of the TWS process. Principal candidates included thoughts on how the TWS could be used as a tool or framework in their role as instructional leader in their TWS project. They identified how useful the TWS would be as they coach teachers, evaluate them, and deliver professional development advice.

Coaching and Conversation with Teachers

- "I will make sure I include much discussion with teachers about the impact of contextual factors and how they must work to overcome barriers to learning."

- "Because what is inspected gets respected, I will informally review preassessments with teachers to ensure they don't assume student prior knowledge or bore students with curriculum they have already mastered."
- "Even if I can't expect teachers to take time to write a TWS yearly, I can at least keep the rubrics in front of teachers as I talk with them. The rubrics clearly identify expectations and standards."
- "I plan to keep the TWS prompt and rubric in my desk drawer and use it during preconferences as a frame for creating my questions to ask teachers during pre- and post-conferences."
- "My principal mantra will be: Remember to link the seven teaching processes!"

Teacher Evaluation and Supervision

- "If we expect teaching to be a true profession, then we should not apologize for asking teachers to document their expertise by writing a TWS yearly. The TWS is more authentic and rich compared to the portfolios we now require of teachers. The time to create a portfolio could be used to write a TWS, and it demonstrates the impact on student learning."
- "In addition to me giving feedback to teachers based on a written TWS every other year, think about how powerful it would be if teachers would read and discuss one another's work samples."
- "I am going to design a shortened version of the TWS for veteran teachers without so much narrative with templates for the seven processes. Teachers will still provide evidence of connecting them, impacting student learning, and reflecting. This will give us opportunities to discuss their practice."
- "The TWS must be used with teachers in need of assistance. The prompt gives a guide for struggling teachers and specifics for mentor guidance. I will keep the prompt and rubric for this purpose."
- "A modified TWS would be a useful evaluation tool because it reflects teaching at its best. It is practical and doesn't require teachers to create anything they don't normally do. Plus, it provides additional insights not gained during observations."

Professional Development

- "I plan to replicate the progression of learning we had in this class for professional development sessions. Teachers will eventually score the same TWS and engage in discussions about what they learned. We must talk more about actual teaching practice."

- "We will use actual work samples from the website during in-services. I will group teachers and have each group read the same TWS and score it. They will compare scores and discuss why they scored as they did. What a great way to engage teachers in real discussions about teaching, learning, and connecting the seven processes. This gets teachers thinking about what factors impact student learning."
- "I am planning to use a modified TWS as I work with teachers as they develop their coteaching model. I will develop a graphic organizer based on the TWS to be used jointly by the special education teacher and the general education teacher."
- "The TWS could be used in collaborative peer coaching during team meetings. This professional development can be documented and would provide evidence that professional development is linked directly to student learning."

Experiencing the TWS will help principal candidates in their future experience as instructional leaders. "Every experience must prepare the learner for a future experience" (Dewey, 1938, p. 47).

CONCLUSION

The use of the TWS in a principal program helps future instructional leaders better understand effective teaching; see the curriculum, instruction, and assessment connection; experience simulated coaching; and link professional development with actual teacher performance and needs. The course format allowed principal candidates to discover for themselves the potential of the TWS and create their own meaningful applications. The self-discovery and personal application provide an ownership of the learning. With this ownership comes a strong possibility that future principals will actually use some form of the TWS in their schools.

Hopefully, as principal candidates graduate and accept leadership positions, they will take the TWS with them into the schools. Where once the TWS was a hidden and untapped treasure, it will be highly visible and an effective tool used in multiple ways by many principals. I thank Del Schalock for his dedicated contributions in developing one idea that has now grown into many. He was a great teacher.

REFERENCES

Bloom, G., Castagna, C., Moir, E., & Warren, B. (2005). *Blended coaching: Skills and strategies to support principal development.* Thousand Oaks, CA: Corwin Press.

Dewey, J. (1938). *Experience and education: The 60th anniversary edition.* West Lafayette, IN: Kappa Delta Pi, 1998.

Reeves, D. B. (2004). Assessing educational leaders. Thousand Oaks, CA: Corwin Press.

5

Connecting Teaching and Learning

Teacher Work Samples in a University-School Partnership Context

Karen S. Wetherill and Diane S. Calhoun

As you have read in previous chapters, the Teacher Work Sample Methodology has been applied in many contexts. This chapter will describe the application of this methodology in a multifaceted and what we believe is a systemic approach that engages the school of education faculty and candidates with school partners to determine the impact of teaching on students' learning. Not only does the partnership afford the scaffold development of new teachers' proficiencies, but it also creates a learning community structure that challenges and supports the continued development of established educators.

THE CONTEXT AND HISTORY WITH TEACHER WORK SAMPLES

The Watson School of Education at the University of North Carolina, Wilmington, (UNCW) is known for its partnerships, technological applications for education, and our longstanding work with evidence-based teacher education. Located on the coast of southeastern North Carolina, the university is committed to supporting the region, and within that capacity educators from across the campus work closely with school districts and schools in the region. The Watson School of Education believes in the power of partnerships! The commitment to form alliances with P–12 education, businesses, and state and national professional organizations has resulted in an exponential growth in our capacity to improve our programs, to offer services to our stakeholders and community, and to inform colleagues in education and related interdisciplinary fields.

Building and sustaining candidate and career educator capacity to impact student learning through a systemic approach has been a determined focus for the Watson School of Education's well-established university-school partnerships. The pilot with two school districts, which began in 1989, was focused on building relationships with individual schools and selected teachers. The success of the inquiry-focused partnership work at that time with a small number of student teachers (called teacher interns), faculty, and elementary teachers was recognized as a better way to ensure that candidates were prepared for their beginning years. It also became an ethical issue, with nonparticipating candidates expressing concerns and strong arguments about why their preparation did not have what was seen as a higher-quality experience. An external evaluation and faculty-led self-study resulted in the decision across all programs that many of the model's features, policies, and practices be incorporated across the entire School of Education. The consensus was that the partnership must move to a much more systemic model of formal relationships established with school districts and the university as a whole versus with individual programs and schools. Therefore, in 1993 the Professional Development System University-School Partnership was established with formal three-year agreements negotiated, signed by school and university leadership (superintendents, school board chairs, the dean, and chancellor), and celebrated with ten school districts across all of southeastern North Carolina. This collaborative alliance between the Watson School of Education and P–12 partners in southeastern North Carolina has grown to over 123 elementary, middle, and high schools in thirteen school districts, two charter schools, and two early college high schools.

With a primary UNCW goal being to "strengthen regional engagement," the Watson School of Education is well situated with long-term, healthy relationships with school districts across the region. These districts reflect the span of demographics, needs, and locations that educators may encounter in their career. Some districts are more urban, while others are rural; some have more financial resources, while others have high poverty levels; some have relatively stable teacher and student populations, while some have highly transient populations and special needs impacted by military base proximity; and some have already encountered dramatic shifts in population demographics, while others are preparing for future impact.

Many university-school partnerships have come and gone across the nation; however, the UNCW partnership has flourished and has expanded to focus far beyond what the early designers had envisioned. Certainly strong relationships were built and sustained, and our collaborative work has become more than building a community of educators engaged in producing effective teachers and administrators. As the partnership matured, energies needed early on to establish relationships, processes, policies, and procedures became less all-consuming. This opened the door for the School of Education and the partnership to focus on our number-one partnership goal—to improve the lives, learning, and opportunities for all students.

COLLABORATIVELY PREPARING AND SUSTAINING QUALITY PROFESSIONALS THROUGH UNIVERSITY-SCHOOL PARTNERSHIPS

Schools and schools of education must engage in assessing the impact of teaching on student outcomes, be it at the preservice or the in-service level (Rivers & Sanders, 2002; Schalock, Schalock, & Ayers, 2006). Many schools of education have recognized the need to establish partnerships with P–12 schools. If the partnership model has not been adopted as of yet, the changes in accreditation standards have provided an even greater impetus for moving to collaborative university-school partnerships in order to provide evidence that links candidates' teaching with P–12 student learning outcomes (NCATE Standard 2).

On the other hand, school partners face the pressure under state accountability programs and the federal legislation of No Child Left Behind to show continuous progress toward helping all students succeed at high levels and to successfully serve an increasingly diverse student body within the challenge of a significant teacher and administrator shortage. Within the reality of high-stakes accountability, school system partners must link all related activities directly to results for students.

In both instances, partnership schools and schools of education are equally obligated to focus on student learning. As was encountered in many university-school partnerships, we were compelled to establish evidence that documented our program quality; our candidate qualifications and impact on student learning in the classrooms; and the outcomes of intentional programs and approaches for preparing and retaining new teachers and improving the quality of career educators. This substantially raised the bar of the partnership, and specific assessment components that link teaching performance to student learning were critical.

Application of the Methodology

The tools of Teacher Work Sampling Methodology (TWSM) have been instrumental in the development of an adapted model that ensures teacher candidates and career teachers have the knowledge and skills necessary to make data-driven instructional decisions to improve student learning (Schalock et al., 2006). For instance, the intentional processes of TWSM, the instructionally linked measures, the resulting evidences, the scoring processes used that require interns to examine the impact of their teaching on the learning of students through pre- and post-testing, and then the subsequent analysis of results across the subgroups of No Child Left Behind have resulted in a greater articulated awareness and accountability for responsive instructional decisions. The use of formative assessment to guide learning as it occurs can be very effective in improving learning for the teacher and the students. Rick Stiggins (2005) cites extensive research that substantiates the power of the effective use of "classroom assessment to support student learning" (p. 67). These processes have proven to be powerful models for shaping the authentic engagement of professional learning community members and are opportunities for embedded supervision by school leaders. This allows them to view evidences of learning and afford support for teachers to ensure a positive effect on student learning.

THE TEACHING AND LEARNING CONNECTION: TEAM-BASED ASSESSMENT TO IMPROVE EDUCATIONAL QUALITY

Teaching is one of the most complex human endeavors imaginable. Costa and Garmston (2002), in their book *Cognitive Coaching: A Foundation for Renaissance Schools*, point out that teachers who work at higher conceptual levels are capable of higher degrees of complexity in the classroom and are more effective with students. Teachers with higher conceptual levels take into account the learners' frame of reference within their own frame of reference for planning, instruction, teaching, and evaluation. The critical dispositions and capacity for assuming multiple perspectives, using a variety of coping strategies, and utilizing a greater variety of teaching methods can be developed through reflection and intentional collegial interactions. To further link this to improvement in schools, Judith Warren Little (1999) states that in high-performing schools, collaboration is the norm. Teacher membership in a learning community was found to be strongly related to student learning as compared to other control groups. Schools are complex organizations where few opportunities exist for building professional relationships based on shared understandings, mutual trust, relevant goals, and collective assessment. Schmoker (2006) asserts, "We don't commonly see teaching, followed by assessment, then adjustment to practice on the basis of assessment results" (p. 24). We have worked hard to integrate this thinking in our model of team-based assessment.

During the past eight years, the Watson School of Education has conducted research on the implementation of a professional development model that includes specifically focused face-to-face sessions, online collaboration, and an innovative cohort-based community of learners. Creating intentional structures for educators to openly expose their thinking and validate their ideas and concerns is a powerful environment for improving performance in any enterprise.

The Power of Higher-Order Instructional Dispositions

Intentionally, a learning-centered (versus learner-centered) model of supervision and coaching was designed in the early years of the partnership to very specifically focus on reflective practice and inquiry, providing the challenge and opportunity for all teachers (in-service and preservice) to understand their own teaching and its impact on student learning in their classrooms. Key components are based on the belief that highly competent professionals recognize that effective teaching requires continuous self-evaluation and reflection, rather than simply a set of techniques to be mastered and applied. They view themselves as learners and as teachers who are accountable for the learning of their students.

NCATE has helped expose the critical need for schools of education to become increasingly sophisticated in examining teacher dispositions and the role of teacher education in shaping them (Sockett, 2006). Believing that there are attributes essential for professional teaching, a model and framework developed at the Watson School of Education, as shown in figure 5.1, has been used to inform the structured environments, processes, and requirements related to the teacher preparation and professional development program of the partnership (Calhoun, 2006).

This framework that is grounded in research and practitioner knowledge was designed to ensure that teacher candidates and career teachers have the knowledge, ability, and dispositions necessary to make data-driven instructional decisions to improve student learning. The higher-order instructional dispositions and the aligned best practices include the following:

- *Recognizing the strengths of metacognition*: Novice teachers are not just involved in teaching as they begin their careers; they also are involved in their own learning about many of the techniques and strategies it takes to be an effective teacher. Mentoring partnership teachers and university supervisors in this program help foster independent learning by encouraging metacognitive thinking as they coach interns to help provide them with tools that take them forward as professionals. Key dispositions that are developed using metacognition are *self-reflection* and *self-regulation*. These can be made visible before teaching through developing the plan of teaching, during teaching through the maintenance and monitoring of the teaching plan, and after teaching through evaluating the process and outcomes (Costa & Garmston, 2002).
- *Using dialogue to reveal "invisible" cognitive skills*: Trained partnership teachers and university supervisors use dialogue to lead candidates

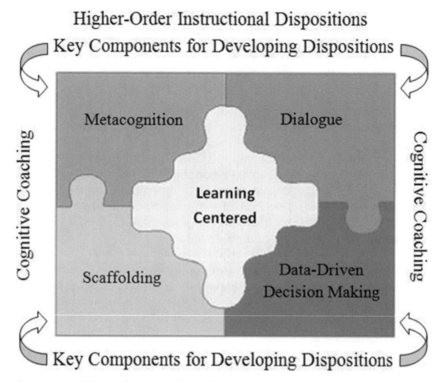

Figure 5.1.　Higher-order instructional dispositions.

through planning, reflection, and decision making, helping both interns and themselves become more aware of their own insights and learning (Lieberman, 1996). Dialogue is key to having learners *hear* their own thinking and begin to make explicit their ideas and beliefs that are the foundation of their behaviors. Asking the right questions is vital for effective coaching that guides the learner through the meta-cognitive thinking that will enhance their teaching and self-reflection (Costa & Garmston, 2002).

- *Scaffolding cognitive maps to refine instructional choices and behaviors*: Using the cycles of clinical supervision (Acheson & Gall, 1992) and the cognitive coaching approach (Costa & Garmston, 2002) results in the development and refinement of cognitive maps. The *planning conference* allows the interns to talk about their thinking and decisions about teaching a lesson and explore a variety of implementation possibilities. The *observation and data collection* process requires the intern to focus on a specific aspect of his or her teaching for the purpose of growth relative to or in terms of placing emphasis on student achievement.

The *reflective conference* helps scaffold and promote teacher reflection by asking questions that will lead to self-regulation and analysis of the lesson and learning based on the data collected. It also helps the candidate to consider how the application of the new insights can be applied to future lessons. This is the critical transformation stage that is necessary to ensure that a teacher's instructional decisions consistently impact student learning.

* *Using data to inform instructional decisions*: Highly competent teachers utilize data from both within and outside their classroom to inform their practices. As inquirers, teachers are always observing and gathering information about their teaching and student learning. Since the data used in the coaching cycle have been requested by the intern, he or she has a much greater sense of ownership for learning, critical analysis, and reflection, leading to more effective instructional decisions and improving student learning (Parsons, 2002).

Combining the tools of using data along with well-designed formats for dialogue and reflective practice create a powerful learning-centered environment.

The Power of Intentional Systemic Processes

Using carefully planned, embedded structures that develop higher-order instructional dispositions has ensured that both new and career educators are engaged in individual and collaborative analysis of teaching and impacts on student learning. The intentional processes of self-assessment and inquiry have been applied in the context of intern, partnership teacher, and university supervisor collaborative efforts. The goal of the supervision model to focus on teaching outcomes is supported through three intentional structured components: (1) site-based seminars or study groups for the cohorts of interns, partnership teachers, school administrators, and university supervisors; (2) the eight to ten reflective coaching cycles focused on building what we call higher-order instructional dispositions in candidates that include objective collection, analysis, and synthesis of data; and (3) the required *Assessment Data Analysis Project* which documents the impact of teaching on student learning. Accountability for improving student learning is realized, modeled, and accepted through such processes as the assessment project. The application of team-based assessment in the teacher preparation program engages the candidates in collecting pre- and post-assessment data and in generating an in-depth analysis of students' learning using the No Child Left Behind subgroups to plot performance. The significance of this and other components in the teacher preparation program is that the beneficial outcomes are not only realized by the intern, but also by the P–12 teacher. One partnership teacher shared the following:

> To me, learning-centered supervision is a way to help a teacher candidate reach their potential in teaching and also helped me reach mine. . . . It is a system to guide the intern and the mentor through strengths and weaknesses and allows for both parties to take an active role in improving themselves and impacting student learning.

The partnership has developed many structures that support the simultaneous learning of P–12 students, school-based faculty, Watson School of Education teacher candidates, and university faculty in an integrated and collaborative approach. The first structure of engaging in collective inquiry is during our internship experience conducted at the school sites and in biannual professional development daylong events for supervising educators. The site-based study-group approach is accomplished through our use of cohort placements and the required on-site seminars. Required weekly *Reflective Site Seminars* are held at each partnership site and are attended by teacher interns, supervising teachers, administrators, and university supervisors. This Reflective Site Seminar structure models professional dialogue, reflective practice, and inquiry focused on evidence of teaching outcomes as assessed by the improvement of student learning. Similarly, biannual *Partnership Conferences* provide a day for dialogue between supervising teachers who are hosting interns, school system administrators, and university faculty to address current educational issues and collect relevant feedback and data informing the practices of the model program and for program improvement. These collaborative approaches are based on the belief that the partnership must engage members in ongoing professional development and open communication and reflection in order to ensure and sustain continuous growth and improvement.

The second structured activity that focuses on inquiry and teaching-learning connections is accomplished through the use of coaching cycles for teacher interns. These cycles are formal and documented in a coaching plan and focus on making instructional decisions based on the objective collection, analysis, and synthesis of data to improve student learning. Recursive in nature, eight to ten formal coaching cycles used by both supervising teachers and university supervisors document and facilitate dialogue to lead interns through planning, reflection, and decision making, helping them become aware of their own insights and learning. Self-discovery is a process of reflection that is built into coaching as a learning disposition, reaching the intern on both an affective and a cognitive level. The coaching cycle is designed around having the supervising teacher use questioning strategies to guide the novice through metacognitive thinking, enhancing his or her teaching and self-reflection now and in the future. By asking the right questions, coaches lead interns through the type of planning, self–reflection, and self-regulation that highly competent teachers practice on a daily basis (Costa & Garmston, 2002). This verbal and written dialogue is a highly effective means of developing and documenting student and candidate learning because it provides a vehicle for candidates to analyze their own decisions about student learning and instruction. The coaching plan used in the weekly coaching cycles, in particular, provides the opportunity to sit with other educators (and alone) to gain some understanding of how students learn and the role of professional decision making and practice in promoting that learning. Both the electronic portfolio and coaching plans help the candidate capture and summarize ideas. The questions raised engage candidates in the critical process of ongoing inquiry necessary for graduates to improve learning in their classrooms.

The third structured activity specifically utilizes Teacher Work Sampling during the internship to engage candidates in the critical process of explicitly examining the impact of their teaching on their students, analyzed for individuals, subgroups, and the whole class. The classroom assessment project includes the following components:

- Classroom demographic data organized into NCLB subgroups
- Student learning impact across NCLB subgroups
- Articulated reflection on the results, reasons for the results, and implications for future teaching

As the interns and their teachers engage in discussions about the formative and summative assessment data, the intent is to further emphasize the critical question in regard to one's teaching, what occurred for the students? The accountability for improving student learning is instilled through analytical thinking about student performance using assessment strategies, analyzing the significance of the findings, and determining and implementing responses that improve the learning of all students in the classroom. This Assessment Data Analysis Project is completed and placed in the candidates' electronic portfolio utilizing Web-based tools. Included in the assessment data are lesson plans for the skills/knowledge taught, student assessment samples, class-assessment analysis graphs, and an in-depth analysis and reflection based on the results. One student stated in her reflection,

> The most important idea that I learned about assessment during my internship was the fact that assessment can be positive if the teacher makes it positive. I noticed that many teachers bombarded their students with paper-and-pencil tests and did not take the time to assess informally. Through firsthand experience, I recognized the importance of using a variety of assessment tools

and applying the results to future lesson planning. Without applying the results, the assessment is not useful.

This candidate's reflection demonstrates that through data collection, analysis, and reflection as applied in this model program, candidates' ability to improve understanding of P–12 pupil learning is positively impacted.

The Power of Evidence

As we consider Teacher Work Sampling, we have adopted a broad view with what we see as two tiers of engagement and analysis: (1) teacher interns' impact on student learning and (2) performance-based assessments that examine the cognitive engagement of interns, partnership teachers, and supervisors in the higher-order instructional dispositions. A comprehensive study was undertaken to assess the impact of the Watson School of Education's model on developing quality teachers that examined data related to these two tiers of Teacher Work Sampling. This study utilized three primary components yielding data on the impact of the model to explicitly connect teaching to student learning. Data were collected and analyzed from the interns' Teacher Work Sampling assessment components, the data from the Performance Evaluation Scale (a summative assessment tool) for teacher interns, and partnership teacher evaluation of the program.

The first source of data for evaluating the model program was the actual intern work products. Throughout the internship, candidates discuss, write, and compile documentation about P–12 student learning for their coaching plans and electronic portfolio. For the assessment of candidates' ability to improve P–12 student learning, we analyzed early childhood, elementary, middle school, and special education interns' Assessment Data Analysis Projects and their pre- and post-assessment analysis of students' performance growth using the No Child Left Behind subgroups. Data were collected through three years of random samplings and indicated the teacher interns' ability to analyze the results of their teaching on all populations in their classrooms, and even more importantly, the positive impact on student learning across these subgroups.

Aggregate data from the exit evaluations of interns were the second component and clearly documented candidate proficiency in the eleven INTASC-related categories depicted in the Watson School of Education's Performance Evaluation Scale. These data are collected at least four times during the final practicum experiences as a component of the formative and summative assessment process. Interns are asked to do a preinternship initial self-assessment; then interns, partnership teachers, and university supervisors each do a midterm formative assessment and a final summative performance assessment using the Performance Evaluation Scale and Rubric. Unitwide data across all program areas indicated that P–12 partnership teachers and university supervisors documented that candidates scored at or above 96 percent in all eleven categories.

The third source of data was obtained through a survey administered to partnership teachers regarding their assessment of the program components and their outcome related to improving candidates' ability to improve student learning. These showed a high correlation with the model and reinforced the marriage of learning-centered supervision and coaching approaches with continuous self-evaluation and structured Teacher Work Sampling.

We strongly believe that the link between P–12 learning and teacher preparation programs can be accomplished if one considers the opportunities across the continuum of teacher development. The main goals of this particular model were (1) to evaluate whether candidates could design and deliver appropriate and accurate assessments, (2) to provide opportunities for candidates and their supporting partnership teachers to evaluate and reflect on their ability to impact student learning, and 3) to require candidates to produce and analyze evidence of student learning as a result of their teaching. While this study reinforced our efforts, it also exposed additional areas for improvement. In keeping with the cyclical model of using data to assess the outcomes and to inform decisions, we will continue to refine and redefine the use of Teacher Work Sampling Methodology in the partnership context.

IMPLICATIONS, ISSUES, AND FUTURE OPPORTUNITIES

Schools and schools of education are in business to cause and promote learning. We must model what it means to be a learning organization that is not only a place where we expect students to learn but is one that engages learning at all levels. The Watson School of Education learning-centered model expects all partnership members to be professional learners and engage in "deep, broad study of the learning they are charged to cause" (Wiggins & McTighe, 2006).

Establishing the evidence base for teacher preparation is a primary need for programs around the country. As teacher education is under increasing scrutiny by accrediting bodies, the public, parents and caregivers, legislators, and state and federal agencies, we, as institutions that prepare educators, must strive to design effective systems to document candidate qualifications and program effectiveness. Future opportunities in teacher preparation programs must provide evidence of work with and impact upon public school students and educational improvements in P–12 settings.

REFERENCES

Acheson, K., & Gall, M. (1992). *Techniques in the clinical supervision of teachers: Preservice and inservice applications.* White Plains, NY: Longman.

Calhoun, D. (2006). *Evaluating the success of a professional development system: Assessing for improving P–12 student learning and higher-order instructional dispositions.* Paper and presentation at the annual Council of Professors of Instructional Supervision (COPIS) Conference, Gainesville, FL.

Costa, A., & Garmston, R. (2002). *Cognitive coaching: A foundation for renaissance schools second edition.* Norwood, MA: Christopher-Gordon Publishers.

Lieberman, A. (1996). Creating intentional learning communities. *Educational Leadership, 54*(3), 51–55.

Little, J. W. (1999). Organizing schools for teacher learning. In L. Darling-Hammond & G. Sykes (Eds.), *Teaching as the learning profession: Handbook of policy and practice.* San Francisco, CA: Jossey-Bass.

Parsons, B. (2002). *Evaluative inquiry: Using evaluation to promote student success.* Thousand Oaks, CA: Corwin Press.

Rivers, J., & Sanders, W. (2002). Teacher quality and equity in educational opportunity: Findings and policy implications. In L. Izumi and W. Evers (Eds.), *Teacher Quality* (pp. 13–23). Palo Alto, CA: Hoover Institution.

Schalock, H. D., Schalock, M. D., & Ayers, R. (2006). Scaling up research in teacher education: New demands on theory, measurement, and design. *Journal of Teacher Education, 57*(2), 102–119.

Schmoker, M. (2006). *Results NOW: How we can achieve unprecedented improvements in teaching and learning.* Alexandria, VA: ASCD.

Sockett, H. (2006). *Teacher dispositions: Building a teacher education framework of moral standards.* Washington, D.C.: AACTE Publications.

Stiggins, R. (2005). *Student-involved assessment FOR learning* (4th ed.). Lebanon, IN: Prentice Hall.

Wiggins, G., & McTighe, J. (2006). Examining the teaching life. *Educational Leadership, 63*(6), 26–29.

6

Practicing Connecting Teaching and Learning Using the *Cook School District* Simulation

Gerald R. Girod and Mark Girod

Gerald R. Girod and Mark Girod

WESTERN OREGON UNIVERSITY'S HISTORY WITH TEACHER WORK SAMPLING

Since the mid-1960s, Western Oregon University (WOU) has been a leader in the conceptualization and development of, first, competency-based teacher education and, later, Teacher Work Sampling (Girod, 2002). In the latter case, after establishing a scholarly framework for program redesign and the research and evaluation efforts to successfully embed work sampling into preparation programs, WOU turned its attention, in part, to the analysis of what was needed to educate teachers to work effectively in standards-based schools. Two principles became apparent.

First, teaching candidates to develop a work sample was not the most important outcome of a preparation program. The ultimate goal was to help prospective teachers learn to connect their teaching decisions to the learning progress exhibited by their students. That meant that not only did prospective teachers need to learn the components of a work sample, but they also needed to learn how to analyze the myriad data available to them regarding their planning and implementation decisions as well as information constantly being collected from students. Preparation program faculty needed not only to teach how to construct a Teacher Work Sample, but they also needed to help candidates learn to think like professional educators. That task of teaching candidates to analyze and reflect is one that required much from the faculty and from the program itself.

Second, expecting candidates to perform and think as professionals requires a different curriculum within a teacher education program.

83

While teaching candidates to connect teaching and learning, we expect them to

- analyze their teaching setting,
- plan to teach significant content or skills,
- implement with structure,
- engage and keep students on task,
- assess logically,
- analyze and reflect on performance with insight,
- adapt instruction as needed to account for all learners,
- select instructional and assessment strategies that are consistent with the content of one's unit and the scholarly research, and
- explain one's choices persuasively to students, parents, and colleagues.

It just isn't reasonable to expect candidates to learn all this without providing authentic practice opportunities that include structured feedback and skill-building opportunities.

To achieve those targets of (1) teaching candidates to connect teaching and learning and (2) providing practice and feedback around the skills necessary to make those connections, faculty at Western Oregon University devised a simulation called *Cook School District*. The *Cook* simulation is used to provide candidates with a practice setting to learn how to conceptually connect their teaching with student learning. This chapter discusses briefly the design, construction, and evaluation of the simulation. We also describe at the end of the chapter our goals for the future as well as lay out for readers how they might review *Cook School District* should they choose to do so.

What Is the *Cook* Simulation and How Do Candidates Use It?

Cook School District is a Web-based classroom simulation in which teacher candidates practice connecting their actions as teachers to the learning and engagement of all students. In the *Cook School District* simulation, candidate users choose a teaching assignment (grade and curriculum area) and then are assigned a randomly drawn set of students. Each student has an accompanying case history detailing the kinds of information that is likely available should the teacher inquire in the guidance or counselor's office (e.g., attendance record, health history, prior achievement record, information about home and family).

After candidates describe what and how they will teach their students, the simulation begins providing feedback on student achievement gains (or losses) and on-task behaviors. Student users can then adapt their goals and/or their instructional and assessment strategies to account for the simulated student performance. The more insightful the candidate is in aligning instruction and assessment to the students' needs, the more the simulated students will learn and the more frequently they will be on task. (An algorithm within the simulation portrays for users these relationships.) Teacher education faculty users have found that these sets of information provided by the simulation form the basis to begin helping candidates analyze and hypothesize about connections between their teaching and student learning.

Though the simulation can be used in many different ways, and with candidates across the range of teacher development (including practicing teachers and administrators), the following bullets highlight the full array of major features.

- As part of the initial contact with *Cook School District*, the users read about the community of Cookvale (the simulated school district), review exemplary work samples, and select or build a lesson plan or unit to use with the simulation.
- Users can select to teach third or ninth graders in any curriculum area in either general or special education.
- Users read the simulated students' case histories and comments from last year's teacher(s) about each student assigned to his or her classroom.
- Users select and describe the number of objectives they will teach. They also state how many class sessions they will need to accomplish their objectives.
- Users select instructional strategies for each of their sessions.
- At various points during the simulation, users are asked to explain their planning, implementation, and reflective decisions. Those explanations (as well as notes they may have chosen to write to themselves) are recorded for printing at the end of the simulation.
- Users design their preassessment, which can be as formal or informal as they choose.
- At any time after users select their objectives, they can adapt their plans, instruction, or assessments for one to four students or groups. They can even differentiate small-group instruction for activities such as lab groups or reading groups.
- After the design of the preassessment, the computer produces a table of results indicating how each P–12 student performed on each item or criterion of the simulated pretest.
- After reviewing the preassessments, if no adaptation is thought necessary, or once the needed adaptations have been made, users begin simulated teaching. On-task behaviors are reported for each of the simulated students for each instructional strategy users chose to use.

- Users are invited to design and administer a formative assessment at any time during the teaching phase, particularly if the number of students who are off task is judged to be too high.
- The formative assessment can be a replica of the pre- or post-assessment or as informal as a single item or even a set of question-and-answer recitations. Once a formative assessment is designed, it is administered, and the results are provided before the user returns to the teaching phase.
- If a user believes the formative assessment provided cues that instruction needs to be changed, the simulation allows the user to adapt the instructional strategies for one, a few, or all students.
- After users have completed the teaching phase, they are invited to provide a postassessment to their students. When they have designed and administered the assessment, the results are provided by the computer for each child and each test/performance item.
- As a final step, users can print copies of the decisions they made as well as the results tables for students' achievement and on-task behaviors.

In summary, the simulation was designed to provide teacher candidates an opportunity to practice the skills necessary to effectively connect the actions of their teaching to the learning of each student.

How Has the *Cook* Simulation Been Used?

To date, the *Cook* simulation has only been used by a small group of teacher preparation programs around the country, most significantly at Longwood University in Farmville, Virginia. At Longwood, teacher candidates use the simulation concurrently with an (1) educational technology course to consider issues of teaching and learning without the actual real-world demands of a classroom, and (2) with an assessment and evaluation class to analyze classroom learning data.

The faculty at Longwood found that early education students are often not confident or adept in classroom management and don't focus their attention on connecting teaching and learning. That doesn't surprise any veteran teacher educator. Allowing student users opportunities to practice connecting teaching and learning free from classroom management issues helps candidates to build confidence and skillfulness in a protected setting. No one, of course, is advocating that the *Cook* simulation be substituted for real-world practica, but when used together, early results from Longwood indicate a simulation such as *Cook School District* can provide a more effective professional preparation experience.

At Western Oregon University, use of the *Cook* simulation is sprinkled across several different courses and instructors who use the practice opportunities of the simulation to highlight key concepts, skills, and teaching demands that correspond to course issues. For example, as candidates early in their preparation programs learn about the community in which they will be student teaching, they work in the simulation to investigate and understand the effect of a wide variety of community, school, and individual student-level variables that may have an effect on teaching and learning. Just as understanding these factors helps candidates develop more effective lessons in the simulated setting, understanding their real-world corollaries helps them to maximize teaching and learning in the real world.

Evidence in Support of the Effectiveness of the *Cook* Simulation

A series of parallel evaluation studies were conducted to assess the efficacy of the *Cook* simulation to effect meaningful change in teacher candidate users (Girod & Girod, 2006, 2008). The outcomes of interest included ratings and associated data on candidate users' (1) perceived skillfulness in connecting teaching and learning, (2) valuing of the skills embedded in connecting teaching and learning, (3) Teacher Work Samples, (4) actual performance teaching in real settings, (5) perceptions of the value of the *Cook* simulation, and (6) descriptions of their own effectiveness in connecting teaching and learning in real classroom settings.

In each of the evaluation studies, an identical design was used, in that a portion of each cohort of master of arts in teaching students from Western Oregon University, a small, regional university, were asked to participate in use of the *Cook* simulation. Unfortunately, simulation use was not substituted for other teacher preparation experiences, so we are unable to account for the unique value added by the simulation, only that the additive effect suggested several advantages over that for nonusers. Again, more detail about the nature of the treatment experiences, the sample sizes and characteristics, and the analytic methods employed to arrive at the following assertions can be found in the sources cited previously. Major findings from each of the six treatment outcomes are described in the remainder of this segment.

Candidate perceptions of skillfulness in connecting teaching and learning. When responding to pre- and post-test surveys of one's own perceptions of skillfulness in each of eleven different skills thought necessary to connect teaching and learning, users of the *Cook* simulation reported statistically significantly higher perceptions of skillfulness for the total factor, with an ANCOVA p value of $< .0001$, $F(1, 70) = 56.99$. Individual items included responses to "I am skillful in my ability to . . ."

- make adaptations;
- align goals and objectives, instructional methods, and assessment strategies;

- assess student learning;
- increase student learning;
- deliver high-quality instruction;
- identify important content;
- gather important information about the context in which teaching and learning will occur;
- reflect on feedback from students and make adjustment during the course of the lesson or unit of instruction;
- articulate clear and compelling rationale for the decisions made in the classroom;
- reflect on multiple sources of evidence to inform future professional development goals; and
- monitor student engagement and modify instruction as appropriate.

Schalock and Myton (2002) identified the skills above as those in which highly skillful teachers are proficient, and, by proxy, are necessary to effectively connect teaching and learning.

Candidate perceptions of value of skills embedded in connecting teaching and learning. Administered at the same time as the pre- and post-test survey of perceptions of skillfulness, parallel value items were written for each of the skills identified above. For example, candidates were asked both before and after use of the *Cook* simulation about the degree to which they valued "making adaptations" as an important part of their job as a teacher. Though mean differences between pre- and post-administrations were not as far apart as for the perceived skillfulness items, the results were still statistically significantly different in favor of the experience of using the *Cook* simulation, resulting in an ANCOVA p value of $<.001$, $F(1, 70) = 11.23$.

Analysis of candidate performance on Teacher Work Samples. Interestingly, teacher candidate participants were required to complete two Teacher Work Samples during the course of their preparation programs, and the *Cook* simulation treatment was situated between the construction of these two performance assessments. Though ratings of the components of the Teacher Work Samples were completed by seven different raters, rater training was provided, and Cronbach's alpha for the total work samples scores was .88, suggesting fairly high internal consistency in ratings. When taken as a whole, the total work sample ratings assigned by supervisors were higher for *Cook* simulation users, demonstrating a p value of $<.05$, $F(1, 5) = 4.56$, when analyzed using ANCOVA.

Ratings of actual teaching performance in real settings. Also, as part of participants' regular teacher preparation program, extensive evaluations of real-world teaching performances were recorded. As with ratings of the work samples above, these evaluations were conducted by a variety of observers, though all were trained in observation techniques and use of the measures. Applying ANCOVA, *Cook* users were rated as performing significantly better on several factors including evidence of planning for instruction, establishing a classroom climate conducive to learning, and ability to evaluate pupil learning.

Perceptions of the value of the Cook *simulation as measured through user interviews.* Upon conclusion of the *Cook* simulation treatment, participants were interviewed regarding their experience using the simulation and the perceived effect on their real-world teaching practices. Interviews were recorded and transcribed, and, using a constant comparative method (Glaser & Strauss, 1967), the following categories of common responses were identified. First, simulation users claimed heightened attention to individual students. Participants claimed that the simulation helped them to quickly track the performance and engagement of each of the students in their simulated classrooms and that this experience encouraged them to strive for the same level of detail for each of their real-world students. Second, simulation users claimed increased understanding of the concept of alignment, a critical instructional issue in work sampling. Users described their efforts to align—not only goals and objectives—but also instructional strategies, assessment practices, and efforts to adapt instruction and materials for learner differences. Third, users described heightened awareness of the role of assessment in learning. Because formative assessment is easy to conduct in the *Cook* simulation, users became accustomed to administering formative tests to judge "in-flight" simulated student learning. In each case, participants speculated that these "refined sensitivities" would likely follow them to real-world practice, and it seems that real-world evaluations of teaching performance, described above, supports this suggestion.

Data from reflective writing found in completed Teacher Work Samples. As a final source of evidence, both treatment and control group participants' Teacher Work Samples were collected and analyzed for potential differences. Simply because of the sheer amount of evidence found in typical work samples, focus was placed on analysis of the reflective essays written at the conclusion of the work sample. Candidates were asked to reflect on their own effectiveness as classroom instructors in their efforts to connect teaching and learning and to consider their own near-term professional development needs as a result. As with the interview evidence described above, these data were coded and analyzed using a constant comparative approach, and the following five categories emerged, each favoring those who used the simulation:

- more sophisticated attention to issues of alignment across a wide variety of contextual factors and teacher actions and decisions,
- deeper concern and analysis of efforts to individualize instruction and/ or assessment to maximize the potential for learning for each student,

- deeper awareness of the teacher's role in affecting student learning including the limitations of teacher effort,
- more systematic reflection about one's own professional needs, and
- deeper reflection on other factors that may impact student learning including those within and beyond the purview of the teacher.

We interpreted the above to mean that simulation users became more introspective regarding their ability to influence pupil learning and behavior, more analytical in that they used a wider array of data to guide their decisions, and more committed to gathering information from their students to help guide their next instructional decisions. We saw those outcomes as worth the effort of teacher educators.

Next Steps for *Cook* and Information about Access and Use

As we completed the development, evaluation, and revision of *Cook School District*, it became apparent that these efforts should be expanded into other media to design practice activities for other areas from which teacher education students would benefit. What follows is an abbreviated list of possible next steps.

Video clips. It is essential for new users (both candidates and faculty) to see the potential of the *Cook* simulation in their learning and instruction. For this reason, we have experimented briefly with the creation of short videos that highlight the use of the simulation. For example, we made one video showing a faculty member and a candidate in a guided discussion of the data the simulation had returned after the candidate had designed and administered a posttest.

We have considered additional videos highlighting (1) analysis of simulated student profiles, (2) the design of instructional adaptations for simulated students with various needs, (3) "in-flight" decision making regarding simulated student on-task behavior, (4) the scope of use of formative assessments, (5) analysis of performance of various simulated student subgroups like those identified in the NCLB legislation, and (6) analysis of candidate user proficiency and professional strengths and weaknesses. These short videos could be stored in an online library of video cases, which could also guide analysis, reflection, and, most powerfully, instructional capacities in teacher preparation settings.

Contrived scenarios. To enable faculty users to develop lessons where students practice skills, such as adapting instruction, we intend to develop contrived settings using appropriate screens from the simulation. For example, one scenario might show a class roster with nineteen students with typical skills, backgrounds, and interests, but the twentieth child would have a marked learning disability. The question to resolve would be how the prospective teacher, as a professional beginner, might develop adaptations to account for that student. With all students in the teacher education class reviewing the same class roster and the same special-needs student, class discussion could be rich and fruitful, particularly for students who have never before thought about how to provide adaptations.

Several kinds of scenarios are being designed to serve as in-class instructional settings. The authors will provide advice, via a manual, to faculty to help them lead a fruitful but appropriate discussion.

ACCESSING THE *COOK* SIMULATION

Those interested in exploring the *Cook School District* simulation more thoroughly can do so free of charge by going to the following URL: http://cook. wou.edu/demo Please direct questions, comments, or further information about use of the *Cook* simulation in your setting to Gerald Girod at Western Oregon University at girodg@wou.edu or to Mark Girod at girodm@wou.edu.

REFERENCES

Girod, G. (Ed.). (2002). *Connecting teaching and learning: A handbook for teacher educators on Teacher Work Sample Methodology.* Washington, DC: American Association of Colleges for Teacher Education.

Girod, M., & Girod, G. (2006). Exploring the efficacy of the *Cook School* Simulation. *Journal of Teacher Education, 57*(5), 1–17.

Girod, M., & Girod, G. (2008). Simulation and the need for quality practice in teacher preparation. *Journal of Technology and Teacher Education, 16,* 307–337.

Glaser, B., & Strauss, A. (1967). *The discovery of grounded theory: Strategies for qualitative research.* New York: Aldine De Gruyter.

Schalock, H. D., & Myton, D. (2002). Connecting teaching and learning: An introduction to Teacher Work Sample Methodology. In G. Girod (Ed.), *Connecting teaching and learning: A handbook for teacher educators on Teacher Work Sample Methodology* (pp. 5–31). Washington, DC: American Association for Colleges of Teacher Education.

7

Sowing the Seeds of Multi-institutional Collaborative Research: A Case Study

Ronald A. Beghetto and Linda Samek

Imagine a group of researchers and teacher educators, representing nearly a dozen different institutions (both public and private), working collaboratively to design a set of focused and meaningful studies. Imagine the tremendous potential for forging new and sustainable connections between the world of research and the practice of teacher education. Consider how meaningful and insightful findings from such studies could be for understanding the shared project of educating future teachers and the impact that education has on student learning.

Such an image is tightly aligned with the vision of collaborative research recently proposed by the National Research Council's (NRC) Committee on Strategic Education Research Partnership (Donovan, Wigdor, & Snow, 2003). The NRC envisions strategic research partnerships as representing cadres of researchers and practitioners working together, in collaborative teams, on coherent, highly focused programs of education research which lead to the forging of new connections between research and practice. The NRC's proposal outlines three key dimensions necessary for creating such partnerships, including (1) "use-inspired" research and development (i.e., placing problems of practice as a central focus of the research); (2) creating the organizational infrastructure necessary to develop, sustain, and implement research; and (3) ensuring that there is a healthy partnership between the research and practice community.

Although the NRC's proposal for establishing strategic research partnerships was not focused on teacher education research, such collaborative projects have great potential for building greater capacity for teacher education research (Zeichner, 2005). At present there are several networks of researchers and teacher educators across the nation already engaged in making this vision a reality. Zeichner (2005) has highlighted a few of these networks, including the Carnegie Corporation's Teachers for a New Era project, the New York City Pathways Study, and multi-institutional studies in Massachusetts and Ohio. Zeichner (2005) has also noted that although these various teacher education research projects differ in important ways, they all involve "networks" of teacher educators and researchers "pursuing focused assessment agendas concerning teacher education and its connections to outcomes including student learning" (p. 754).

One such network, the Oregon Collaborative Research Initiative (OCRI), has formed in the state of Oregon. The OCRI group, made up of researchers and teacher educators representing nearly a dozen public and private teacher education institutions, has the stated goal of

> [Engaging] Oregon's teacher preparation institutions in the collaborative study and dissemination of a meaningful and sustainable set of research projects. *Meaningful* in that the projects address questions of common interest, are aimed at improving teacher preparation, and have real-world implications for teacher development and PreK–12 student learning. *Sustainable* in that the research projects do not overburden participants but rather offer feasible and rewarding opportunities to engage in and disseminate the findings of collaborative inquiry. (Beghetto, *OCRI Work Plan*, 2006, p. 1)

That researchers and teacher educators have the capacity to establish strategic research partnerships is without question. Still, many questions remain. For example, under what conditions do such partnerships develop? How do collaborative groups develop and carry out their research agendas? What seems to support such efforts? What challenges do such efforts face? Our purpose in this chapter is to provide an initial attempt at addressing these questions by providing a brief introduction and overview of the genesis and development of the OCRI group. Specifically, we start by briefly describing the historical context out of which the OCRI emerged—highlighting how the process was seeded and grew into what is now a set of three robust, interrelated studies. We then introduce the goals of each project and close with a brief discussion of key supports and challenges.

HISTORICAL CONTEXT

One might ask how a diverse set of institutions of higher education has come to a collaborative stance with the ability to work together in a process that could be daunting for just one institution to organize and operate. After all, in Oregon there are currently twenty-one institutions with state-approved teacher preparation programs. Included in the collection of institutions are six public, fourteen nonprofit private, and one for-profit. The public institutions span research, urban, regional, and rural motifs. The nonprofit private colleges and universities include six religious and six secular institutions. This diversity alone could preclude options for collaboration. But in addition to these differences, the program sizes vary from hundreds of completers of initial programs each year to as few as twenty completers in a year. Finally, one institution began preparing teachers in the 1880s, and the newest program commenced in fall 2007.

A number of events over the last decade have come together to make Oregon ripe for a collaborative project. Precursors to the OCRI project include the NSF-funded project, the Oregon Collaborative for Excellence in Preparation of Teachers (OCEPT) housed at Portland State University. This collaborative involved most of the teacher preparation programs, math and science departments, and many of the two-year community colleges in the state through the late 1990s. A second large grant-funded project, the Oregon Quality Assurance in Teaching (OQAT) program, housed in the Oregon University System's chancellor's office, included all sixteen institutions that had state-approved programs in 1998–2002. Both OCEPT and OQAT were highly successful in gathering faculty, higher-education administrators, PreK–12 participants, and teacher candidates in working toward the common goal of preparing excellent teachers for Oregon schools.

In 2005, a small group of individuals who shared a vision for ongoing collaborative research projects around teacher preparation came together to propose the OCRI project. This group included members from both the Oregon Association of Colleges for Teacher Education (OACTE) and the Oregon Association of Teacher Educators (ORATE). In considering an appropriate research agenda, several important contextual factors were instrumental in the final decision for the project focus. These factors included the following:

- Leaders from all institutions have common goals in preparing excellent teachers.
- The Oregon Teacher Standards and Practices Commission requires that candidates provide evidence of competent performance and ability to foster student learning for licensure recommendations.
- All candidates are required to produce at least two Teacher Work Samples during their student teaching experience.
- More Oregon institutions have become interested in and are pursuing NCATE accreditation.

- The decentralized education enterprise in Oregon leaves most programs underfunded.
- The OACTE has treasury funds that need to be used.

The decision to undertake the OCRI research project as a statewide collaborative is ambitiously extensive and long-term. Each institution that has
committed to participating will be expected to provide funding for campus
data collection and dissemination. Leaders of the project desired that the
details of the project be carefully designed to maximize impact on learning
and minimize impact on campus workload for all involved. Thus, the combination of a rich history of collaboration, shared goals and accountability
structures, and limited resources seemed to create a fertile ground from
which the OCRI network could emerge. Finally, the role of *research design
coordinator* was created by the OACTE and ORATE group (and filled by the
first author) to assist in development of a collaborative research network.

FROM BLUEPRINTS TO REALITY

In reflecting on how the vision of the collaboration moved into a reality, it became clear that the key to building a project of this scale and
complexity was to leverage the already existing commitment and spirit
of collaboration among participants. In this particular case, it involved
starting with a small "core" group of highly motivated and interested representatives from several institutions in which the project's collaborative
mission and initial research project could be identified. In this case, a *core
research team* (CORT) was identified (made up of key teacher education
faculty and leaders from public and private institutions around the state)
that would work closely with the research design coordinator in developing a strategy and work plan.

The CORT identified, as its first focus of inquiry, the Teacher Work Sample Methodology (TWSM). TWSM was mandated by the Oregon Teacher
Standards and Practices Commission in 1986 as one of the required means
of documenting the effectiveness of teacher preparation programs and
teacher candidates' ability to foster student learning. Consequently, TWSM
has had a major impact on how prospective teachers are prepared and
licensed in Oregon. The Teacher Work Sample Methodology is the one
consistent component in every teacher preparation program in the state.
As such, the Teacher Work Samples (TWSs) have served as a focal point for
establishing the collaborative research group—creating opportunities for
participants from public and private, large and small, research and teaching institutions to participate on equal footing in conversations around the
teacher preparation enterprise.

The next phase of establishing the OCRI network involved holding an open meeting at a statewide teacher education gathering to be facilitated by OCRI's research design coordinator and members of the CORT. The idea of establishing a meaningful and sustainable collaborative research initiative, centered on studying the Teacher Work Sample Methodology, was presented to potential participants. Key questions surrounding TWSM were elicited from participants and synthesized into three strands of inquiry: (1) the *evolution* of the TWSM, (2) the *experience* with the TWSM, and (3) the *effect* of the TWSM. The goals and a brief overview of these projects are displayed in table 7.1.

Planning tools were created and used to help support the development of project goals within research strands, to identify and align research questions to those goals, and to develop a plan for identifying and collecting data sources and analyzing those data sources (example planning tools are included in appendix C).

Participants who were predominantly faculty members involved in teacher preparation then organized themselves into the research strand that most interested them and nominated *project strand leaders* who would then manage all subsequent communication within and across the three OCRI work teams. The development and enactment of the OCRI project represents an iterative, multistage process of planning and activity. A schematic of this process is illustrated in figure 7.1.

The three OCRI research project strands are currently underway. Data collection instruments and procedures have been developed. The three research teams have engaged in data collection and preliminary data analysis. The progress, challenges, and initial insights from these three interrelated projects were documented in the Oregon Collaborative Research Initiative symposium papers presented at the fifty-ninth annual meeting of AACTE.

Table 7.1. Project strands, goals, and overview

Project Strand	Goal	Brief Overview
Evolution of TWSM	Examine how TWSM has been implemented and has evolved.	Using a "Theory of Action" framework, juxtapose the enactment of TWSM with the state's TWSM theory of action.
Experience with TWSM	Document the perceptions of teacher educators and candidates regarding TWSM.	Participants' perceptions (representing public and private institutions) regarding the meaningfulness, usefulness, and applicability of the TWSM.
Effect of TWSM	Examine how TWSM has impacted PreK–12 learners.	Analysis of completed work samples to examine how work samples are impacting PreK–12 learning.

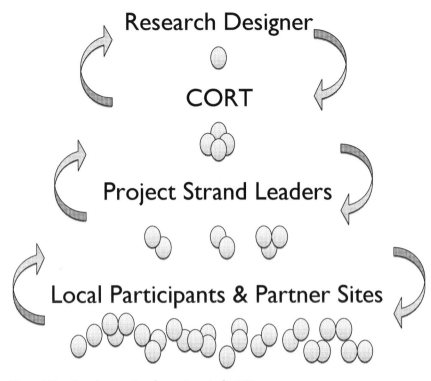

Figure 7.1. Development and enactment of OCRI.

SUPPORTS AND CHALLENGES

Engaging in a multi-institutional, collaborative research initiative is a rare opportunity, filled with many rewards and challenges. Although the Oregon group is still in the early stages of this process, the project has already attained no small measure of success. Indeed, it has brought together a diverse range of teacher education institutions in a focused effort to better understand, communicate, and strengthen the shared project of preparing teachers. Of course, such a large-scale and complex endeavor does not come into existence without key supports and its share of challenges.

In reflecting on the supports and challenges faced along the way, we have identified two key supports (and accompanying challenges) that have been instrumental in the development of the OCRI project. The first support is what we call *cyclical scaffolding*. This concept is an elaboration of the metaphor originally developed by Wood, Bruner, and Ross (1976). We define cyclical scaffolding as

Skilled others (i.e., individuals and groups within or outside of the OCRI network) providing reoccurring, temporary support to various project teams such that those teams can develop the capacity to move forward in carrying out some aspect of the collaborative research agenda.

An example of cyclical scaffolding would be the research design coordinator meeting with strand team members (e.g., the evolution group) to provide support around the use of a particular theoretical orientation (e.g., theory of action, Argyris & Schon, 1976) for framing the methodological work necessary for attaining the goals of the strand (e.g., examining differences between the state's TWSM theory of action and various institutions' TWSM theory in use). A key challenge of cyclical scaffolding is anticipating and providing "just-in-time" support for teams as they engage in the work.

The second support is what we call *loose coupling of parallel efforts*. We define loose coupling of parallel efforts, within the OCRI project, as

Providing each of the three project strands with sufficient autonomy to pursue their particular research agenda while at the same time ensuring that each project strand maintains a sufficient level of relatedness to the larger OCRI network.

For instance, we found that in order for each of the three project strands to move forward they needed to have the autonomy to establish their own project-particular priorities, procedures, and timelines for carrying out their focus of inquiry. This, for instance, included the responsibility for drafting and attaining approval for conducting human-subjects research (from their respective institutional review boards). At the same time, each project strand also needed to maintain an active connection with the larger OCRI network so as to share information about progress and procedures, receive timely information and support, and work through shared challenges.

One shared challenge surrounded the issue of intellectual property. Indeed, an overarching goal of the OCRI network is to share information, instruments, and, when appropriate, data sources such that all institutions could benefit from what is learned within and across particular research strands. The issue of intellectual property is one that will need to be continually revisited; however, an initial step toward addressing this challenge was to have the research coordinator work with members of the CORT to draft a data use-and-release agreement (which provides proper acknowledgment and expectations regarding the development, ownership, and use of data sets). This agreement can then be disseminated by strand leaders to individuals or groups who are interested in using data sources for their own work.

Finding the right balance between autonomy, connection, and support is an ongoing and dynamic process. Within the OCRI network, the establishment and use of an OCRI listserv and having strand leaders also serve on the core research team has gone a long way in striking this balance.

CONCLUSION

At this point, only time will tell what the Oregon group is able to accomplish in this ambitious endeavor. However, we are highly optimistic and indeed energized by the idea that researchers and teacher educators from nearly a dozen institutions can come together in the spirit of forging a strong link between the research and practice of teacher education and ultimately work toward enhancing teacher preparation, and in turn K–12 student learning.

REFERENCES

Argyris, C., & Schon, D. A. (1974). *Theory in practice: Increasing professional effectiveness.* San Francisco: Jossey-Bass.

Beghetto, R. A. (2006). *Oregon Collaborative Research Initiative: Work plan.* Unpublished document. Eugene, OR.

Donovan, M. S., Wigdor, A. K., & Snow, C. E. (2003). *Strategic education research partnership.* Washington, DC: National Academies Press.

Wood, D. J., Bruner, J. S., & Ross, G. (1976). The role of tutoring in problem-solving. *Journal of Child Psychology and Psychiatry, 17,* 89–100.

Zeichner, K. M. (2005). A research agenda for teacher education. In M. Cochran-Smith & K. M. Zeichner (Eds.), *Studying teacher education: The report of the AERA panel on research and teacher education.* Mahwah, NJ: Erlbaum.

III

RESEARCH

8

Using TWS Methodology to Establish Credible Evidence for Quality Teacher Preparation

Antony D. Norman, C. Samuel Evans, and Roger Pankratz

The national discussion about issues related to evidence of teaching quality, and in particular accounting for teacher impact on student learning, shows no sign of abating. Just within the last few years, several books and reports have been published drawing various conclusions about these issues. Work by the National Academy of Education's Committee on Teacher Education outlines concepts and strategies toward the goal of establishing teaching as a profession (Darling-Hammond & Bransford, 2005). Another report by the American Educational Research Association (AERA) Panel on Research and Teacher Education concludes that there is still little evidence that clearly connects teacher characteristics and student outcomes (Cochran-Smith & Zeichner, 2005). Even more recently, Levine (2006) calls for a major re-structuring of how to carry out the business of teacher preparation. Increasingly, as teacher preparation institutions process the ideas of these multiple voices, they also must respond to greater demands by education accrediting agencies, such as the National Council for Accreditation of Teacher Education (NCATE) and the Teacher Education Accreditation Council (TEAC), and even by regional accrediting agencies, to become more evidence-based and outcome-oriented. Within this framework and with an eye to the national climate, the present chapter represents how Western Kentucky University's teacher preparation programs are using Teacher Work Sample Methodology to establish credible evidence that teacher candidates meet standards of teaching quality and in consequence make an impact on student learning.

It is important to note that the present chapter represents a continuation of foundational work begun by several of the authors and described in two recent publications (Denner, Norman, Salzman, Pankratz, & Evans, 2004; Evans, Daniel, Mikovch, Metze, & Norman, 2006). A brief discussion of this work follows to provide a context for the present chapter.

Denner et al. (2004) described several multi-institutional research efforts to establish the validity and reliability of the Renaissance Teacher Work Sample (TWS) as a tool for measuring teacher candidate impact on P–12 student learning. We found that education experts, composed of university faculty, university administration, and school practitioners, deemed the TWS to be a valid measure of relevant Interstate New Teacher Assessment and Support Consortium (INTASC) standards and that the TWS components were strongly related to crucial and frequent teacher behaviors. Furthermore, given sufficient training, scorers could achieve reasonable levels of interrater reliability to make "high-stakes" decisions about teacher candidate proficiency. Finally, we found a strong positive relationship between candidates' TWS performance and the quality of the assessments they used to measure student learning.

Our second publication (Evans et al., 2006) described efforts to build a comprehensive Web-based electronic accountability system that includes not only state-required teacher candidate admission and exit information but also electronic portfolio data, including the TWS, used to document candidate progress toward state teacher standards. In the electronic portfolio portion of the system, faculty developed key assessments to measure one or more state teacher standards, as well as to prepare candidates for various components of the culminating assessment, the TWS. As faculty added assessments to the system, candidates were able to upload completed assignments that faculty then reviewed and scored electronically.

Clearly, Denner et al. (2004) make a compelling case that the TWS is a valid measure of candidate performance relative to standards and that highly trained, independent scorers *can* score TWS reliably. Such research, however, raises another question: what evidence can we gather to ascertain whether *our faculty who score TWS as an assignment within the context of their course* are doing so in a reasonably consistent manner? After a brief overview of WKU's Teacher Work Sample, we will first describe how we have sought to answer this question. Likewise, second, although Evans et al. (2006) describe the conceptualization and early development of an electronic accountability system, we will describe how we use TWS data in the system to evaluate the quality of our various preparation programs and to explore the relationship of TWS to other essential admission and exit data within the system. Third, we will describe and discuss the results of our preliminary efforts to measure candidate impact on P–12 student learning from data within the TWS. Finally, we will conclude with limitations and lessons learned from our efforts to use the TWS to establish the quality of teacher preparation programs.

WKU'S TEACHER WORK SAMPLE

The TWS prompt and rubrics used at WKU are those developed as part of the Renaissance Teacher Work Sample materials (Renaissance Partnership for Improving Teacher Quality, 2001). The prompt represents guidelines for candidates to follow as they develop the TWS based on their classroom experiences during student teaching. The analysis rubrics correspond to seven targeted TWS components:

- Contextual Factors (CF)—using information about the learning/teaching context and student individual differences to set learning goals, plan instruction, and assess learning.
- Learning Goals (LG)—setting significant, challenging, varied, and appropriate learning goals.
- Assessment Plan (AP)—using multiple assessment modes and approaches aligned with learning goals to assess student learning before, during, and after instruction.
- Design for Instruction (DFI)—designing instruction for specific learning goals, student characteristics and needs, and learning contexts.
- Instructional Decision Making (IDM)—using ongoing analysis of student learning to make instructional decisions.
- Analysis of Student Learning (ASL)—using assessment data to profile student learning and communicate information about student progress and achievement.
- Reflection and Self-Evaluation (RSE)—analyzing the relationship between instruction and student learning in order to improve teaching practice.

On each of these rubrics, the multiple targeted indicators for each component are rated on a three-point scale: 1 = *standard not met*, 2 = *standard partially met*, and 3 = *standard met*. The number of indicators per TWS component range from three indicators (Instructional Decision Making) to six (Design for Instruction).

Average scores for each component can be computed by totaling scores for each indicator and dividing by the number of indicators per component. Combining scores across the thirty-two total indicators creates a total score that can vary from 32 to 96 points. In addition, after scoring the entire TWS, faculty or other scorers provide a holistic score as a measure of the overall quality of each TWS based on the following scale: 1 = *beginning*, 2 = *developing*, 3 = *proficient*, 4 = *exemplary*. For purposes of unit- and program-level evaluation, candidate scores are categorized as to whether they meet proficiency at both the analytic and holistic levels. At the analytic level, candidates are considered to demonstrate proficiency on a given component if their average score across indicators is 2.5 or higher. At the holistic level, candidates who score either a 3 or 4 are considered to meet proficiency.

As the Commonwealth of Kentucky requires teacher preparation programs to provide evidence that their candidates demonstrate proficiency on the Kentucky Teacher Standards (KTS), WKU faculty have worked to develop a matrix to demonstrate the alignment between TWS components and indicators and the state standards (see table 8.1). Although the TWS does not align to all standards, other accompanying evaluations during student teaching work together to ensure that candidates are evaluated on all standards during the culminating student-teaching experience.

As will be described later, knowledge of this alignment allows us to consider candidate proficiency through the lens of not only the TWS components, but also the Kentucky Teacher Standards.

ESTABLISHING FACULTY SCORING RELIABILITY

Anyone who has been touched by accrediting organizations over the last decade has witnessed a revolutionary shift from a focus on "inputs," i.e., the courses that candidates completed toward a degree, to a focus on "outputs," i.e., what candidates know and are able to do based on their preparation experiences. Furthermore, an accompanying shift in emphasis has been from candidates demonstrating knowledge and skills in isolation to how knowledge and skills translate into student learning. As the *target* language of NCATE Standard 1 (2006) reveals, teacher candidates must be able to "accurately assess and analyze student learning, make appropriate adjustments to instruction, monitor student learning, and have a positive effect on learning for all students" (p. 16).

Table 8.1.   TWS component and KTS alignment

TWS Components	Kentucky Teacher Standards
Contextual Factors	2 – Designs/plans instruction
Learning Goals	2 – Designs/plans instruction
Assessment Plan	5 – Assesses/communicates learning results
Design for Instruction	1 – Demonstrates content knowledge 2 – Designs/plans instruction 6 – Implements technology
Instructional Decision Making	4 – Implements/manages instruction
Analysis of Student Learning	5 – Assesses/communicates learning results
Reflection and Self-Evaluation	7 – Reflects/evaluates teaching/learning 9 – Implements professional development

As we prepared for our 2002 accreditation visit, we felt confident that our Teacher Work Sample results provided evidence that our candidates where making an impact on student learning. Yet, as we began preparing to report TWS score results *by program*, we were troubled by patterns that emerged wherein some program categories were not faring as well as others. Until that point, our approach to meeting NCATE criteria that assessments be fair, accurate, and consistent was to cite cross-institutional research (Denner et al., 2004), as well as internal studies that followed similar procedures and found comparable results. However, it became clear that answering the question, *can* TWS be scored reliably? was not the same as answering the question, *are* TWSs being scored consistently? Until we were able to compare results of faculty scoring to those of independent scorers, we would not be able to discern whether apparent program differences on TWS scores were the result of program issues or faculty issues.

To date, we have conducted multiple "mass scorings" of TWS to ascertain the level of agreement achieved between and among independent scorers and faculty. Although the data allow for multiple ways of exploring these relationships, ultimately, in a high-stakes environment, the question becomes, does the overall candidate performance on the TWS meet proficiency or fall short of it, and are scorers able to agree on the level of proficiency? Table 8.2 is an example of the ways we are able to review scoring results.

These and several semesters of additional results demonstrated that there are reasonable levels of agreement among independent scorers and faculty. More importantly, further investigation revealed that a few faculty members who tend to score more leniently accounted for most of the disagreement between independent scorers and faculty.

EXPLORING RELATIONSHIPS BETWEEN TWS AND OTHER KEY TEACHER QUALITY DATA

Given the evidence that candidate TWS are scored in a reliable manner, we were prepared to revisit the differing patterns of success across our various teacher preparation program categories, in particular, the elementary program, middle grades program, secondary education programs, primary-to-twelfth-grade programs, and fifth-to-twelfth-grade programs. Table 8.3 presents the results of two TWS scoring sessions where independent scorers judged the quality of the TWS performances. These scores do not include the faculty scores used to calculate candidates' course grades. "Passing" represents those candidates who scored a holistic score of 3, "proficient," or 4, "exemplary."

Table 8.2.   Interrater agreement on level of TWS proficiency

	A/B[1]	A/Faculty	B/Faculty	A/B/Faculty[2]	A or B/Faculty[3]	AB/Faculty[4]
Agreement	83%	72%	74%	65%	81%	77%
Disagreement	17%	28%	26%	35%	19%	23%
Total	100%	100%	100%	100%	100%	100%

[1]A/B should be read, "If A scorer chooses a level of proficiency, does B scorer agree?"
[2]A/B/Faculty should read, "Do A, B, and faculty scorers all agree on the level of proficiency?"
[3]A or B/Faculty should read, "Does faculty agree with the level of proficiency chosen by A or B?"
[4]AB/Faculty should read, "If A and B scorers both agree on level of proficiency, does the faculty agree?"

Table 8.3.   TWS pass rates by program

TWS "PASS" RATES	OVERALL		ELED		MGE		P–12		SECED		5–12	
	N	%	N	%	N	%	N	%	N	%	N	%
Fall 2006 Candidates	151		95		28		2		21		5	
Holistic Score 3 or 4	107	81%	77	81%	14	50%	0	0%	14	67%	2	40%
Spring 2007 Candidates	211		107		34		20		32		18	
Holistic Score 3 or 4	155	73%	83	78%	21	62%	15	75%	20	63%	16	89%

These and other results presented below are now shared annually with program coordinators so they may discuss with their colleagues what the findings suggest about their candidates' preparation. Data over several semesters of scoring sessions indicate persistent differences across preparation programs, with elementary education program candidates typically scoring higher than candidates in other programs. A ready explanation for this finding is that elementary education program faculty have surpassed other programs in developing course-embedded assessments that allow candidates to practice the various TWS components prior to student teaching.

By using data collected within the electronic accountability system, we have also been able to explore program differences at the TWS component level. Figure 8.1 is based on faculty scoring data and depicts the percentage of candidates by program who averaged at least 2.5 (considered "proficient") on the indicators for each TWS component.

Furthermore, based on a faculty mapping of the alignment between the TWS and the Kentucky Teacher Standards, figure 8.2 depicts the percentage

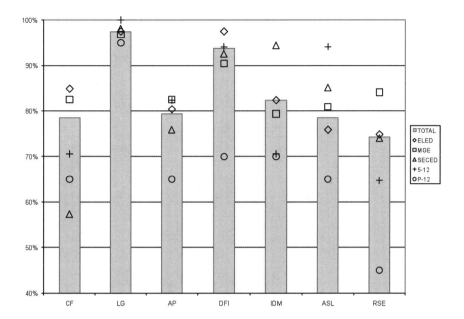

Figure 8.1. Percentage of Program[a] Candidates Passing Teacher Work Sample Components[b]
Footnotes:
[a] Program Abbreviations: ELED – Elementary Education, MGE – Middle Grades Education, SECED – Secondary Education, 5-12 – 5th-12th Grade Education, P-12 – Primary-12th Grade Education
[b] Teacher Work Sample (TWS) Component Abbreviations: CF – Contextual Factors, LG – Learning Goals, AP – Assessment Plan, DFI – Design for Instruction, IDM – Instructional Decision-Making, ASL – Analysis of Student Learning, RSE – Reflection and Self-Evaluation

of candidates by program who averaged at least 2.5 on indicators related to each Kentucky Teacher Standard measured by the TWS.

Because other key candidate data are stored along with TWS data within our centralized electronic accountability system, we were also able to explore the relationship between TWS performance and other achievement data gathered during teacher preparation admission and exit. These include ACT scores and GPA, collected at admission, and Praxis Content and Principles of Learning and Teaching scores, collected as candidates exit the program and seek certification. Because of delay between graduation and gathering of Praxis II exit data and the desire for data reporting consistency, table 8.4 reports admission data, and table 8.5 reports exit data on candidates who completed teaching preparation programs during the 2005–2006 academic year.

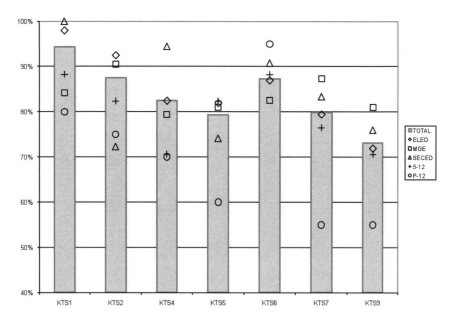

Figure 8 2.   Percentage of Program[a] Candidates Passing Each Kentucky Teacher Standard[b]
Footnotes:
[a] Program Abbreviations: ELED – Elementary Education, MGE – Middle Grades Education, SECED – Secondary Education, 5-12 – 5th-12th Grade Education, P-12 – Primary-12th Grade Education
[b] Kentucky Teacher Standard (KTS) Abbreviations: KTS1 – Demonstrates Content Knowledge, KTS2 – Designs/Plans Instruction, KTS4 – Implements/Manages Instruction, KTS5 – Assesses/Communicates Learning Results, KTS6 – Implements Technology, KTS7 – Reflects/Evaluates Teaching/Learning, KTS9 – Implements Professional Development

INVESTIGATING TWS EVIDENCE FOR
IMPACT ON P–12 STUDENT LEARNING

It is arguable that many institutions have adopted TWS methodology because of its potential to capture teacher candidate performance on multiple teaching standards. We would be remiss, however, if we did not acknowledge our attraction to the assessment as a means to capture newly required NCATE evidence—candidate impact on P–12 student learning. Within the TWS, candidates report student pre- and post-instruction assessment results that clearly demonstrate their impact on learning. However, the challenge for us has been twofold: (1) how to extract such data embedded within the TWS, and (2) how to calculate and analyze learning gains.

A discussion of the pros and cons associated with various methods for calculating learning gains is beyond the scope of this chapter. Our recent decision was to conduct a preliminary analysis of a small sample ($N = 22$)

Table 8.4. TWS relationship to admission data

		Admission GPA	ACT
TWS holistic average	Pearson *R*	.293**	.087
	N	319	247
TWS grand average	Pearson *R*	.264**	.072
	N	319	247

** Correlation is significant at the .01 level (2-tailed).

Table 8.5. TWS relationship to exit data

		TWS grand average	Praxis content average[†]	Praxis PLT
TWS holistic average	Pearson *R*	.803**	.106	.142*
	N	335	275	272
TWS grand average	Pearson *R*		.077	.051
	N		275	272

** Correlation is significant at the .01 level (2-tailed).
* Correlation is significant at the .05 level (2-tailed).
† Candidates typically take more than one content test. This score represents the average percentage across these tests. Percentages were used because not all tests have the same scaling.

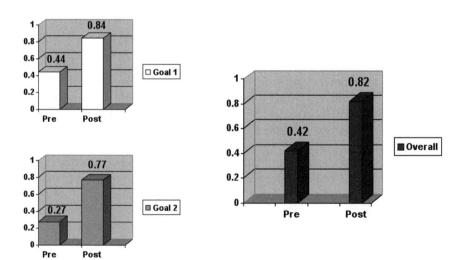

Student Teacher N = 22
P – 12 Student N = 464

Significant Student Gain (Controlling for Student Teacher Effects)

Figure 8.3. Impact on Student Learning Results

of TWS to ascertain how easily we could extract pre- and post-data based on the learning goals established in the TWS. Thus, we avoided overall pretest–posttest gains for gains reported for each learning goal (typically, two learning goals per TWS). The results in figure 8.3 indicate that a more concerted effort to collect these data would be worthwhile. However, we are still contemplating the best means to collect these data in an efficient manner.

LIMITATIONS, LESSONS LEARNED, AND NEXT STEPS

Western Kentucky University has adopted the TWS as a viable tool for instruction and performance assessment in its teacher education programs. Furthermore, WKU has demonstrated consistent holistic scoring of student Teacher Work Sample exhibits; had linked performance on the TWS to seven Kentucky Teacher Standards; has incorporated TWS performance data into its teacher preparation data management and accountability system; has collected TWS data of student teachers and related performance scores to different internal preparation programs, admission data, and other program performance data; and has investigated the pre-post K–12 student assessment data on instructional units developed and taught by student teachers.

The cutting edge of data use, analysis, and reflection at WKU is understanding the meaning of TWS data as it relates to overall candidate and program performance and obtaining credible evidence that teacher graduates can produce learning with the children they teach. In this endeavor, the most obvious limitation of TWS data is the internal consistency and validity of the specific components of Teacher Work Samples. We need to know more clearly what is both best practice and acceptable practice for teacher candidates relative to using context, designing instruction and student assessments, analyzing student learning, and reflecting on teaching and learning. While faculty and school practitioners can agree on holistic ratings of work sample exhibits, they have not addressed the issues of best practice and acceptable practice for individual work sample components. Without teacher education, arts and sciences faculty, and school practitioners debating and reaching agreement on these issues, each professional who mentors and judges TWS performance will make decisions based on their own perceptions rather than established standards.

Until there is greater internal consistency of TWS scoring across all programs and scorers, performance data, no matter how well analyzed, will not provide good guidance for candidates' feedback and improvement. Furthermore, until agreement is reached among faculty and school practitioners about best and acceptable practice of TWS components, candidates are left to guess what individual university instructors and clinical supervisors regard as performance that will be judged as proficient or above. Attention to best practice and scorer consistency of TWS components, especially unit goal setting, design of instruction, and assessment of learning, is also critical to producing credible evidence of a teacher candidate's ability to produce learning using the pre-post assessment data of students over a unit of instruction.

Obtaining the resources and finding the time to address best-practice issues of TWS components and establishing unitwide agreement will no doubt be an arduous, if not a formidable, task. However, it is an essential process that we must have the will and commitment to achieve. It is the logical next step in developing the usefulness of the TWS process for good instruction, feedback on performance, program improvement, and obtaining credible performance data.

REFERENCES

Cochran-Smith, M., & Zeichner, K. M. (Eds.). (2005). *Studying teacher education: The report of the AERA Panel on Research and Teacher Education.* Mahwah, NJ: Erlbaum.

Darling-Hammond, L., & Bransford, J. (Eds.). (2005). *Preparing teachers for a changing world: What teachers should learn and be able to do.* San Francisco, CA: Jossey-Bass.

Denner, P. R., Norman, A. D., Salzman, S. A., Pankratz, R. S., & Evans, C. S. (2004). The Renaissance Partnership Teacher Work Sample: Evidence supporting score generalizability, validity, and quality of student learning assessment. In E. M. Guyton & J. R. Dangel (Eds.), *Teacher education yearbook XII: Research linking teacher preparation and student performance.* Dubuque, IA: Kendall/Hunt.

Evans, S., Daniel, T., Mikovch, A., Metze, L., & Norman, A. D. (2006). The use of technology in portfolio assessment of teacher education candidates. *Journal of Technology and Teacher Education, 14,* 5–27.

Levine, A. (2006). *Educating school teachers.* Washington, DC: Woodrow Wilson National Fellowship Foundation.

National Council for Accreditation of Teacher Education. (2006). *NCATE 2006 Unit Standards.* Washington, DC: Author.

Renaissance Partnership for Improving Teacher Quality. (2001). *Teacher Work Sample: Performance prompts, teaching process standards, scoring rubrics.* Retrieved from http://edtech.wku.edu/rtwsc/resources.htm.

9

Generalizability of Teacher Work Samples across Occasions of Development

A Research Case Study

Peter Denner, Julie Newsome, and Jack Newsome

To warrant the use of Teacher Work Sample (TWS) assessments for the purpose of making decisions about teacher candidates' performance levels, and to claim that TWS scores reflect teacher candidates' capabilities with respect to institutional and state teaching standards, it is important for teacher preparation institutions employing a TWS assessment to obtain evidence supporting the validity and reliability of their TWS scores. Recent research (Denner, Salzman, & Bangert, 2001; Denner, Salzman, Newsome, & Birdsong, 2003) has supported the content validity of the Idaho State University TWS assessment and its match to state and national standards. The research has also provided support for the dependability of the total scores obtained from the TWS when judged by mixed panels of qualified raters—both from within (Denner et al., 2001; Denner et al., 2003) and across (Denner, Norman, Salzman, Pankratz, & Evans, 2004) teacher education institutions. The purpose of the present investigation was to gather additional evidence with respect to the generalizability of TWS performances across occasions of development.

An important consideration for any complex performance assessment, like a Teacher Work Sample (TWS), is whether performance levels on one occasion generalize to performance levels on other occasions. To claim that TWSs measure teacher candidates' abilities to meet program and state teaching standards, the candidates should show performance similarly across similar performance occasions (Medley, 1982; Shavelson & Webb, 1991). Stuffelbeam (1997) has criticized the lack of evidence for the predictive validity of TWS assessments across teaching contexts and outcomes.

Messick (1989) has identified generalizability as one of the core components of validity. Because many contextual factors can influence complex
performances, and because the performances of even highly skilled people
tend to fluctuate from one occasion to the next, some fluctuation in TWS
performance levels across teaching occasions is to be expected. On the other
hand, "To the extent that behavior is inconsistent across occasions, gener-
alization for the sample behavior collected on one occasion to the universe
of behavior across all occasions of interest is hazardous" (Shavelson &
Webb, 1991, p. 7). Hence, it is vital to obtain an estimate of the amount
of variance attributable to teaching occasions and to examine the degree
of dependability of TWS performance scores across different occasions of
TWS development. In other words, to what extent can we expect TWS performance levels to be replicated by teacher candidates?

This study applied generalizability theory (Brennan, 2001; Shavelson
& Webb, 1991) to investigate the dependability of TWS scores across two
assessment occasions when the same teacher candidates taught different
topics to different students during different internship experiences in separate semesters. The dependability of the scores made by separate panels of
qualified raters was also examined. The central question addressed was, do
TWS total scores demonstrate sufficient generalizability across raters and
development occasions to warrant their use in high-stakes decisions about
the quality of candidates' teaching abilities?

METHODS

Participants

At Idaho State University, teacher candidates complete two TWSs during the
teacher education program. The first TWS is completed during a half-time
preinternship (junior level), and the second is completed during a full-time
student-teaching internship (senior level). The TWS sets in this study were
collected from teacher candidates at Idaho State University who completed
their half-time internship during a spring semester and completed their
student-teaching internship the following fall semester during the same
year. From this population of teacher candidates, two sets of twenty TWSs
were established.

First, the TWSs with a matching TWS from the subsequent fall semester
were identified. Second, the instructor ratings for the preinterns' TWS
collected during the spring semester were used to sort the TWSs into four
categories along a developmental continuum of 1 = *beginning*, 2 = *developing*, 3 = *proficient*, and 4 = *exemplary*. The category scores were assigned
by applying the established teacher education program cutoff scores for

the TWS total scores for each category. Then, within the four categories, the TWSs were randomly assigned to TWS Set A (ten TWSs) or Set B (ten TWSs). This resulted in two beginning, two developing, four proficient, and two exemplary TWSs in each set. This distribution reflected the available distribution of the identified candidates' TWS performances. The matching TWSs from the subsequent fall semester for these same ten teacher candidates were then added to each set to bring the total to twenty TWSs in each set. Thus, both Set A and Set B consisted of ten preinternship TWSs and ten matching TWSs from the student-teaching internships of the same candidates in the set.

The Set A TWSs contained six TWSs produced by secondary education teacher candidates and four TWS produced by elementary education teacher candidates. The Set A TWSs were from two male and eight female teacher candidates. The Set B TWSs consisted of five TWSs produced by secondary education teacher candidates and five TWSs produced by elementary education teacher candidates. The Set B TWSs were from three male and seven female teacher candidates. The TWSs in both sets varied in the subject matter taught by the teacher candidates. Also, because the teacher candidates were required to complete their student-teaching internships in settings different from where they taught during their preinternships (for secondary education teacher candidates, the placements were middle school and high school, and for elementary education teacher candidates, the placements were primary grades and upper elementary grades), the two separate TWSs developed by each of the teacher candidates assessed their abilities to teach different topics, to different students, at different grade levels, typically in different schools, and during different school semesters.

The TWS guidelines given to the teacher candidates in this study were an updated version of the ones employed by Denner, Salzman, Newsome, and Birdsong (2003). The modifications were made to increase clarity and to increase alignment with the newer indicator-level scoring rubric (see description of the scoring rubric below). The guidelines established the standards to be demonstrated, specified the tasks to be performed, and directed the teacher candidates through the steps of the required documentation (see http://ed.isu.edu/depts/assistdean/assistdean_index.shtml for the targeted TWS standards, current TWS guidelines, and current TWS scoring rubric). The tasks required by the TWS included (1) description and analysis of the learning-teaching context, (2) specification of achievement targets for the instructional sequence that were aligned with state achievement standards, (3) development of an assessment plan that included both formative and summative assessment of the achievement targets, (4) documentation of lesson plans aligned to the achievement targets for at least six learning activities used in teaching an instructional sequence, (5) use of formative assessment data to make modifications to instruction, (6) aggregated and disaggregated analysis of student learning that occurred as a result of the instructional sequence for at least two of the achievement targets, and (7) evaluation and reflection on the success of the instructional sequence with regard to student learning and future practice. The guidelines also specified other requirements, such as document formatting and effective written communication throughout.

TWS Scoring Rubric

The TWS sets were scored by separate panels of trained raters using an analytic scoring rubric. Each indicator on the rubric was rated on a three-point scale of 0 = *indicator not met*, 1 = *indicator met acceptably (partially met)*, and 2 = *indicator met at target*. Scores for the eight standards can be determined by summation of the indicator ratings of the standard. A total score for each TWS was computed by summing the indicator scores across all indicators. Total scores could vary from 0 to 82 points. The total scores were the focus of the present study.

TWS Raters

The TWS raters were six teacher education faculty members (five female and one male). Four of the six teacher education faculty members had previous experience scoring TWS. Three of the raters held doctoral degrees, and three of the raters held masters or educational specialist degrees. The raters averaged 7.7 years (SD = 6.6) of college teaching experience and 14.5 years (SD = 10.0) of public school teaching experience. All of the raters attended two training sessions during the study (see procedures below). The raters were first blocked by TWS rating experience and then randomly assigned to the two TWS sets (Set A or Set B). Thus, each panel of raters consisted of two experienced raters and one inexperienced rater.

Procedures for Rater Training

An initial rater training session was held for all of the Idaho State University teacher education faculty members who mentor teacher candidates and assess TWS performances. This was done to ensure all faculty members were familiar with the current guidelines and rubric, and to ensure scoring alignment across sections and courses. A second TWS training session was held for the raters who volunteered to participate in this study. The initial rater training covered the TWS standards, the guidelines the teacher candidates' used to develop their work samples, and an extensive review of the scoring rubrics. The second training session thoroughly reviewed the standards, guidelines, and scoring rubric. The second training session also included bias-reduction training for uncovering potential scoring bias due to personal preferences regarding an ideal TWS. This training followed the same procedures employed by Denner, Salzman, and Bangert (2001) and Denner, Salzman, Newsome, and Birdsong (2003). Both training sessions included practice scoring of two previously rated TWSs. As a final part of the training preparation for the benchmarking activities, the raters were given additional directions regarding respect for the confidentiality and security of the teacher work samples used in the study, the importance of avoiding halo and pitchfork effects in scoring, and the importance of searching for evidence in all specified locations (as guided by a matrix table for finding the evidence).

Before releasing the raters to score, the raters were told the importance of scoring their assigned set of TWSs independently without any discussion with the other raters. All raters reported that they heeded this instruction. They were also advised to review their list of potential biases each time they began to score (from the bias-reduction training described above). Finally, all of the raters were asked to return their completed TWS set within two weeks. The raters were required to score the TWS in a quiet setting with no distractions. All of the raters reported following these instructions. The order of the TWSs within each set was random and different for each rater. All raters scored their assigned set of TWS and returned the set within the allotted period.

Design

To investigate the generalizability of TWS scores across two occasions of development, we employed design concepts from generalizability theory (Brennan, 2001; Shavelson & Webb, 1991). The multifaceted design employed in this study followed an example presented by Shavelson and Webb (1991, pp. 32–35) and treated persons as crossed with raters and occasions. The person, rater, and occasion facets were analyzed as random effects. The design was analyzed separately by TWS set (Set A and Set B). All statistical analyses were conducted using SPSS 11.0 for Macintosh GLM procedures and ANOVA Method III Sums of Squares. This resulted in quasi-F ratios for the tests of main effects based on Satterthwaite's (1946) method for approximating the degrees of freedom for the denominator of the F' ratios. However, in keeping with generalizability studies, the statistical analyses were performed mainly to obtain variance estimates for use in computing the variance components for this design. The variance components, in turn, were used to compute dependability coefficients, in accordance with the formulas for this design supplied by Shavelson and Webb (1991).

Dependability coefficients were calculated for both sets of TWS scores. These same formulas were also adjusted to provide estimates of dependability coefficients for different-sized rater panels. Dependability coefficients estimate the proportion of score differences that are generalizable (in this case, generalizable across comparable raters and occasions) when performance scores are used to make absolute (criterion-referenced) decisions about teaching performance levels. "Absolute interpretations address decisions about 'how well' an individual can perform, regardless of the performance of his or her peers" (Shavelson & Webb, 1991, p. 95). Previous studies (Cronin & Capie, 1985; Erlich & Borich, 1979; Erlich & Shavelson, 1978; Smith, Waller, & Waller, 1982) have used .70 as a minimum criterion of acceptability for generalizability coefficients. This criterion was also suggested as a minimum criterion by Ingersoll and Scannell (2002) in their book on performance-based teacher certification. Taking into consideration the size of the TWS sets employed in this study and the addition of the occasion facet in this design, we decided to adopt this same criterion for acceptable generalizability.

RESULTS

Variance Components

Table 9.1 presents the variance components for the multiple facets of the design for the total score performances of the teacher candidates for both TWS sets (Set A and Set B). Notice that the variance component attributable to persons is larger for Set B than Set A (42 percent of the total variance for Set A compared to 68 percent for Set B).

Effect of Person

As anticipated, the person facet was statistically significant for both the Set A TWS total scores, $F(9, 13.85) = 3.74$, $MSE = 86.37$, $p = .01$, and the Set B TWS total scores, $F(9, 15.27) = 8.93$, $MSE = 52.78$, $p < .001$. These results indicate the teacher candidates' TWS performances varied significantly in both TWS sets, which is not surprising because the TWS sets were composed of TWSs selected from four performance levels along a developmental continuum from beginning to exemplary performances.

Effect of Occasion

The effect of TWS development occasion was not statistically significant for either Set A, $F'(1, 2.97) = .18$, $MSE = 125.21$, $p = .70$, or Set B, $F'(1,$

Table 9.1. Estimates of variance components from Set A and Set B TWS total scores

Source of variation	df	MS	Variance component	%	MS	Variance component	%
		Set A			Set B		
Person (P)	9	323.04	45.19	42	471.19	73.12	68
Rater (R)	2	123.80	3.66	3	261.12	1.16	1
Occasion (O)	1	22.82	-0.64	0	28.02	0.84	0
P × R	18	60.63	17.33	16	44.38	14.71	14
P × O	9	51.71	8.58	8	23.35	2.80	3
R × O	2	99.47	7.35	7	13.62	-0.13	0
Residual (P × R × O)	18	25.97	25.97	24	14.95	14.95	14

2.93) = 1.27, MSE = 22.02, p = .34, for the total TWS performance scores. The occasion by rater interaction was statistically significant for Set A, $F(2, 18)$ = 3.83, MSE = 25.97, p = .04, but not for Set B, $F(2, 18)$ = .91, MSE = 14.95, p = 42. In addition, the occasion by person interactions were not statistically significant for either the Set A TWS, $F(9, 18)$ = 1.99, MSE = 25.97, p = .10, or for the Set B TWS, $F(9, 18)$ = 1.56, MSE = 14.95, p = .20. The results show that the TWS performance levels of the teacher candidates generalized across the two occasions of TWS development. However, the significant interaction effect for Set A between rater and occasion means that judgments of TWS produced on different occasions can be affected by rater differences.

Effect of Rater

The rater facet was not statistically significant for Set A, $F'(2, 3.47)$ = .92, MSE = 134.13, p = .48, but it was statistically significant for Set B, $F'(2, 8.64)$ = 6.07, MSE = 43.04, p = .02, for the total TWS performance scores. Unfortunately, the rater by person interactions were statistically significant for both Set A, $F(18, 18)$ = 2.34, MSE = 25.97, p = .04, and for Set B, $F(18, 18)$ = 2.97, MSE = 14.95, p = .01. Post hoc mean comparisons of the raters' scores for Set B revealed the inexperienced rater assigned higher scores ($p < .05$) on average compared to the two experienced raters. However, experience was not the only source of the scoring differences among the raters, since the interaction of person and rater was also statistically significant for both TWS sets. This meant there were also variations in the raters' applications of the scoring criteria to particular TWSs. Still, the interactions also reflected differences in rater experience.

Generalizability

Using the variance components from table 9.1 to compute dependability coefficients for the TWS total scores produced three-rater dependability coefficients of .73 for the Set A TWS total scores and .88 for the Set B TWS total scores. The negative variance components shown in table 9.1 were set to zero for these calculations in accordance with the recommendation of Shavelson and Webb (1981). Both dependability coefficients showed evidence of acceptable score dependability, even though the number of TWSs rated by each panel was quite small. Despite the significant difference among the Set B raters, the dependability coefficient for Set B was higher than for Set A. Dependability coefficients are reliant upon the size of the score variations among persons, so this was due largely to the smaller variance component for the person facet for the Set A scores. Table 9.2 presents estimates of total score dependability for different-sized panels of raters across two occasions of TWS development.

DISCUSSION

To claim that Teacher Work Sample scores reflect teacher candidates' abilities with respect to targeted teaching standards, teacher education programs must show support for the generalizability aspect of the validity of their candidates' TWS performances, including both the generalizability of the scores across raters and the generalizability of the scores across teaching occasions. The results of the present study indicate that TWS total scores can be generalized across raters and occasions of TWS development with sufficient dependability to warrant their use in making decisions with respect to teacher candidates' overall performance levels and to demonstrate program accountability for the candidates' overall ability to teach.

Table 9.2.   Dependability coefficient estimates for TWS total scores by number of raters for Set A and Set B TWS across two TWS development occasions

	Dependability coefficients	
Number of raters	Set A	Set B
5 raters	.79	.92
4 raters	.77	.91
3 raters	.73	.88
2 raters	.66	.84
1 rater	.52	.74

In the present study, the dependability coefficients for three-member rater panels were found to be .73 and .88 respectively for the two TWS sets when the TWS performances of teacher candidates were rated across two occasions of TWS development. Both dependability coefficients met the minimum criterion of .70. This same criterion has been employed by previous investigations that applied generalizability theory to teacher performance assessments (Cronin & Capie, 1985; Erlich & Shavelson, 1978; Erlich & Borich, 1979; Smith, Waller, & Waller, 1982). The magnitudes of the dependability coefficients are also in concert with the findings of Denner, Salzman, and Bangert (2001) and Denner, Salzman, Newsome, and Birdsong (2003), when a different, modified-holistic scoring rubric was used. Taken together with the previous research findings, the evidence supports the generalizability of TWS total scores for panels of three or more qualified raters. The results for the Set B TWSs also suggest the possibility of reducing the number of needed raters to only one or two experienced raters, assuming careful rater selection and training.

Rater Experience

The effect of rater was not found to be statistically significant for total scores for one of the TWS sets, but it was found to be statistically significant for the other set. Surprisingly, the scoring differences among the raters in the second set did not result in a lower dependability coefficient for that set compared to the first set. Nonetheless, this result confirmed that rater differences can be a source of measurement error and must be carefully monitored when TWS performances are used for the purpose of high-stakes decisions with respect to teacher candidate performance levels. Importantly, rater inexperience was determined to be the central factor associated with the inconsistency of the ratings. This supports the findings of Denner et al. (2003, p. 44), who reported that "when the effect of rater was statistically significant, it was always the least experienced rater who stood out from the others." Hence, teacher candidate TWS performances must be evaluated not only by raters who are well qualified and trained, but also by raters who are experienced at rating TWSs as well.

Generalizability across Performance Occasions

The fact that occasion of development was not found to be statistically significant for either of the TWS sets (Set A or Set B) is an important finding. This finding suggests that candidates' performance levels are generalizable across teaching occasions when teacher candidates teach different topics to different students at different grade levels, typically in different schools, and during different semesters. This also means that the TWS assessment measures important standards-linked aspects of teaching ability. One of the important implications of this finding is that TWS performance levels during preinternship experiences can be used as one source of evidence for determining whether teacher candidates are ready for placement in a full-time student-teaching internship. A second implication is that TWS performance levels demonstrated during student teaching are likely to generalize to initial teaching situations after graduation. Of course, entry-level teachers continue to learn from their teaching experiences, so further research is needed to determine the extent to which TWS performance levels demonstrated during teacher preparation actually generalize to teaching after graduation. Another issue worthy of future investigation is the extent to which TWS performances can serve as a measure of the professional development of teachers as suggested by Denner et al. (2001).

REFERENCES

Brennan, R. L. (2001). *Generalizability theory*. New York: Springer.

Cronin, L. L., & Capie, W. (1985, March). *The influence of scoring procedures on assessment decisions and their reliability*. Paper presented at the annual meeting of the American Educational Research Association, Chicago, IL. (ERIC Document Reproduction No. ED 274 704).

Denner, P. R., Norman, A. D., Salzman, S. A., Pankratz, R. S., & Evans, C. S. (2004). The Partnership teacher work sample: Evidence supporting score generalizability, validity, and quality of student learning assessment. In E. M. Guyton & J. R. Dangel (Eds.), *Teacher education yearbook XII: Research linking teacher preparation and student performance*. Dubuque, IA: Kendall/Hunt.

Denner, P. R., Salzman, S. A., & Bangert, A. W. (2001). Linking teacher assessment to student performance: A benchmarking, generalizability, and validity study of the use of teacher work samples. *Journal of Personnel Evaluation in Education, 15*(4), 287–307.

Denner, P. R., Salzman, S. A., Newsome, J. D., & Birdsong, J. R. (2003). Teacher work sample assessment: Validity and generalizability of performances across occasions of development. *Journal for Effective Schools, 2*(1), 29–48.

Erlich, O., & Borich, G. (1979). Occurrence and generalizability of scores on a classroom interaction instrument. *Journal of Educational Measurement, 16*, 11–18.

Erlich, O., & Shavelson, R. J. (1978). The search for correlations between measures of teacher behavior and student achievement: Measurement problem, conceptualization problem, or both? *Journal of Educational Measurement, 15*, 77–89.

Ingersoll, G. M., & Scannell, D. P. (2002). *Performance-based teacher certification: Creating a comprehensive unit assessment system*. Golden, CO: Fulcrum.

Medley, D. M. (1982). *Teacher competency testing and the teacher educator*. Charlottesville: University of Virginia, Bureau of Educational Research.

Messick, S. (1989). Validity. In R. L. Linn (Ed.), *Educational measurement* (3rd ed., pp. 13–103). New York: Macmillan.

Satterthwaite, F. E. (1946). An approximate distribution of variance components. *Biometrics Bulletin, 2,* 110–114.

Shavelson, R. J., & Webb, N. M. (1991). *Generalizability theory: A primer.* Newbury Park, CA: Sage.

Smith, P. L., Waller, M. I., & Waller, S. P. (1982). Generalizable observations of the teaching process. *Educational and Psychological Measurement, 42,* 467–478.

Stuffelbeam, D. L. (1997). Oregon teacher work sample methodology educational policy review. In J. Millman (Ed.), *Grading teachers, grading schools: Is student achievement a valid evaluation measure?* (pp. 53–61). Thousand Oaks, CA: Corwin Press.

10

Research on First- and Second-Year Teachers Using the TWSM and Pathwise Observation Form B

Tracy Fredman, Kathleen McKean, and Kyle Dahlem

National and state teacher preparation program accreditation and federal reporting requirements have created the need for higher education teacher preparation programs to collect, compile, and analyze long-term data on their teacher candidates and graduates and their impact on student learning. The National Council for Accreditation of Teacher Education (NCATE) standards specify that a graduate "from an accredited department of education should be able to help all pre-kindergarten through twelfth grade (P–12) students learn." The Oklahoma Teacher Enhancement Program (OTEP) was designed to develop a set of assessments based on the Oklahoma Teaching Competencies to demonstrate the impact of teacher preparation and teacher performance on student learning.

The Oklahoma State Regents for Higher Education (OSRHE) partnered with several state agencies (the Oklahoma State Department of Education, the Oklahoma Education Association, and the Oklahoma Commission for Teacher Preparation) in this Title II Teacher Quality Enhancement state grant. Only state institutions participated in the grant in the first year, but in the second year, private institutions were added.

OTEP developed and piloted an assessment system with first- and second-year teachers who had completed a performance-based teacher education program to determine the impact of teacher preparation on student learning. Initially, the assessment system triangulated three assessments: (1) the Teacher Work Sample, (2) Pathwise Induction Program observations, and (3) portfolios maintained by first- and second-year teachers.

Two questions guided the study: (1) do the Teacher Work Sample, the Pathwise Induction observations, and the portfolio comprise valid and reliable measures of the impact of teacher preparation and teacher performance on student learning? and (2) what is the impact of that performance?

METHODOLOGY

OTEP participants included two cohorts of residency teams. Each team consisted of a first- or second-year teacher, a mentor, an administrator, and a higher-education faculty member. The first-year cohort comprised eighty-three teachers and their residency teams; forty-six completed all aspects of the program. Teachers from all grade levels, large and small schools, and urban and rural districts were represented. Higher education was represented by a variety of schools including large and small state universities as well as private colleges.

The second-year cohort comprised seventy-two teams: forty-nine first-year and twenty-three second-year teachers. Two participants were members of the initial cohort. Of the seventy-two teachers, forty-nine completed the TWS portion of the program, and seventy completed the Pathwise component.

Instruments

Oklahoma Teacher Work Sample

The Oklahoma Teacher Work Sample (OTWS) is composed of two sections, the prompt and the rubric. Developed by a committee of three higher-education faculty members and administrators, the OTWS is a modified version of the Emporia State University (a Renaissance Partnership Institution) work sample and addresses the fifteen Oklahoma Teaching Competencies and NCATE standards. The prompt provides instructions and explanation on completing the six factors. The rubric has two parts: a checklist section to designate what should be included in each factor and a varied number of demonstration components (Fredman, 2002).

Using the prompt and rubric and working through the six factors of the OTWS, the teacher develops, implements, and documents a multiweek teaching unit. The OTWS comprises six sections with a set amount of points assigned to each factor:

Factor 1   Contextual Information: research about the students, class-room, school, and community (15 points).

Factor 2   Learning Goals: the unit goals and objectives presented in accordance with Bloom's Taxonomy of Learning (18 points).

Factor 3   Assessment Plan: the unit assessment design, including a description of all assessments used and their relation to the learning objectives (21 points).

Factor 4   Instructional Design: a written plan for teaching the unit, including a table displaying the unit activities and their relationship to the goals and objectives (18 points).

Factor 5   Analysis of Learning: student pre-post scores and learning gains accompanied by the teacher's analysis of the gains (8 points).

Factor 6   Reflection of Learning: the teacher writes a reflection addressing specific questions about his or her teaching of the unit, professional growth, and student learning (20 points).

The teacher summarizes, interprets, and reflects on each step of the teaching process and analyzes student growth in comparison to where students were when the unit began and where they are at the end of the teaching unit. The OTWS yields six factor scores that total one hundred points. To make the OTWS score range comparable to the Pathwise Form B, the range was defined as follows: distinguished, 76–100; proficient, 51–75; basic, 26–50; and unsatisfactory, 0–25.

The OTWS was scored by a team of three trained raters. Estimates of the validity and interrater reliability of the OTWS were published for both years and were similar. Using a two-way repeated-measures design that yielded a generalizability coefficient (G coefficient), the scale was determined to have reliability values of approximately .91 in both years. Thorough training of scorers was found to be critical to the reliability of the instrument.

Pathwise

OTEP used the Pathwise Induction Program which is based on Charlotte Danielson's *Frameworks for Teaching*. Pathwise emphasizes four domains of teaching, (1) planning and preparation, (2) instruction, (3) classroom environment, and (4) professional responsibility, as one of the assessments. Each domain was measured by five to six indicators. To improve reliability of the data, OTEP extended the Pathwise training to include all members of the participating RYC. The training centers on collecting evidence on what the RYT knows and is able to do in the classroom and on how to record the evidence on the observation form. A four-point scale is assigned to a holistic rubric of (1) unsatisfactory, (2) basic, (3) proficient, and (4) distinguished to quantitatively rate RYTs on the four domains.

Form B was thus a 64-point scale (16 items × 4 points possible = 64 total points). Note that the rating of "distinguished" was "reserved for teachers who show a high level of expertise and teaching effectiveness in the classroom." Ratings of "proficient" on all items yielded a score of 48, and ratings of "basic" on all items yielded a score of 32. The lowest possible score was 16.

An analysis of the interrater reliability of the Pathwise Form B scale was conducted. Because it is a lengthy observation form, a great deal of the data were missing, both within forms (e.g., items for which no rating was recorded) and across forms (i.e., individuals who were not rated by all three raters). A total of fifty-eight individuals had three sets of scores, using data from the fall administration. SPSS software calculated intraclass correlations (ICC), using a one-way random model.

The reliability of the Pathwise Form B was less than that of the TWS. The averaged ICC coefficient was .638. Combining the fall and spring administrations to increase the sample size did not increase the ICC; this analysis had a sample size of 116 and an ICC of .626. The ICC of .638 is applicable *only* when multiple raters are used. When one rater is used, the reliability estimate dropped to .358, clearly an unacceptable level. Thirty of the second-year participants had Pathwise Form B scores from three raters in the fall and three raters in the spring. For the first-year participants, complete data were available for only twenty-eight participants. Data for the remaining participants could not be regarded as reliable and were not used in later analyses.

Form B was an observation instrument, and its utility was not limited to the scores yielded by applying the rubric. A major use of the instrument is the initiation of dialogue with the resident teacher and for providing structured formative feedback and initiating plans for improvement.

Portfolio

The OTEP portfolio was originally designed to include a comprehensive set of data that supplemented the OTWS and Pathwise assessments. During the program recruitment phase, project staff determined that the portfolio requirements would require too much time and would be overwhelming to first-year teachers. The instrument was revised, but the purpose appeared to be different from that of the other two instruments. Both time consuming and providing little useful information, this instrument was not used with third-year teachers.

FINDINGS

Table 10.1 summarizes basic descriptive information from all administrations of the Pathwise Form B and Teacher Work Sample instruments. The mean rating on the Pathwise observation forms was at the top of the basic range on the fall assessment and in the proficient range on the spring assessment. (A total score of 48 is required to reach the proficient range). The Teacher Work Samples, all conducted during the spring semesters, were at the top of the proficient range in 2001–2002 and at the bottom of the distinguished range in 2002–2003. (A TWS score of 75 is required to be rated as distinguished.) No statistically significant differences were noted in total scores across years or across semesters.

The instruments were developed with factor or domain structures. The Pathwise Form B was designed to measure three factors, while the OTWS has six. Since no differences were noted across years, the data were aggregated for examination of the factor structure. This increased the sample sizes, compensating to some degree for the lower reliability of the Pathwise scores. The larger *N* gained by aggregating the scores allowed detailed analyses to be conducted.

A principal components analysis was conducted to determine (1) whether the instruments measured separate constructs and (2) the degree to which scores on the instruments were related to student achievement gains, as hypothesized in the grant proposal. The results, although based on a relatively small sample size, revealed three unambiguous factors that could clearly be defined as (1) a Teacher Work Sample factor, (2) a Pathwise factor, and (3) a student gain factor. Table 10.2 shows that these three factors accounted for nearly two-thirds of the total variance.

The Oklahoma Teacher Work Sample subscales alone defined the first variance component; this component was named *OTWS*. The second component was just as clearly defined by high loadings from the three Pathwise domain scores (see figure 10.1 and table 10.3). The third factor was defined by the achievement gains of the resident teachers' students.

The scores from the two assessments are clearly grouped, indicating that these two instruments measure different aspects of teaching. This confirms the research hypothesis upon which the OTEP program was based. These two measures contributed unique information; in fact, the lack of redundancy was surprising. None of the Pathwise domain scores loaded on the TWS component, and only one TWS factor loaded on the Pathwise compo-

Table 10.1. Descriptive statistics, Pathwise TWS data by year

Measure	Statistics	Year 2	Year 3
	Mean	*45.24*	*46.28*
Pathwise Form B, fall	Std. deviation	6.48	5.98
	N	43	73
	Mean	*48.70*	*48.51*
Pathwise Form B, spring	Std. deviation	7.36	6.28
	N	43	72
	Mean	*70.89*	*75.38*
Teacher Work Sample	Std. deviation	16.56	15.40
	N	42	47

Table 10.2.   Principal components analysis, total variance explained

Component	Initial eigenvalues			Rotation sums of squared loadings		
	Total	% of variance	Cumulative %	Total	% of variance	Cumulative %
1	3.10	31.04	31.04	2.96	29.64	29.64
2	2.47	24.69	55.73	2.48	24.84	54.48
3	1.00	10.04	65.77	1.13	11.29	65.77
4	0.96	9.61	75.38			
5	0.69	6.87	82.25			
6	0.56	5.57	87.82			
7	0.44	4.36	92.18			
8	0.32	3.21	95.39			
9	0.30	2.96	98.35			
10	0.17	1.65	100.00			

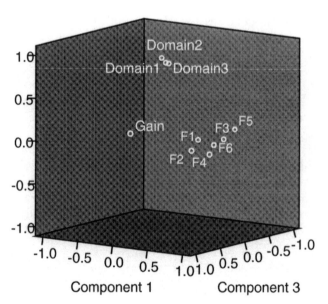

Figure 10.1.   Component Plot in rotated space, using Fall Pathwise scores

nent. The student gain component, however, contained moderate loadings from both of the instruments. Figure 10.1 shows the ten variables in three-dimensional space; the clear delineation of the components is noteworthy. Also noteworthy is the placement of the Student Gain component—between the OTWS and Pathwise components. This confirms the research hypothesis upon which the OTEP program was based: the TWSM and the

Table 10.3. Rotated component matrix (varimax).*

Variable	Component		
	1	2	3
TWS Factor 3: Assessment Plan	.794		
TWS Factor 4: Instructional Design	.790		.273
TWS Factor 5: Analysis of Learning	.770	.131	-.275
TWS Factor 6: Reflection of Learning	.653		
TWS Factor 2: Learning Goals	.594		.359
TWS Factor 1: Contextual Information	.566		.184
Pathwise Domain 2: Classroom Environment		.932	
Pathwise Domain 3: Instruction		.897	.138
Pathwise Domain 1: Planning and Preparation		.862	
Average Student Gain	.100	.181	.891

*Note that correlations less than .10 are not displayed.

Pathwise Observation form together demonstrate the impact of teacher preparation and quality on student learning.

The variable with the highest loading on the Student Gain factor was the TWS Learning Goals score. A positive loading from the TWS Instructional Design score and an inverse loading from the TWS Analysis of Learning score were next, followed by minor loadings from the TWS Contextual Information score and the Pathwise domain 3 (Instruction) score. Student Gain loaded on the Pathwise factor, so the variance shared by these two instruments was "already used" before the third component was generated. The relationship between the Student Gain score and the Pathwise scores tended to be general, across all three domains, rather than specific.

Because of the small sample size and the low reliability of the Pathwise scores, a second principal components analysis was conducted, replacing the fall Pathwise domain scores with those from the spring observations. The results were similar to those of the first analysis, as illustrated in figure 10.2.

Effect on Student Achievement

Two analyses were conducted using the 2001–2002 OTWS scores: (1) the first analysis was conducted to determine whether a relationship existed between the quality of the residency year experience and OTWS scores, and (2) the second analysis was conducted to determine whether student achievement, as measured by the OTWS, was related to teacher quality as measured by the other instruments used as a part of OTEP.

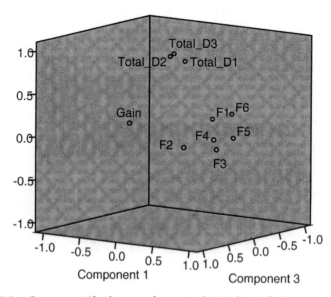

Figure 10.2.   Component Plot in rotated space, using Spring Pathwise scores

Analysis 1: Quality of Resident-Year Experience and Student Achievement

The implementation levels were not the same for all residency teams. This discrepancy in implementation levels permitted an assessment of the effect of the PDI on student achievement as defined by pre-post analyses of the student achievement data included in the OTWS. Trainers identified two groups of participating teams: (1) "ideal" or "excellent" implementations of the mentoring program, and (2) "unsatisfactory" or "poor" implementations. Comparisons of these two groups' OTWS student achievement data were conducted. The research hypothesis was that resident teachers whose teams fully participated in the program would earn higher OTWS scores and demonstrate a greater degree of student improvement (pre-post).

A repeated-measures ANOVA was conducted to determine whether the implementation level (satisfactory vs. unsatisfactory) was related to the pre-post change in students' achievement scores. No significant difference was noted; however, the small sample size resulted in an analysis that had low power to detect such a relationship, $F(1, 26) = 4.106$, $p = .053$, power = .497). The results suggested that this is a promising area for further study.

Analysis 2: Relationship between Student Achievement and Teacher Quality

The second analysis was conducted to determine whether student achievement, as measured in the OTWS, was related to teacher quality as measured by the other instruments used as a part of OTEP. The OTEP process utilized three separate measures of teacher quality: a portfolio assessment, the Pathwise assessment, and the Teacher Work Sample. Analysis 2 was conducted to determine whether these "teacher quality" scores were related to pre-post change in student achievement, as measured by class average scores included in the OTEP. The correlation matrix shows the degree of relationship across these measures (see table 10.4).

Two outliers artificially inflated the pre-post correlation because these teachers did not compute student scores on a percentage-correct basis—they had very low ceiling scores. When these two outliers were removed from the pre-post student achievement data, the correlation between pre and post changed from an (inflated) value of .527 to a more accurate .319.

A linear regression analysis was conducted, using the forty-one remaining subjects. The student pretest and the three teacher measures were used to predict student posttest scores. The pretest and teacher quality measures accounted for 72.3 percent of the variance in posttest scores ($R = .850.$). Significant predictors were the pretest (nearly always the best predictor of posttest scores), the TWS, and the Pathwise total score (spring). The portfolio score was not significantly related to the pre-post difference. Without the pretest, scores on the three instruments were still significantly related to the pre-post gain ($R = .474$, $R^2 = .225$). In other words, students whose teachers scored higher on the Pathwise and TWS demonstrated greater gains in achievement.

A replication study, using 2002–2003 data, resulted in statistically significant findings; however, the magnitude of the R and R^2 values was much smaller, and the influence of the instruments was reversed (see table 10.5). In the 2002–2003 study, the Pathwise instrument was a better predictor of student achievement than the OTWS. A number of factors were differ-

Table 10.4. 2001–2002 OTEP measures, Pearson *r* correlations (*N* = 43 in all cells)

Measure	Student gain	Student posttest	Student pretest	Work sample	Pathwise (spring)	Portfolio
Student pre-post gain	1.00					
Student posttest scores	0.43**	1.00				
Student pretest scores	-0.53**	0.53**	1.00			
Work sample total	0.24	0.08	-0.17	1.00		
Pathwise (spring)	0.18	-0.04	-0.20	-0.06	1.00	
Portfolio score	0.17	-.32*	-.46**	0.14	0.20	1.00
Total teacher score	0.31*	-0.03	-.34*	.86**	0.38**	.47**

** Correlation is significant at the 0.01 level (2-tailed).
* Correlation is significant at the 0.05 level (2-tailed).

ent including a smaller number of instruments, differences in the range of student pre-post scores, and a greater number of instruments rated by only two raters.

The sample sizes for all analyses were very small, and these should be regarded as pilot investigations. Larger sample sizes will yield more reliable results and facilitate more detailed analyses of these phenomena, including an analysis of the factors related to teacher improvement and of those related to changes in student achievement. Learning what these sets of factors have in common should prove of interest to teacher preparation professionals.

GRANT COROLLARY

In 2000, during initial meetings of the partners, discussions centered on developing assessments that would benefit the state colleges of education. Since data collection was fragmented at best, the goal of developing statewide assessment tools was enticing. In fact, the revised NCATE standards, the impending No Child Left Behind law, and the Title II report card all contained overtones of strengthened accountability measures which included directly linking student achievement to teacher preparation programs. Ironically, the deans of education were not particularly thrilled with the proposal even though the assessments were intended to provide relevant data to inform programs as well as to document graduate effectiveness. There was a suspicion that unfunded and unmanageable mandates would be the result. Despite the lack of consistent support from the state colleges, deans of education from the private institutions asked to be included in the pilot.

Throughout the four-year implementation, monthly meetings of the partners and representatives from the Oklahoma Association of Colleges of Teacher Education provided a vehicle for input and feedback. Additionally,

Table 10.5.   2002-2003 OTEP measures, Pearson r correlations (N = 45 in all cells)

Measure	Student gain	Student posttest	Student pretest	Work sample	Pathwise (spring)
Student pre-post gain	1.00				
Student posttest scores	0.54**	1.00			
Student pretest scores	-0.47**	0.28	1.00		
Work sample total	0.14	0.02	-0.02	1.00	
Pathwise (spring)	0.36*	0.08	-0.22	0.17	1.00

** Correlation is significant at the 0.01 level (2-tailed).
* Correlation is significant at the 0.05 level (2-tailed).

monthly reports from the OTEP coordinator evidenced a sincere effort to be as transparent as possible in the creation of a system that had the potential for serious ramifications.

The success of the program is evidenced by the findings of the research and the resultant professional development. Even further is the fact that fourteen of the twenty-four colleges of education have embedded the TWS in methodology courses. Teacher Work Sample data is also being used in annual reports and NCATE documents.

CONCLUSIONS

The Pathwise Form B provided valuable, observable evidence of the teacher's performance in the classroom and was complemented by the Oklahoma Teacher Work Sample, which contributed a written plan of instruction, practice, analysis, and reflection by the teacher on his or her performance. A principal components analysis demonstrated that the instruments complemented each other, were not redundant, and showed a relationship to student learning as measured by the unit pre-post scores. Participants' mean scores on these instruments showed that teachers had reached a proficient level of teaching by the end of their induction experience.

The TWSM, one of the most relevant, informative, and valuable tools for teacher preparation programs, can be used in determining and recording evidence of teacher candidate preparedness and program quality and linking it with student learning. The inclusive nature of the TWSM distinguishes it from other teacher preparation program assessments used in documenting program and teacher quality and encompasses an essential piece of evidence in the assessment puzzle linking teacher preparation to student learning and the assessment of students. If the TWSM rubric and scoring sheet are composed to distinguish specific knowledge and skills, the TWSM has the capability to pinpoint areas for improvement in a preparation program and, most importantly, in a teacher's practice. Coupling the TWSM with an observation assessment when implementing the work sample strengthens the assessment process and truly creates a performance-based teacher assessment system promoting dialogue between teacher and evaluator and helping teachers improve practice, and preparation programs meet realistic needs for all levels of teachers.

REFERENCES

Fredman, T. (2006, February). *The TWSM: An essential component in the assessment of teacher performance and student learning.* Paper presented at the AACTE conference, New York, NY. ERIC, ED 464046.

Girod, G. (Ed.). (2002). Connecting teaching and learning: A handbook for teacher educators on teacher work sample methodology. Washington, DC: AACTE Publications, 5–31.

McKean, K. E. (2004, January). *Oklahoma Teacher Enhancement Program: Effectiveness of the training model.* Report prepared for the Oklahoma State Regents for Higher Education, Oklahoma Technical Assistance Center, Cushing, OK.

11

Contextualizing the Teacher Work Sample: An Evolving Early Childhood Perspective

Karen S. Buchanan and Mary Johnson

One of the beauties of the Teacher Work Sample (TWS) is that it employs a common framework that is applied across all licensure levels and specialty areas (Brodsky & Schalock, 2001). The one-size-fits-all structure, however, has potential to be problematic for programs committed to providing opportunity for their teacher candidates to demonstrate specialty competence. For example, candidates preparing to teach in Oregon's early childhood licensure level (age three to the fourth grade) receive specialized training that addresses the tremendous physical, cognitive, and social/emotional growth that occurs in young children. Teachers need to be well versed in child development and use that knowledge to select developmentally appropriate practices, learning goals, and age-appropriate assessments. Demonstrating this type of specialty competence is critical for our candidates and necessary for institutions seeking NCATE accreditation.

Arthur Wise, in NCATE's spring 2006 issue of *Quality Teaching*, set the expectation that teacher candidates must demonstrate content and content-specific pedagogical knowledge. He illustrates this point by stating that NCATE "expects science teachers to be able to teach according to the standards of the National Science Teachers Association" (p. 7). NCATE also expects early childhood teachers to teach according to specialty standards as defined by the National Association for the Education of Young Children (NAEYC) Standards for Early Childhood Professional Preparation in Initial Licensure Programs (2003).

At George Fox University (GFU), both undergraduate and graduate (master of arts in teaching—MAT) candidates recommended for initial teaching licensure are required to complete two teacher work samples in two different classroom settings. This program expectation is reflective of Oregon licensure requirements. For most George Fox candidates, this requirement is met during each of their student teaching experiences, one at each authorization level. In Oregon, authorization levels are available in early childhood (age three to grade four), elementary (grade three to grade eight), middle-level education (grade five to grade ten), and high school education (grade seven to grade twelve). The intent of the licensure levels and the dual student teaching experience is to ensure that teachers have specialized knowledge and skills and demonstrate competence in working with children at each licensure level. The TWS is one tool that we use to document a candidate's ability to demonstrate the required knowledge, skills, and competencies at each authorization level.

At George Fox, the majority of teacher candidates are recommended for licensure in dual early childhood and elementary authorization levels. As early childhood specialists, we have a vested interest in ensuring that the candidates we recommend for licensure are demonstrating not only state standards but also NAEYC standards for initial licensure. Since the TWS serves as a key assessment tool for the demonstration of early childhood competence, we have taken the opportunity to carefully examine our expectations for candidates and their performance. The purpose of this chapter is to describe our journey studying and improving our practice as it relates to early childhood Teacher Work Samples.

REVIEW OF THE LITERATURE

As we began to wrestle with the notion of the TWS allowing candidates to demonstrate specialty competence, we became curious if other colleagues in the field were dealing with similar struggles and found that this aspect of TWSM is in its infancy. Schepige (2006), a professor at Western Oregon University, talks about her journey developing science-specific TWS requirements for her secondary-level preservice educators. Her project grew out of the frustration she encountered scoring science work samples based on generic TWS requirements. Her candidates' lack of evidence around sound scientific pedagogy in their Teacher Work Samples inspired her current work in progress. Hegler (2003) describes the use of the TWS to evaluate his special education teacher candidates. The TWS requirements are designed to evaluate general education outcomes as well as special education outcomes. Ernest Pratt (2002) collected a sample of fifty mathematic work samples from elementary through high school teacher candidates that had been prepared with general TWS requirements. He was interested in whether the general TWS requirements were successful at encouraging candidates to apply the National Council of Teachers of Mathematics (NCTM) national standards in their classroom practice. His study showed weak alignment with NCTM standards for all the work samples.

Pratt's (2002) work, coupled with anecdotal evidence from our own experience with early childhood candidates, inspired our inquiry project investigating whether George Fox early childhood Teacher Work Sample requirements in undergraduate and graduate initial licensure programs are adequate indicators of competence as defined by the NAEYC Standards for Early Childhood Professional Preparation in Initial Licensure Programs (2003). The NAEYC standards were created from a solid body of research regarding effective practices in early childhood education, and guide teacher preparation institutions seeking to align their program with early childhood outcomes. These initial licensure standards are organized around the five broad statements below; each standard is further defined by a set of accompanying key elements (NAEYC, 2003). Explanations of these standards are in appendix C.

Standard 1: Promoting child development and learning
Standard 2: Building family and community relationships
Standard 3: Observing, documenting, and assessing to support young children and families
Standard 4: Teaching and learning
Standard 5: Becoming a professional

EXAMINING GFU TWS TOOLS AND STUDENT OUTCOMES

Our self-study, conducted in three phases, began by drawing a convenience sample of fifty from a pool of eighty-five undergraduate and graduate early childhood Teacher Work Samples. The sample included eleven kindergarten, ten first-grade, ten second-grade, ten third-grade, and nine mixed-age work samples created and taught during the candidates' student teaching experience from 2003 to 2005. First, an alignment of the George Fox Teacher Work Sample requirements and NAEYC standards was completed. Missing NAEYC standards in the Teacher Work Sample requirements became variables of interest for further study. Second, a scoring rubric was created to investigate these variables of interest within the Teacher Work Samples. Third, the sample was examined for the variables of interest. Finally, results were analyzed reported, and recommendations for retooling our requirements and enhancing our course content were set forth.

Alignment of NAEYC Standards and GFU TWS Requirements

The first phase of the self-study aligned the key elements of each NAEYC standard with the GFU requirements for undergraduate and graduate Teacher Work Samples. Along with expectations of professionalism, cultural proficiency, and technology, both departments divide the Teacher Work Sample into five sections:

Section 1: Description of school, setting, students, curriculum, and self
Section 2: Mapping, standards, and assessments
Section 3: Lesson plans and daily reflections
Section 4: Learning gains data
Section 5: Final unit reflection

Departmental TWS handbooks provide guidance to all teacher candidates as they complete each of the five sections. These guidelines were created to be applicable for Teacher Work Samples from pre-K to grade twelve.

The alignment of TWS requirements and NAEYC standards revealed three categories of significant elements either missing or not reflective of the depth required by the NAEYC standards. These missing elements, which became our variables of interest, were especially evident in NAEYC Standard 1 and Standard 2.

1. Understanding and application of child development to learning
   Standard 1: Promoting child development and learning: candidates use their understanding of young children's characteristics and needs.

2. Creating environments that promote learning
   Standard 1: Promoting child development and learning: candidates create environments that are healthy, respectful, supportive, and challenging for all children.

3. Involving families and communities in children's development and learning
   Standard 2: Building family and community relationships:
   candidates know about, understand, and value the importance and complex characteristics of children's families and communities. They use this understanding to create respectful, reciprocal relationships that support and empower families, and to involve all families in their children's development and learning. (NAEYC, 2003, p. 29)

Variables of Interest

During phase two, a rubric was created that included these three key elements of the NAEYC standards, as well as the work sample section where we would expect to find that element (the rubric is included in appendix C). For example, evidence of the understanding and application of child development should be found in sections 1 and 2.

First Key Element: Understanding and Application of Child Development

In section 1 of the TWS, we looked specifically for a candidate's ability to describe and reference developmental characteristics associated with the given age group. This could include references to cognitive, social, emotional, and/or physical characteristics that should be considered when designing a teaching and learning unit. Additionally, we expected to see descriptions of children whose development might differ from generic age group characteristics. In section 2, candidates demonstrate their understanding of development by selecting appropriate state benchmark and learning goals.

We expected to see evidence of the application of knowledge of child development in sections 2 and 3. In section 2, the rationale for why the unit is appropriate for this group of students provides an opportunity for evidence, as well as developmentally appropriate and educationally significant assessments. In section 3, the rubric investigates candidate lesson plans and lesson reflections for evidence of the application of knowledge regarding child development.

Second Element: Creating Environments That Promote Learning

A second missing element to be investigated was *creating environments that promote learning*. The rubric we created looks for evidence of this element in sections 2 and 3. In section 2 of the TWS, candidates have an opportunity to show how their unit plans address the use of/or modification to the environmental setup. In section 3, lesson plans and daily reflections, the rubric looks for ways candidates have planned to modify or enrich the environment through their daily lesson plans.

Third Element: Involving Families and Communities in Children's Development and Learning

The final missing element, *involving families and communities*, is examined in sections 2 and 3. In section 2, candidates have an opportunity to not only demonstrate ways that they have communicated with families about the learning in the TWS, but they also have a chance to show how they might collaborate with families in the learning process. Section 3 allows candidates to explain how they might involve parents and the community in the learning experience.

INVESTIGATING VARIABLES OF INTEREST IN TEACHER WORK SAMPLES

The last phase of our project involved reviewing a sample of TWS using the rubric referenced above. We were interested to see if the variables of interest, though missing in the guidelines, were present in the candidates' finished work. If evident, did they meet the target descriptors cited on the rubric? Fifty work samples, randomly selected from a pool of eighty-five early childhood work samples completed during the last two years, were divided between the two researchers, analyzed, and scored. To provide interrater reliability, the professors came together midway through the scoring and cross-scored samples, sharing supporting evidence for their scoring to date. Strong scoring commonality was revealed.

Results

Not surprisingly, table 11.1 shows that our teacher candidates clearly identify state benchmark standards as the foundation for their curricula design. Our program places great emphasis on students demonstrating knowledge of state benchmark standards. However, in their planning, our students did not explicitly talk about development regarding their student's age group or the development of individual children. When candidates spoke about individual development, it was typically in reference to a child's reading level, or they saw a lower level of development as a disability.

Daily reflections are required in section 3 of the TWS where candidates reflect on successes and failures in the daily teaching and learning process. Of particular interest were the reflections relating to development where candidates attributed their successes or failures to the developmental levels of the students. The ability to reflect in this way leads us to believe that our teacher candidates do, in fact, have the developmental knowledge that we have sought to teach them in their early childhood coursework. However, our work sample requirements did not encourage candidates to think proactively about their practice when they are planning for instruction.

In the second section of the Teacher Work Sample, we looked for *use of* or *modification to* the environmental setup in the planning of the overall unit. In section 3 we searched daily lesson plans looking for modifications made

Table 11.1.   Understanding and application of child development

Evidence of understanding and application of child development	None	Evident	Target
Developmental stages	44	5	1
Describes individuals	22	24	4
Appropriate benchmarks	0	6	44
Rationale for these students	38	8	4
Appropriate/significant assessment	17	29	4
Lesson plans varied/balanced	14	28	8
Reflections relate to development	11	29	10

to alter or enrich the daily learning environment. Table 11.2 shows that in their overall unit plan, our teacher candidates rarely considered environmental setup. But greater attention was paid to modifying and enriching the environment in their individual lesson plans.

Still only about half of the candidates paid attention to this element. In our early childhood course sequence, we talk about the Reggio-inspired notion of the environment as a third teacher (Curtis & Carter, 2003). Teacher candidates do not seem to be translating this classroom theory into practice.

The third variable, involving families and communities, proved to be interesting. Table 11.3 clearly indicates that our candidates have included some form of communication with parents about their TWS content. This is not surprising, given the fact that our work sample requirements include a brochure or newsletter sharing the purpose and content of the Teacher Work Sample.

The NAEYC guidelines, however, reach far beyond communicating with parents to building reciprocal relationships with families and empowering them as partners in their child's development. The standard includes involving community as well. Only 20 percent of our samples showed evidence of this, and none of the work samples were on target.

IMPROVING OUR PRACTICE

This self-study project has convinced us that Teacher Work Sample Methodology can be an accurate assessment of "learning to teach" and "teaching to learn" in early childhood education. Our experiences have led us to improve our practice so that our candidates have the opportunity to document the learning and growth of young children in the TWS. Our improvements include retooling our TWS requirements and enhancing course content in our early childhood course sequence.

Table 11.2. Attention to environment

Evidence showing attention to environment	None	Evident	Target
Unit plan attends to environment	46	4	0
Daily plans attend to environment	20	28	2

Table 11.3. Involving family and community

Evidence involving family and community	None	Evident	Target
Family/community communication	7	42	1
Family/community collaboration	38	12	0
Family/community involvement	40	10	0

Retooling Teacher Work Sample Requirements

The work of our candidates shows they are receiving sufficient content regarding variable 1: *understanding and application of child development*. We want our candidates, however, to spend time in the planning phase of their lessons thinking critically about development. After teaching their lessons, we hear candidates reflecting on the developmental appropriateness of their plans. It is most obvious to them when their planning was not appropriate for the developmental age of the children. Therefore, we have taken steps to retool both undergraduate and graduate TWS guidelines to require candidates to focus on and preplan based on developmental considerations.

Variable 2 study results, *creating environments that promote learning*, were weak, particularly in how candidates planned to use the environment from a unit planning perspective. We chose to address this by retooling our TWS expectations in chapter 2 as candidates create their unit plan. They are required to write a section regarding how the environment will be created and/or modified to enhance and extend the learning of students.

Variable 3 results, *involving families and communities in children's development and learning*, indicated that candidates were fairly proficient at producing a communication piece for families describing the TWS content. This finding was not surprising since the TWS guidelines clearly required it. But NAEYC standards go far beyond communication to collaboration with families. Therefore, we retooled our expectations to require candidates to demonstrate collaboration with families and communities.

We have implemented these retooled guidelines for almost a year and a half. After raising our expectations and aligning with NAEYC standards, we see more consistent results demonstrating early childhood specialty competence.

Enhancing Course Content

The results of our study not only led us to retool TWS requirements, but also to reexamine our course content and delivery. A recent end-of-program survey revealed that our graduates did not feel prepared to work with families. This finding, combined with our TWS self-study results, troubled us because we had assumed that this content was embedded in coursework and that instructors even infused this content throughout all program coursework. Our data tells us that our assumptions were incorrect. We chose to redesign the module of our Early Childhood Education course focused on collaborating with families and communities. We even chose to teach it first, as a foundation for other course modules. When we begin with this key component of early childhood education, candidates tend to see it as a thread that runs through all early childhood content.

Variable 2 results challenged us, as instructors, to find ways to bring the environmental piece alive in our early childhood coursework. Previous course content had emphasized environment but had not helped candidates translate that theory into practice. We have enhanced our content by providing more focused experience in field observations, and we are experimenting with a collaborative project where candidates create a "model" early childhood environment on campus.

SUMMARY

Marilyn Cochran-Smith (2006), in her editorial "Taking Stock in 2006: Evidence, Evidence Everywhere," reminds us that the current research, policy, and practice climate is focused on evidence. This inquiry project has not only helped our program take needed steps toward requiring our candidates to demonstrate evidence of their specialty competence, but it has also provided us with the stimulus to improve our own practice by redesigning our coursework and retooling our TWS requirements. Initial results from our piloted changes indicate that adjustments in TWS requirements around specialty competencies offer great promise for providing the evidence needed to certify competence in a specialty area. Our efforts will continue to be studied over the next few years as we seek to better prepare future teachers for the challenges of the early childhood classroom.

REFERENCES

Brodsky, M., & Schalock, D. (speakers). (2001). *Teacher Work Sample Methodology: An introduction to connecting teacher work to P–12 student progress* (CD-ROM). Monmouth, OR: Western Oregon University.

Cartwright, D. D., & Blacklock, K. K. (2003). *Teacher Work Samples and struggling readers: Impacting student performance and candidate dispositions.* (ED472395). Paper presented at the annual meeting of AACTE, New Orleans, LA.

Cochran-Smith, M. (2006). Taking stock in 2006: Evidence, evidence everywhere. *Journal of Teacher Education, 57,* 6–12. Retrieved January 5, 2006, from jte.sage.com/current.dtl.

Curtis, D., & Carter, M. (2003). *Designs for living and learning: Transforming early childhood environments.* St. Paul, MN: Redleaf Press.

Hegler, K. L. (2003). *Evaluating the use of Teacher Work Samples to describe teacher candidate competence and PK–12 learning.* Paper presented at the annual meeting of AACTE, New Orleans, LA.

National Association for the Education of Young Children. (2001). *NAEYC standards for early childhood professional preparation: Initial licensure.* Washington, DC: Author.

Pratt, E. O. (2002). Aligning mathematics Teacher Work Sample content with selected NCTM Standards: Implications for preservice teacher education. *Journal of Personnel Evaluation in Education, 16*(3), 175–190.

Schepige, A. (2006, February). *Generic or subject specific Teacher Work Samples as evidence of teacher effectiveness?* Paper presented at the annual meeting of AACTE, San Diego, CA.

Wise, A. (2006, Spring). The role of research in NCATE accreditation. *Quality Teaching, 14*(2), 7–8.

Wright, D. (2002). Teacher Work Sample Methodology in early childhood and elementary preparation: A case study. In G. Girod (Ed.), *Connecting teaching and learning: A handbook for teacher educators on Teacher Work Sample Methodology* (pp. 361–374). Washington, DC: American Association of Colleges for Teacher Education.

12

Using Teacher Work Sample Data for Program Improvement

John Henning and Frank Kohler

In this chapter, we describe an approach to establishing a line of research around Teacher Work Sample (TWS) Methodology for the purpose of improving a teacher education program. Our approach to using the TWS as a source of data could best be described as programmatic; that is, it involves collecting data in multiple stages over an extended period of time. In contrast to individual investigations, programmatic studies are sequential or build upon one another in a logical fashion and often become more complex over time. For example, a series of five to six investigations might examine the same research questions, look at the same dependent variables, or institute the same instructional methods to improve student learning. The overall goal of programmatic research is to achieve outcomes that would not be possible with studies that occur in isolation or independently of one another (Roane, Fisher, & McDonough, 2003; Strowig & Farwell, 1966).

Programmatic research approaches can differ depending on the nature of the topic or area under investigation. In this chapter, we will describe and illustrate three different types of research studies that apply to the TWS methodology. These studies are presented in the order in which they might logically occur during a process of adopting and implementing the TWS into a teacher education program. We refer to the first type of study as implementation and impact studies. These types of studies might occur very early in the acclimation process and focus on issues related to feasibility and logistics of implementation, as well as the impact of the TWS on existing practices. The second type of research involves analyzing TWS scores. These studies can reveal trends and areas of strength and weakness in student teachers' performance and are most informative after a stable system of scoring Teacher Work Samples has been implemented. The third type of research involves analyzing the TWS contents. A content analysis investigates questions that extend beyond the limits of a scoring analysis. For example, this type of study might entail an in-depth examination of student teachers' assessments or the quality of their reflections in the TWS. In the following sections, each of these will be described more thoroughly and illustrated with examples. We include a number of previously published studies for the benefit of readers who would like to examine individual studies more thoroughly.

IMPLEMENTATION AND IMPACT STUDIES

The TWS was initially adopted at the University of Northern Iowa (UNI) in the spring of 2000. Our initial concern was learning how to successfully incorporate and implement the TWS during these early stages. To address these concerns we conducted a series of pilot studies to explore the feasibility and logistics of implementing these new practices. These studies focused on questions such as "How can TWS methodology best be implemented?" or "To what degree has TWS methodology been incorporated into various aspects of our program?"

One of our first implementation studies occurred immediately after adoption when our faculty had no experience with the TWS. This pilot study included approximately fifteen student teachers, fifteen cooperating teachers, and thirty UNI faculty members. This group of participants was divided into ten teams that included a student teacher, a cooperating teacher, a faculty member from the college of education, and a faculty member from a content area who taught a core methods course. The primary goal or impetus was to learn about the feasibility and specific steps involved in completing a TWS. The cooperating teacher and the two faculty members on each team worked together to examine and facilitate the student teacher's completion of a TWS. Each team met on a weekly basis to discuss the various processes and guide the student teacher through each individual step. In addition, the two faculty members also completed a TWS for a unit of their own teaching. This research activity produced valuable information about the process of completing a TWS. All four team members were able to gain a richer understanding of the steps required for the seven processes. In addition, the university instructor and cooperating teacher also gained knowledge about the types and level of support that student teachers might require to complete a TWS. Other outcomes included the development of specific directions or prompts for completing each TWS process and a plan to incorporate the TWS into two student-teaching centers.

Closely related to implementation studies are investigations designed to examine the impact of implementing the TWS. These studies often consist of surveys or interviews of stakeholders involved in the implementation process. Typically, they ask, "What changes have occurred as a result of implementation?" or "What impact have these changes had on teaching, learning, or other aspects of the program?" For example, shortly after the TWS was implemented, we surveyed student and cooperating teachers by asking them to do the following: (1) rate the importance of each TWS process for effective teaching (on a 1-to-5 scale); (2) rate how skilled they believed themselves to be at incorporating that process into teaching; and (3) provide a specific example of how each process was implemented throughout the course of teaching. Results indicated that many student teachers provided higher ratings of importance and skill from pre- to post-administration. In addition, the data indicated that many cooperating teachers were actively involved in implementing the TWS along with their student teachers. Finally, we gained many excellent examples of how the various TWS processes were being incorporated into teaching practice. These were later incorporated into supporting materials for guiding student teachers through the process of completing a TWS.

Impact studies often follow and build upon implementation studies. For example, two years after implementing the TWS, we conducted a pilot study to implement an abbreviated version of the TWS in an early field experience. (For a more thorough treatment of this study, refer to Henning, DeBruin-Parecki, Hawbaker, Nielsen, Joram, & Gabriele, 2005.) The adapted TWS was incorporated into a twenty-five-hour field experience that all teacher education majors are required to take early in their program. This field experience is housed in the university laboratory school, which provided easy access and a high degree of coordination between laboratory school teachers and university faculty. All preservice teachers have the opportunity to interact with teachers, conduct classroom observations, and teach two individual lessons.

This study was conducted with twenty-one teacher candidates who were placed with ten cooperating teachers at the University Laboratory School. After completing their field experience, each candidate and their cooperating teacher completed a survey and participated in a focus group. These assessments addressed teachers' and candidates' perceptions about the implementation and impact of the modified TWS. Implementation questions focused on the workload of the modified TWS, as well as on the level of support that candidates needed to be successful. Questions about impact focused on the effectiveness of the modified TWS for enhancing candidates' overall learning, lesson plan organization, and ability to make connections between course work and teaching and to conduct high-quality assessments and reflection. Results of this study demonstrated that the student-teaching work sample could be modified to fit an early field experience, which led to the full implementation of the adapted TWS.

After implementation, we conducted an impact study involving all 270 teacher candidates. Following completion of this field experience, each participant completed a twenty-item survey that related to the requirements, support, and impact of the adapted TWS. Field experience participants and cooperating teachers both reported that the adapted TWS was effective for promoting reflection and assessment and provided benefits that alternative assignments did not. In addition, both groups also believed that the workload was appropriate and that students received adequate levels of support. These findings convinced us to retain the modified TWS as an integral requirement for this field experience.

We have continued to employ implementation and impact studies as our work with the TWS has evolved. For example, in the spring of 2006, we piloted several revisions to the Renaissance TWS prompt over a period of several semesters. This study provided information that led us to make significant changes in the way student teachers analyzed student learning, as well as minor changes in the Contextual Factors, Assessment Plan, and Reflection and Self-Evaluation teaching processes. Both implementation and impact studies continue to provide valuable information for us regarding TWS methodology.

In summary, implementation and impact studies serve several integral functions in the process of acclimating the TWS methodology into a teacher education program. These studies address issues that exist very early in the development of a program, such as concerns about feasibility, logistics, extent of implementation, and perceptions of key users or stakeholders. The studies described above also produced results that paved the way for larger-scale implementation of the TWS and enabled research that addressed the next two stages of investigation.

ANALYSES OF TWS SCORES

A second form of TWS research involves analyzing TWS scores. Each TWS at the University of Northern Iowa is scored to determine if student teachers have attained a minimal level of competency before receiving licensure (Schalock & Myton, 1988). The scoring is done by a diverse group of teacher education faculty members, including professors, student teacher supervisors, and cooperating teachers. Preferably, each Teacher Work Sample is read and scored by at least two faculty members. Faculty members consult criterion-referenced standards and analytic rubrics developed by the Renaissance Group for each of the seven teaching processes. Each rubric standard is based on descriptions of key indicators and scored analytically on a three-point scale with a 3 meaning "standard met," a 2 meaning "standard partially met," and a 1 meaning "standard not met." In addition, an overall score of 1, 2, or 3 is assigned to the TWS itself. The numerical scales described above were derived from the Renaissance TWS prompt, but they can vary among teacher education programs (for an example of an analysis of TWS scores using a different numerical scale, see Fredman, McKean, & Dahlem, this volume).

The scores from Teacher Work Samples can be used for a variety of analytical purposes, such as establishing reliability of scoring processes (for an example, see Denner, Newsome, & Newsome, this volume). TWS scores can also be used to chart areas of strength and weakness in the program over time, to track student-teacher performance, or to compare two or more instructional approaches. For example, Henning and Robinson (2004) presented four semesters of TWS scores at UNI from 2002 and 2003. The data showed a continual improvement in TWS scores with increasing familiarity of TWS methodology. It also revealed the Contextual Factors, Analysis of Learning, and Self-Evaluation and Reflection as the three lowest-scoring teaching processes. The two highest-scoring sections were Learning Goals and Instructional Decision Making. In another study utilizing TWS scores, Watkins and Bratberg (2006) compared the TWS scores for Learning Goals, Assessment Plan, and Design for Instruction between students in the arts (theater arts, visual arts, and music) and students in the content areas (math, social studies, and English). Their findings indicated that the mean summative scores for students in the arts were consistently higher than students in the content areas. The authors explained the difference by suggesting that the teacher candidates in the arts engage students in a more authentic and open curriculum.

TWS scores have also been used to track the effectiveness of an instructional approach in physical education. For example, Philips and Marston (2008) conducted a preliminary analysis of TWS scores for student teachers in physical education during the spring and fall semesters of 2002. Their analysis showed that physical education majors received lower TWS scores than a comparison group consisting of all majors in teacher education. Based on this analysis, the faculty designed a strategy that modified the prompts for Learning Goals, Design of Instruction, Instructional Decision Making, and Self-Evaluation and Reflection. Following the intervention, TWS scores from fall 2004 and spring 2005 were analyzed. Findings indicated statistically significant gains in the following teaching processes: Learning Goals, Design for Instruction, Instructional Decision Making, and Reflection and Self-Evaluation. Although, the all-majors group still outscored the physical education majors group, the physical education majors showed more improvement from 2002 in every area except Analysis of Student Learning.

In summary, the analysis of scores can accomplish important functions in the development of a TWS program. The process of examining scores is necessary to determine whether student teachers have attained a minimal level of competency before receiving licensure (Schalock & Myton, 1988). TWS scores can also be analyzed and tracked over time to identify student teachers' areas of strength and weakness. Once trends are established, then faculty can examine the impact of program differences or changes in TWS scores. Recently, we began using TWS scores as part of a collegewide mapping activity to examine how well we address the ten INTASC standards in our program.

ANALYSIS OF TWS CONTENTS

Typically, the analysis of the TWS contents involves a careful reading of selected parts of the TWS to address more specific questions about the thinking of student teachers, such as, "In what way can an analysis of Teacher Work Samples inform us about the teaching and thinking skills of student teachers?" A content analysis of the TWS can range from the very informal approach of simply reading a TWS and taking notes on interesting aspects of student performance to more formal, published studies. While more informal approaches to analyzing the TWS contents can occur during an early phase of the implementation process, more complex studies depend on having established a stable cycle of completing and scoring a TWS. Addressing the initial issues associated with implementation reduces concerns about the legitimacy of the process and the validity of the results.

More formal studies are usually characterized by research designs that target specific teaching skills. For example, Devlin-Scherer, Daly, Burroughs, and McCartan (2007) examined the Teacher Work Samples of four male and four female students in secondary math, science, English, and history. Their analysis highlighted descriptions of changes designed to improve student learning and engagement, including the assessment strategies and modifications used by student teachers. The selected descriptions were coded into four categories: planning, delivery of instruction, evaluating instruction, and reflection.

Findings indicated that student teachers used both formal and informal assessments, but that most student teachers did not consider multiple sources of data when making changes. All but one candidate used paper-and-pencil tests as part of their preassessment plan, and observation was the primary form of informal assessment. Using variety and providing more frequent supports for secondary students were the most frequently reported strategies. In addition, knowledge of community factors did not influence planning for any of the student teachers. The findings were used to suggest several program improvements, including managing the TWS process better, demonstrating for student teachers how the community context can be helpful, providing more examples for student teachers on how to vary assignments to foster individual learning, and expanding the assessment options for teacher candidates.

In another study (Henning, Robinson, Herring, & McDonald, 2006), the Teacher Work Samples of 197 student teachers were examined to discover how many student teachers planned to integrate technology during student teaching, how they planned to integrate technology during student teaching, and what prevented them from including technology in their instructional design. Findings indicated that many of the student teachers planned to use some form of technology, but fewer than half of the student teachers included computers in their instructional design, 40 percent planned to include computers for their personal use, and fewer than 20 percent planned for the student use of computers. The barriers to technology integration were most often related to instruction (e.g., the technology did not serve the learning goals, and the technology was not developmentally appropriate) rather than lack of available resources or time. The authors concluded by suggesting that preparation prior to student teaching should alert preservice teachers to the barriers they will face, help them distinguish legitimate barriers from misconceptions, coach them on how and under what conditions they can overcome barriers, and provide guidance as to where they can seek professional support.

The content analysis described above achieved multiple outcomes. First, it informed our teacher education program about the ability of our student teachers to integrate technology into their teaching units. Second, it demonstrated the usefulness of the TWS as a source of data. Third, it made a contribution to the research literature on technology integration during student teaching. This level of content analysis should be framed by a research question that targets a specific portion of the TWS and is based on previous research relevant to a specific skill or ability associated with student teaching.

To illustrate these points, the remainder of the chapter will examine a study that investigated the instructional decision making of student teachers (Kohler, Henning, & Usma-Wilches, 2008). Instructional decision making involves assessing students' learning and then modifying one or more aspect of instruction (Corno & Snow, 1986). Prior research indicates that novice teachers are challenged by both of these processes. For example, in a study examining how preservice teachers learn to assess student learning, Kusch (1999) found that participants were influenced more by their cooperating teachers than by their assessment of students' actual needs and characteristics. Similarly, Bachor and Baer (1999) found that preservice teachers' instructional decisions were often based on their intuition rather than student learning. Other studies indicate that experienced teachers are more likely than novices to modify or adjust their instruction when students' display difficulties with learning (Fogarty, Wang, and Creek, 1983; Housner & Griffey, 1985; Westerman, 1991). The challenges that novice teachers experience with instructional decision making have led numerous research-ers to recommend that this process become part of the teacher education curriculum (e.g., Borko & Livingston, 1989; Westerman, 1991). Therefore, the purpose of this study was to examine the Teacher Work Samples of 150 student teachers to determine their ability to make instructional decisions.

Instructional decision making is specifically addressed in the Instruc-tional Decision Making section of the Renaissance Partnership TWS prompt, which requires a three-step response from student teachers: (1) an initial formative assessment of student learning, (2) an instructional modi-fication, and (3) a rationale that justifies the modification:

> Think of two times during your unit when a student's learning or response caused you to modify your original design for instruction (the resulting modi-fication may affect other students as well). Cite specific evidence to answer the following: (1) Describe the student's learning or response that caused you to rethink your plans. The student's learning or response may come from a planned formative assessment or another source (not the pre-assessment); (2) describe what you did next and explain why you thought that this would improve student progress toward the learning goal. (Suggested length of 3 to 4 pages.) (Renaissance Partnership, 2002)

The following TWS excerpt from a third-grade reading class provides an exemplar of an instructional decision that includes an initial assessment, three instructional modifications, and a follow-up assessment. The initial assessment is presented in sentences 4 through 7, in which the student teacher discusses specific examples from a single student's writing and talk to identify his difficulties with meeting the learning objectives. Three in-structional modifications follow: in sentences 9 and 10, the student teacher provides an example for the student; in sentences 11 and 13, she employs a questioning strategy; and in sentences 13 through 15, she creates a graphic organizer. A rationale for the modifications is provided in sentences 18–20, and in sentences 21 and 22, the student teacher reports that her student's learning was enhanced.

> [1] My first instructional decision was with a student named Jeff. Jeff has always struggled with school due to his ADD and is at a reading level of 1.4. [2] He usually needs extra assistance in all tasks, and this assignment was no exception. [3] In order for him to achieve my second learning goal, I needed to rethink my plans. [4] His response in the paragraph writing was very poor. [5] There was no structure to his paragraph, poor spelling, and no punctuation. [6] He attempted to use the topic sentence from the board, but did not success-

fully copy it correctly. [7] Jeff could not describe why his character George had those feelings. [8] Based upon his writing, I knew Jeff would need additional assistance in order to be successful with this particular assignment. [9] Therefore, I chose to give Jeff a sample paragraph example to look at and use as a guide. [10] It was a sample I had already created, and gave to him to use at his own desk. [11] While the other students were working, I had the opportunity to work through the directions and expectations with him for the assignment. [12] I asked questions to clarify what he needed to do to make sure he did not have any problems. [13] Then I made a list of the feelings Jeff wanted to use in his paragraph in his notebook. [14] In another column, he told me why he thought his character felt that way. [15] This would be a graphic organizer for the simple paragraph he was to construct. [16] At this point, I left him alone to do his work while I checked on the other students. [17] One of Jeff's biggest challenges is focusing on a task, so writing his four-sentence paragraph took a lot of time and effort. [18] I felt this strategy would improve Jeff's understanding of a proper paragraph and lead him toward accomplishing the learning goal. [19] I think having a concrete example in front of him helped to guide his writing. [20] This would eliminate frustration and keep him from feeling helpless in a task he thought was too big for him to figure out correctly. [21] These few adaptations proved successful for Jeff and really improved the writing of his paragraph. [22] Through this activity, he made great strides toward meeting Learning Goal 2.

The findings from this study indicated that student teachers were more likely to implement some elements of the instructional decision-making process than others. The formative assessment strategies of observing students' performance and listening to talk were reported most frequently. In addition, nearly all student teachers were able to make adjustments in their teaching. The modifications of altering instructions and students' tasks were reported most frequently. We also found numerous instructional decisions (30 percent) where two or more modifications were combined.

However, several methods of formative assessment were rarely reported, such as examining writing or products, administering tests or quizzes, and having students engage in self-assessment. Many student teachers used the more accessible approaches of observing and listening to student talk. The majority of modifications involved altering instructions or tasks, and there were few occasions of modifying grouping arrangements, materials, learning objectives, or methods of assessment; providing supplemental enhancement; or teaching students to use cognitive strategies. Finally, over three-quarters of the modifications were implemented with the entire class rather than focusing on a small group or individual student.

The findings also indicated that only 40 percent of participants provided specific examples of the student cues that precipitated their instructional decisions, perhaps implying that recognition of student cues is important to instructional decision making. Similarly, only 40 percent of student teachers gave a rationale explaining why their modification would improve students' learning, even though the TWS gave a specific prompt to do this. Moreover, some of the explanations they did provide were ambiguous, poorly developed, or not based on theory. The paucity of rationales may also indicate that student teachers were unable to establish a logical connection between the results of their formative assessment and their instructional modification.

The findings from this study support prior research by indicating that novice teachers have difficulty adjusting to unexpected student responses and by verifying previous recommendations suggesting that some aspects of instructional decision making can be learned during the course of teacher preparation (Borko & Livingston, 1989; Fogarty, Wang, & Creek, 1983; Housner & Griffey, 1985; Westerman, 1991). This study also extended the previous literature by using previous research on instructional decision making, teacher learning, and reflective practice as a basis for analyzing student-teacher decision making. The analysis in this study addressed measures of instructional decision making that have been lacking in many prior investigations, such as the types of formative assessment used to identify student cues, the modifications made to facilitate student learning, the presence of a rationale for those modifications, and the type of follow-up assessment used to reevaluate student learning, These findings suggest that assessing these experiences with performance-based artifacts (such as the TWS) can provide a rich and viable source of data for analyzing the instructional decisions of student teachers.

In summary, the analysis of contents is a critical part of TWS research in teacher education. These studies can provide valuable information about student teachers' performance in specific areas such as use of technology, assessment, reflection, and instructional decision making. This information is integral for revealing the depth of student teachers' knowledge, thinking, and skill with the various TWS processes. Content analysis studies build upon the examination of TWS scores by providing a more thorough illustration of student teachers' strengths and weaknesses and by suggesting directions for program revision and improvement.

CONCLUSIONS

In this chapter, we recommended a programmatic approach to conducting research surrounding the use of TWS methodology. A key characteristic of programmatic research is the sustained examination of a series of research questions that unfold over time. We have suggested an approach that utilizes three different types of studies conducted in a sequence relative to the implementation of TWS methodology. They are summarized below.

Implementation and impact studies help establish and justify new practices. They can provide valuable information early in the process of implementation about the feasibility, logistics, and impact of the TWS. They are also helpful later whenever a new TWS process is implemented in the program, for example, revising the TWS based on changes in program goals. Analyses of TWS scores can begin when the implementation and the scoring process stabilize. These types of studies can provide insight into reliability, program strengths and weaknesses, and the efficacy of instructional strategies. Analyses of TWS scores can enable faculty to monitor or evaluate program effectiveness and examine the impact of programmatic changes. The third type of study to emerge in our description of programmatic research is an analysis of TWS contents. These studies enable a much closer examination of specific teaching skills, such as planning, technology integration, instructional decision making, assessment, and reflection. They also offer the potential to inform educational research about the thinking processes of student teachers.

Two important points are suggested by the research studies that we have presented in this chapter. First and foremost, these studies all provide information that is integral to the refinement and improvement of teacher education programs. Second, these studies can be conducted in a sequential way that enables one study to build upon a previous one. An overall goal of programmatic research is to achieve outcomes that would not be possible with studies that occur in isolation or independently of one another (Roane, Fisher, & McDonough, 2003; Strowig & Farwell, 1966). We believe that establishing a programmatic line of research has contributed significantly to the implementation and refinement of TWS methodology in our teacher education program.

REFERENCES

Bachor, D., & Baer, M. R. (1999). An examination of preservice teachers' simulated classroom assessment practices. *Alberta Journal of Educational Research, 3*, 244–258.

Borko, H., & Livingston, C. (1989). Cognition and improvisation: Differences in mathematics instruction by expert and novice teachers. *American Educational Research Journal, 26*(4), 473–498.

Collier, S. T. (1999). Characteristics of reflective thought during the student teaching experience. *Journal of Teacher Education, 50*(3), 173–181.

Corno, L., & Snow, R. E. (1986). Adapting teaching to individual differences among learners. In M. C. Wittrock (Ed.), *Handbook of research on teaching* (3rd ed., pp. 605–629). New York: Macmillan.

Devlin-Scherer, R., Daly, J., Burroughs, G., & McCartan, W. (2007). The value of the Teacher Work Sample for improving instruction and program. *Action in Teacher Education 29*(1), 51–60.

Fogarty, J. L., Wang, M. C., & Creek, R. (1983). A descriptive study of experienced and novice teachers' interactive instructional thoughts and actions. *Journal of Educational Research, 77*(1), 22–32.

Henning, J. E., DeBruin-Parecki, A., Hawbaker, B. W., Nielsen, C. P., Joram, E., & Gabriele, A. J. (2005). The Teacher Work Sample: A tool for scaffolding and assessing preservice teachers' early field experiences. *The Teacher Educator, 40*(3), 188–207.

Henning, J. E., & Robinson, V. (2004). The Teacher Work Sample: Implementing standards-based performance assessment. *The Teacher Educator, 39*(4), 231–248.

Henning, J. E., Robinson, V. L., Herring, M. C., & McDonald, T. (2006). Integrating technology during student teaching: An examination of Teacher Work Samples (TWS). *Journal of Computing in Teacher Education, 23*(2), 71–76.

Housner, L. D., & Griffey, D. C. (1985). Teacher cognition: Differences in planning an interactive decision-making between experienced and inexperienced teachers. *Research Quarterly for Exercise and Sport, 56*, 45–53.

Kohler, F. W., Henning, J. E., & Usma-Wilches, J. (2008). Preparing preservice teachers to make instructional decisions: An Examination of data from the Teacher Work Sample. *Teaching and Teacher Education, 24*(8), 2108–2117.

Kusch, J. W. (1999). The dimensions of classroom assessment: How field study students learn to grade in the middle school classroom. *Journal of Educational Thought, 33*, 61–88.

Phillips, C. L., & Marston, R.E. (2008, September 22). Using the Teacher Work Sample to assess the impact of PETE program changes upon student teachers' performance. *The Physical Educator*, September.

Renaissance Partnership for Improving Teacher Quality Project. (2002). *The Teacher Work Sample.* Retrieved from http://fp.uni.edu/itq.

Roane, H. S., Fisher, W. W., & McDonough, E. M. (2003). Progressing from programmatic to discovery research: A case example with the overjustification effect. *Journal of Applied Behavior Analysis, 36*, 35–46.

Schalock, H. D., & Myton, D. V. (1988). A new paradigm for teacher licensure: Oregon's demand for evidence of success in fostering learning. *Journal of Teacher Education, 39*(6), 8–16.

Strowig, W., & Farwell, G. F. (1966). Programmatic research. *Review of Educational Research 36*, 327–334.

Watkins, P., & Bratberg, W. (2006). Teacher Work Sample Methodology: Assessment and design compatibility with fine arts instruction. *National Forum of Teacher Education Journal, 17*(3), 1–10. Retrieved from www.nationalforum.com/Journals/National%20Forum%20of%20Teacher%20Education%20Journal/National%20Forum%20of%20Teacher%20Education%20Journal/TOCte8e3.htm.

Westerman, D. A. (1991). Expert and novice teacher decision-making. *Journal of Teacher Education, 42*(4), 292–305.

IV

POLICY

13

"Student Learning" in Accreditation

Emerson Elliott

The National Council for Accreditation of Teacher Education (NCATE) prescribes a standard for schools, departments, and colleges of education:

> Candidates preparing for professional education positions must have knowledge, skills, and professional dispositions "necessary to help all students learn."

Such a standard may seem an obvious and simple prescription for an accreditation organization. But in the life of NCATE, crafting this standard, and expecting evidence to demonstrate its accomplishment, is relatively recent.

This is a case study of student learning as the focus of teacher preparation, applied in accreditation by NCATE. It begins with the evolution of accreditation as a quality assurance process in higher education and traces important developmental periods in NCATE. It concludes with NCATE's current perspective on student learning in the context of teacher preparation—a perspective that seems congruent with views about preparing to teach, and the purposes of teaching, that were given prominence for a third of a century by Del Schalock.[1]

ACCREDITATION IN HIGHER EDUCATION

Accreditation in American higher education is an independent function rather than a government one. It is intended as both a quality assurance mechanism for the public, and as a means for improvement. Accreditation is built around individual institutional missions and self-study in relation to "standards" created by accrediting agencies. It has historically been concerned with "inputs"—the quality or currency of facilities, the degrees and research productivity of faculty, the volumes in the library, the quality of laboratories, the ratio of faculty to students, and the like. More recently the focus has moved to the curriculum of study—the content of syllabi and the learning experiences of students. And now, with the insistence of the U.S. Department of Education and policy officials who seek to adapt strategies from elementary and secondary "reform" efforts, the emphasis is shifting to student learning. Institutions under review by regional accrediting agencies, as well as programs seeking specialized accreditation, must offer evidence that college students have demonstrated their proficiencies through assessments. These might be end-of-course or graduate admissions tests, certification, or any of a variety of achievement measures.

This move to performance in accreditation is quite recent. The U.S. Department of Education oversees accreditation agencies, a function linked to eligibility for federal student financial aid programs. For several years it has pressed for assessments of student learning as part of the accreditation process in both regional and specialized accreditation (such as law, engineering, or teaching). The typical response of regional accreditors has been to insist that *institutions* have assessments in place so *they* can measure student performance in their own way. These accreditors have not, themselves, established assessments, nor the levels of performance, nor the specific standards on which the assessments are based; instead, they have left those responsibilities to institutions. The practices of specialized accreditation associations are varied, with several stating standards that require demonstration of college student learning through a licensure test or some other measure of performance. Such provisions are found, for example, in accreditors for schools of business, architecture, engineering, nursing, law, and physical therapy.

ACCREDITATION IN NCATE

Since its founding in 1954, NCATE has traversed this same historical path, evolving through input and curriculum-based accreditation reviews, then moving on to performance. NCATE's early accreditation visits examined teacher preparation programs in different specialties, such as elementary education, secondary education, or special education, and visiting teams were typically large and unwieldy. By the 1970s and early 1980s, there were growing criticisms that education accreditation duplicated a role that states have played in education, unlike other professions, through their approval of instructional programs for teachers and other professional educators. NCATE responded to this challenge by designing a completely different approach, approved in 1985[2] (NCATE, 1992, p. 11) and first implemented in 1987[3] (NCATE, 1995, p. 11). The principal feature of this redesign was that each institution would base its programs on established and current research findings and sound professional practice (NCATE, 1992, p. 45). Clinical and field-based experiences were to provide opportunities for candidates to observe, plan, and practice in a variety of settings appropriate to the professional roles for which they were preparing (NCATE, 1992, p. 51). Collaboration with K–12 schools was to develop inquiry strategies with the joint involvement of practicing teachers and education faculty that would extend professional knowledge bases (NCATE, 1992, p. 52). The standards would extend across all programs offered by the education "unit"—the school, or college, or department of education (NCATE, 1992, p. 45)—and the focus of site visits would be on the unit rather than individual programs. The full process did include reviews of programs, in those states that required them, and specialized professional associations wrote standards in the form of curriculum guidelines. However, the programs were reviewed on the basis of "folios" of information, on paper, off-site, rather than as part of the NCATE institutional visit. The evidence was intended to show the *conformity of the program's syllabi with the specialty area guidelines*[4] (NCATE, 1991, p. 10).

The 1987 NCATE standards represented significant changes, especially in their intent to base accreditation on research and the wisdom of practice (the term in NCATE's standards is "knowledge bases"). Those standards also encouraged "regular and systematic evaluations," follow-up studies of graduates, and use of the results to modify and improve programs (NCATE, 1992, p. 52), all tending toward a more performance-oriented accreditation process. Still, those standards featured several more traditional accreditation requirements, such as minimum length of student teaching experience, faculty course load, practicum supervision load, and also in reference to such inputs as adequacy of resources, physical facilities, and library holdings (NCATE, 1992, pp. 59–60).

Additional modifications were made in NCATE's revised standards of 1995, giving greater emphasis to knowledge bases that undergird the unit, stated in a "conceptual framework" that could be articulated and applied by faculty and candidates alike (NCATE, 1995, p. 11). Several new elements of performance evidence were introduced in these standards. Prospective teachers were expected to demonstrate specific skills as a result of their preparation, and the unit was to play a monitoring role in candidates' progress throughout the program of study. A variety of performance measures were expected to be employed (NCATE, 1995, p. 12). The education unit was to establish "criteria/outcomes for exit from each professional education program" (NCATE, 1995, p. 23); candidates were to be "monitored through authentic performance-based assessments"; and candidate progress was to be based on multiple data sources, including "grade point average (GPA), observations, the use of various instructional strategies and technologies, faculty recommendations, demonstrated competence in academic and professional work (e.g., portfolios, performance assessments, and research and concept papers), and recommendations from the appropriate professionals in schools" (NCATE, 1995, p. 22).

A PERFORMANCE-BASED SYSTEM

During the 1990s, NCATE's president, Arthur E. Wise, elaborated his conception of the field of teaching. He foresaw that organizations and experiences associated with preparation, entry, and advancement in other professions (such as medicine, law, engineering, nursing, and architecture) might serve as instructive models for adaptation to the education profession. He gathered ideas from the experience of the first President Bush's meeting with the nation's governors at the Charlottesville "summit" in 1989 and the subsequent formulation of national goals, as well as from the then-developing National Board for Professional Teaching Standards (NBPTS). These ideas formed the basis for an NCATE grant proposal in 1991 that described plans for a "true national system of teacher education accreditation" (NCATE, 1991, p. 9). Those plans would sort out functions in a way that paralleled other professions. States would administer "performance measures to determine a teacher's competence" (NCATE, 1991, p. 11), and state teacher licenses would attest to that. Schools would build and operate preparation programs, following the leading consensus in the field, and the accreditor would examine the overall institutional operations and attest that they were in accord with the national consensus standards. The NCATE plan for this common national system of teacher education accreditation would attempt to replace the dual state and NCATE reviews with one in which states effectively delegated program review and accreditation functions to NCATE—similar to what happens in other professions.

NCATE prepared another grant proposal in 1993 that referenced "three quality assurance mechanisms to distinguish" a profession: national accreditation of professional schools, state licensing of the new practitioners, and advanced board certification of the experienced practitioners[5] (NCATE, 1993, p. 8). The three organizations that, together, encompassed these mechanisms for education were NCATE, the Council of Chief State School Officers (CCSSO) and state teacher licensure boards, and NBPTS. Each of these organizations was embarked on standards writing—for teacher candidates, for newly inducted teachers, or for accomplished teachers. NCATE asserted that graduates must be able to meet performance-based state licensing standards, and some graduates who enter teaching might eventually aspire to meet national board certification standards. Master's level preparation programs offered by schools, departments, and colleges of education could help prepare them to be successful in attaining board certification.

The proposal signaled a shift in NCATE's specialty organization standards. Each organization was to write its teacher preparation standards *focusing on outcomes and consistent with standards for students* (NCATE, 1993, p. 10). Subsequently funded by several foundations, the proposal promised that NCATE would work with its constituent member professional specialty associations to develop outcome-based expectations. These standards would describe *"what teachers should be able to do as a result of their education"* (NCATE, 1993, p. 17). NCATE would establish an advisory group to assist specialty associations with guideline development (NCATE, 1993, p. 21).

Due to foundation funding and NCATE start-up cycles, it was well into 1996 when NCATE convened the promised advisory group, although converting it to a single exploratory and planning endeavor. NCATE then adopted, as its vehicle to shape this new form of standards, a committee charged with writing a "model" for elementary teacher preparation. That committee represented many of the NCATE constituents: specialty professional organizations; representatives from crosscutting education fields such as elementary, early childhood, and special education; individuals with experience on teacher standards and assessments at the state level and with INTASC (the Interstate Assessment and Support Consortium, a CCSSO project); representatives of school and college of education leadership; and individuals from organizations outside NCATE, such as arts education and the Council for Basic Education. Several of the committee members were conversant with the student content standards of their own organizations and helped other members understand those perspectives. One had been a participant in leading work of the State of Connecticut to write a description of skills that newly prepared teachers needed.[6] The breadth of experience, collected across this committee, was therefore broad.

While there was a clear understanding that the model elementary preparation standards would describe, not the content of the curriculum, but what teacher candidates completing their preparation should know and be able to do, there were contextual circumstances in the middle to late 1990s that surrounded the committee's work and helped to shape it. INTASC, NBPTS, and several national standards efforts then underway or recently completed (such as those of the National Council of Teachers of Mathematics, or standards on science from the National Research Council) had all followed a similar path. They wrote standards as explicit descriptions of what teachers or P–12 students should know and be able to do, and then either created assessments to demonstrate mastery of those standards or defined the characteristics of appropriate assessments. The NBPTS framed its standards around a set of "core propositions" for experienced and highly performing teachers and set out to apply them first to standards and then to linked assessments used for certification purposes. INTASC adopted general "principles" and then moved on to write standards and devise portfolio assessment models to fit, all of which were available for state adaptation or adoption.

ASSESSMENTS AND STUDENT LEARNING

Two additions to performance-based concepts set out in the 1993 grant proposal and NCATE's 1995 standards were initiated by the NCATE elementary preparation standards committee in 1997–1999. These significantly refashioned NCATE's new unit accreditation standards in 2000 and its guidelines for all other program standards. The first of these was to insist that a performance-based system is not complete with the statement of standards, even standards that describe what candidates should know and be able to do. Standards must be paired with *evidence that candidates exhibit, through their performances in assessments, that they are proficient in those standards.* The committee's framework for a standards- and assessments-based performance system would adapt, for teacher preparation, the model followed by many states in their standards for P–12 students, as well as by INTASC for newly hired teachers, and NBPTS for high-performing teachers.

The second contribution from the elementary preparation standards committee was to insist that *the focus of teaching is learning by students in P–12.* The goal of teacher preparation is not a collection of techniques, but a steadfast insistence that *the measure of accomplishment must be whether students learn.* Brilliant teaching is not an end, but a means. That was viewed as a preposterous assertion by some. At this time, there were still faculty in schools of education who denied any responsibility whatever for learning by their own teacher candidates, and could not imagine that they had even the most remote responsibility for P–12 learning in American schools.

Pauletta Brown Bracy, then associate professor in the School of Library and Information Sciences, North Carolina Central University, served as a member of the elementary standards drafting committee, and she had raised the concept of student learning as the goal of teaching at one of the early meetings of the committee. Recalling that experience in a recent interview,[7] she spoke of two factors that influenced her action. One was accountability, not as much discussed in 1997 as now, but even then becoming a more insistent demand from policy makers. The second was this:

> What we do is ultimately for children. We work with children, and for children. You cannot just attest to teacher competencies—it is the learning that matters. True educators do not stop with teaching, they go on to child learning. That is what it is all about.

Dr. Bracy prepared a synthesis of research literature for the committee,[8] drawing attention to various references from such authors as Jere Brophy, Edward Haertel, Jason Millman, and Richard Stiggins, and especially from a 1988 Del Schalock and David Myton article in the *Journal of Teacher Education*, "A New Paradigm for Teacher Licensure: Oregon's Demand for Evidence of Success in Fostering Learning." The committee was influenced by such ideas as these:

- Student learning is evolving as a viable measure of teacher competence.
- Teacher-made tests used on a daily basis can determine areas for student improvement.
- Del Schalock and David Myton wrote that Oregon's approach to initial licensure differed from most other states. It required use of pupil achievement data as evaluative evidence that prospective teachers were able to apply knowledge and skills acquired in teacher education programs.
- Beginning teachers need to move beyond a concern for acquisition of knowledge and skill to a concern about what students are to learn, how to help them learn, and how to assess and remediate their learning. Oregon encouraged this move in teacher preparation programs by setting four objectives that candidates are to meet upon completion of approved programs: planning for instruction, establishing a classroom climate conducive to learning, implementing plans for instruction, and evaluating pupil achievement.
- Beginning teachers' ability to foster learning in their students can be documented in a "work sample," and several institutions are experimenting with ways to create and evaluate them, including Western Oregon University.

The resulting publication of elementary preparation standards[9] made an unequivocal, visible, and precedent-setting commitment to student learning as the focus of teacher preparation, and to assessments as the basis for judging whether standards had been met. An extended supplement to the standards described the committee's perspectives and included the following:

> Student learning is the goal. The process for quality review of teacher preparation programs should focus clearly on preparation of new elementary teacher candidates who help students learn. The previous practice, basing program review decisions on course offerings and experiences of candidates, is remote from elementary student learning, and only indirectly—although instrumentally—related to what teachers of elementary students need to know and be able to do to foster student learning. (NCATE, 1999 and 2000, p. 43)

The report went on to describe the current state of assessments for teacher licensure, and among other references included this one:

Another development over this same period is found in the State of Oregon, which asks that teacher candidates demonstrate "student progress in learning" as one of five standards for an initial teaching license. For many years, Western Oregon University has been developing assessment technology to assess student learning during teacher preparation.

Such findings made the committee optimistic that "large advances in measurement of teaching competencies . . . have occurred over the past decade" and would likely continue over the coming five to ten years. They concluded that performance-based program review answers the question, "Is the institution preparing elementary teacher candidates with appropriate knowledge, teaching strategies, and dispositions to teach elementary students so those students learn and achieve standards?"

The committee's model was formally approved in October 1999, and its influence on NCATE's accreditation was wide. Quite quickly the model was adopted as policy for all specialty organization standards by the NCATE Specialty Areas Studies Board in October 2000. It was adapted to the NCATE Unit Standards as the "power" feature of NCATE's revisions of 2000. Unit Standard 1 states that candidates must "know and demonstrate the content, pedagogical, and professional knowledge skills, and dispositions necessary to *help all students learn.*" Two of the "elements" for this standard are evaluative rubrics that define "student learning for teacher candidates" and "student learning for other school professionals." Unit Standard 2 requires an assessment system with capacity to provide evidence of candidate accomplishments for Standard 1, and also to inform the program and unit about areas of strength and weakness. More recently, NCATE has made a major shift in program review procedures, first implemented as a pilot in the fall of 2004, that introduced greater consistency in evidence that program standards are met. NCATE now requires six to eight assessments that collectively represent the requirements for each set of specialized professional association standards. Five are explicitly identified. The first four of these—content knowledge represented by a state licensure test in the specialty field, an additional assessment of content knowledge, evidence of ability to plan and conceptualize, and ability to teach effectively in the classroom—are brought to conclusion with an assessment of the candidate's ability to have a positive influence on student learning.

SUMMING UP

NCATE has written numerous guidelines, instructions, and technical assistance papers that explicate the intent of its references to student learning appearing throughout NCATE standards and policies. An NCATE summary paper on this topic, "'Student Learning' in NCATE Accreditation," explains NCATE's interpretation of teacher preparation with a "focus" on P–12 student learning.[10] That paper describes a goal to assure that "subject content knowledge, teaching skills, and dispositions will effectively advance student learning, not be ends in themselves." NCATE stands for continuing assessment activities in teacher education in which the candidate takes responsibility for a significant unit of instruction, then evaluates students' prior learning, plans instruction based on that evaluation, teaches in meaningful and engaging ways appropriate to students' background knowledge and needs, assesses student learning, and then analyzes the results of the assessments and reflects on changes in teaching that could improve results.

NCATE recognizes there are significant implications for faculty in such an approach. Among other things, faculty must prepare candidates to be assessment literate—to know about, create, and use appropriate and effective assessments in teaching. "Assessment literacy" cannot be achieved through just a brief course on measurement! Faculty must provide opportunities in preparation programs for candidates to develop and practice their skills in teaching so that students learn—using assessment "for learning." And faculty must include provisions for evaluating effects that teacher candidates have on P–12 student learning as they design unit assessment systems and assessments for each program.

Accreditors set standards as the basis for quality assurance and to improve programs. The education profession, as a coalition of thirty-five member organizations, has come together to develop and sanction NCATE's standards. As education reform efforts have evolved over the past three decades, NCATE's standards have as well. It is a great distance from standards that define the nature and size of the library collection to standards that describe what candidates should know and be able to do. It is a farther leap to shift the form of program quality evidence from a tally of books in the library to a display of candidate proficiency assessments. But Del Schalock insisted on the ultimate standard: teacher preparation must focus on student learning, and evidence of effective teacher preparation must, in turn, focus on learning by the students that candidates teach. The NCATE goal is to gauge teacher preparation programs by multiple measures, but always including ones that address whether a program's candidates are having positive effects on P–12 student learning.

NCATE's day-to-day accreditation activities create repeated and numerous opportunities for examination of evidence that institutions compile to demonstrate they have met the NCATE standards. The NCATE Board of Examiner teams, and program reviewers for specialized professional programs, see evidence of Del Schalock's initiatives repeatedly in their work. Sometimes Del's influence is found in assessments and various forms of "portfolios" from the institutions with which Del collaborated personally.

Sometimes it is from the extension of Del's efforts that came through the federally supported Renaissance Partnership for Improving Teacher Quality project (a subject of other chapters in this book). And sometimes evidence that student learning is the focus of teacher preparation is observed by NCATE reviewers in other institutions whose faculty have located the Western Oregon University–AACTE–ERIC Clearinghouse "handbook," *Connecting Teaching and Learning*, in which Del played a substantial role with Gerald Girod.[11] Whatever the source, it is evident that Del's legacy is a widespread acceptance of the idea that teacher preparation must focus on student learning. When we want evidence that teacher candidates are effectively prepared, we must sample the actual work of those candidates with students. The key questions, finally, are ones that candidates must be prepared to address themselves: Have my students learned? And how could I improve my teaching so they could learn more?

14

Teacher Work Samples in Louisiana's Teacher Assistance and Assessment Program

Russell French, Gary Skolits, and George Malo

POLICY CONTEXT

After ill-fated attempts to develop and implement a statewide teacher evaluation program in the late 1980s and early 1990s and several years of work by the Louisiana Department of Education, a team of consultants led by Drs. Russell French (University of Tennessee) and George Malo (Tennessee Board of Regents), and a series of panels composed of Louisiana educators, the Louisiana legislature enacted in 1994 legislation mandating a statewide new-teacher assessment program and parameters for local evaluation of experienced teachers. The results of the new-teacher assessment program would become the deciding factor in a teacher's attainment of permanent certification. The Louisiana State Board of Elementary and Secondary Education (SBESE) was authorized to promulgate the legislation, to be implemented by the Louisiana Department of Education (LDE). The act (Act 1/Act 838) was amended in 1997.

As legislated, new teachers in Louisiana are defined as "any person employed as a full-time employee of a local board who is engaged to directly and regularly provide instruction to students," and teachers required to participate in the assessment program are those who hold standard certificates (type C, level 1); those who hold nonstandard certificates (temporary authority to teach, out-of-field authorization to teach, practitioner license, or temporary employment permit); teachers moving for the first time from Louisiana nonpublic schools to public schools; and new teachers from out-of-state who do not bring with them appropriate (comparable) evaluation results from their immediate previous teaching assignments[1] (Part XXXVII, Bulletin 1943—Policies and Procedures for Louisiana Assistance and Assessment).

Pursuant to the 1994 legislation, the New Teacher Assessment Program was originally designed for implementation during the new teacher's first year in a Louisiana public school classroom. Assessment was carried out by a team of three LDE-trained assessors: a teacher's immediate supervisor or designee, an external assessor, and an appropriate faculty member from a Louisiana postsecondary institution.

The foundation for the assessment process was and still is the Louisiana Components of Effective Teaching (LCET). The components, a three-level set of standards for teacher performance (i.e., domains defined by Components, defined in turn by Attributes) were developed by the consultant team with assistance and input from several panels of Louisiana educators and validated through a statewide process. The components are based upon (1) research and best practice, (2) a state-adopted job description for teachers, and (3) agreement among stakeholders (teachers, administrators, teacher educators) regarding their appropriateness and importance. They have been updated twice since their original acceptance (with appropriate panel and stakeholder input) to encompass new research-based knowledge of teaching and learning, and new state and national concerns, like focus on student outcomes. These adjustments are important to an understanding of the application of Teacher Work Sample Methodology introduced into the New Teacher Assistance and Assessment Program in 2002.

Teacher Work Sample Methodology was not a part of the original Louisiana Teacher Assessment Program. Methods of data collection originally employed to assess a new teacher's competence included a classroom observation and a structured interview conducted by each member of the three-person assessor team. (It should be noted that a structured interview differs from a conference in that interview questions are standardized, and teacher responses which are focused on practices and behaviors defined in the teacher standards are scripted by the assessor and scored—a procedure similar to that used in scripting and scoring observation data.)

By the late 1990s, the need for new-teacher induction and mentoring had become a primary concern to the State Board of Education, the Louisiana Department of Education, the education associations, and local educators. Interest in a statewide, state-developed, state-supported induction and mentoring program was strong and was underscored by reports that many external assessors who were often retired teachers and administrators were returning on their own time, without compensation, to assist new teachers in improving instruction after the assessment process was completed. (The assessor team developed with each teacher a professional growth plan during the assessment process and another at the conclusion of the process.) The assistance of these experienced educators was highly regarded by the new teachers.

While interest in a formal induction and mentoring program was high, few state fiscal resources were available to support it. The consultant team was asked to conduct a statistical analysis of existent new-teacher assessment data to determine the impact that reduction in the number of assessors from three to two would have on final scores awarded to a teacher. The study revealed little or no impact. However, these findings may have been influenced by the fact that the rating scale adopted by SBESE at the recommendation of the educator panels and the state superintendent, but against the recommendation of the consultant team, is a two-point scale (2 = competent, 1 = needs improvement, NO = not observed). A limited scale such as this provides limited differentiation regarding performance.

The results of the consultant team study suggested to policy makers that the number of members on an assessment team could be reduced from three to two, thereby freeing some state fiscal resources to be used in induction and mentoring. This modification in assessment procedures was further supported by the fact that requiring the inclusion of a higher-education faculty member on every assessor team had proven unworkable because of lack of geographic proximity and scheduling problems. These factors led to reconstruction of the Louisiana Teacher Assessment Program. It became the Louisiana Teacher Assistance and Assessment Program (LaTAAP), approved for statewide implementation by SBESE in 2002. (See Louisiana Administrative Code, Bulletin 1943, for detailed information.)

THE LOUISIANA TEACHER ASSISTANCE AND ASSESSMENT PROGRAM

There are many details of LaTAAP that cannot be explained in the space available for this case study. Far more than most readers will want to know can be found on the Louisiana Department of Education website where appropriate sections of Bulletin 1943, assessor and mentor manuals, a "Guide for New Teachers," all data collection forms and guides, and the "Louisiana Components of Effective Teaching" can be found. Only those aspects of the program pertaining in some way to the use of Teacher Work Sample Methodology are explicated here.

When LaTAP became LaTAAP, several substantive changes took place:

1. The program was lengthened to two years (four semesters) with a continuing mentor/mentor team in place throughout.
2. The assessment team was reduced to two members—immediate supervisor or designee and external assessor (one option being a higher-education faculty member).

3. Assessment took place in the third semester, allowing for reevaluation in the fourth semester if a teacher did not meet certification standards in the first evaluation.[2]

4. The assistance program, like the assessment program, has as its centerpiece the "Louisiana Components of Effective Teaching" (LCET). This program can be called a "targeted" mentoring program, designed to assist the new teacher in acquiring or improving the behaviors and practices defined as standards of competence/performance required for certification. In essence, the assistance and assessment components are carefully aligned. The mentoring program focuses on the knowledge, skills, behaviors, and practices that will be assessed.

5. Mentors are not members of their mentees' assessment teams. However, they are thoroughly trained in the assessment system, in the same way assessors are.

6. Data collection instruments in the revamped assessment program are observations by each of the two assessment team members and a portfolio, one component of which is a Teacher Work Sample. The portfolio is scored independently by each assessor.

7. Mentors and principals each conduct at least one observation of the new teacher during year one (first two semesters) using the observation record which will be used by assessors in year two. Data from these observations are used in the mentoring process.

8. Mentors are encouraged to have mentees develop "practice components" of the work sample in year one (first two semesters) for critique. The work sample submitted to assessors during the third semester must be one developed and implemented during that semester without assistance/intervention by the mentor.

9. The training for both assessors and mentors is extensive (a week or more for each group), and assessors must meet reliability standards for scripting and rating observational data and for scoring portfolio entries, including the several components of the Teacher Work Samples. Rubrics for synthesizing raw data into scores have been developed. (The two-point rating scale previously mentioned is still used.)

10. At the conclusion of the assessment process (independent observations and scoring of portfolio entries by the two members of the assessment team), team members compare and combine their scores to create the final summary report. If there is substantive disagreement, a third, trained assessor completes an observation and scores the portfolio. Her or his scores are then combined with those of the two previous assessors.

11. For teachers beginning in the fall of 2006 or thereafter, performance standards for certification were raised. Now, a score of 2 must be attained on all eleven components of the LCET. Prior to this time, a

score of 2 was required only on the eight components included in the domains of Planning, Classroom Management, and Instruction.

12. The assessment program is not perceived to be a "gotcha" program, even though a final product is a set of scores used summatively (i.e., to render a decision about certification and employment). The first goal of the assistance and assessment components of the program is instructional improvement (a formative assessment function). Both during and at the conclusion of the assessment process, professional growth plans are developed from the data available. Implementation of the plans is monitored, and results are assessed.[3]

13. In the redesign process culminating in the current LaTAAP program, the Louisiana Components of Effective Teaching were expanded to encompass current educational emphases and concerns. Most of the additions are at the third level (Attributes). Their inclusion at this level influences component scores, but they are not the sole source of component scores. For purposes of this case study, the most notable additions are those that focus on integration of technology into instruction, strengthened emphasis on accommodation of individual differences, and required "evidence of student academic growth under her or his instruction."

A few of the changes outlined above need explanation, especially those related to the substitution of the portfolio for the former structured interview, and the particular role of Teacher Work Samples within the portfolio.

The Portfolio

The portfolio, as the structured interview preceding it, is part of the LaTAAP as an instrument to collect and organize data pertaining to desired elements of teacher performance (Components, Attributes) that cannot be assessed via classroom observation (e.g., elements of teacher planning, assessment, professional development). The Louisiana Components of Effective Teaching consists of five domains: (1) Planning, (2) Management, (3) Instruction, (4) Professional Development, and (5) School Improvement. As previously mentioned, eleven components define the five domains, and thirty-six attributes define the eleven components. The portfolio provides evidence of teacher practices in twenty of the thirty-six LCET attributes:

- all data required for assessing teacher performance in attributes which comprise the Planning domain (domain 1) and its single component (The teacher plans for effective instruction);
- data needed to assess teacher performance in six attributes within three components of domain 3 (Instruction);

- all data required for assessing performance in the two attributes defining component B (The new-teacher plans for professional self-development) of domain 4 (Professional Development);
- all data needed for assessing performance in the six attributes defining components A (The teacher takes an active role in building-level decision making) and B (The teacher creates partnerships with parents/caregivers and colleagues) of domain 5 (School Improvement).

The portfolio is divided into three sections: Teacher Work Sample, Professional Development, and School Improvement. All entries in all sections are provided on a series of forms and necessary attachments to reduce paperwork and ensure uniformity of product—a necessity since this is a high-stakes evaluation. Attention in the remainder of this case study will be limited to the work sample portion of the portfolio.

THE LOUISIANA TEACHER WORK SAMPLE

The Louisiana New Teacher Work Sample contains all of the elements found in the original version of Teacher Work Sample Methodology (TWSM) developed at Western Oregon University. However, it has been shaped to meet the needs of in-service teachers (minimization of paperwork) and the requirements of the assessment system (assessment of performance in the Louisiana Components of Effective Teaching).

Once it was decided to replace the structured interview component of the assessment system with a portfolio, TWSM was a natural fit. The content of a work sample, as defined at Western Oregon University, was already focused on many of the teacher behaviors and practices identified in the Louisiana Components of Effective Teaching. In the Louisiana Teacher Work Sample (TWS), evidence of teacher competence is provided for fourteen LCET attributes, within five different components, and three domains (Planning, Instruction, and School Improvement). These relationships are outlined in table 14.1, where alignment between domain components and attributes contained in the LCET are shown. Table 14.1 also references a series of seven forms which constitute the work sample. Copies of these forms can be found in the appendixes, but some explanations are warranted.

One of the ground rules established by the educator panel overseeing the redesign of LaTAAP and the Louisiana Department of Education was that paperwork for the new teacher would be minimized. In effect, both contents and format of the portfolio, including the work sample, had to be streamlined. Teachers could not be asked to develop lengthy narratives. This mandate actually worked in concert with the requirements of a high-stakes, summative evaluation system (i.e., comparable amounts and

Table 14.1. Alignment of Louisiana's Components of Effective Teaching with Teacher Work Sample elements (and forms/appendixes)

LCET DOMAINS, COMPONENTS, and ATTRIBUTES	WORK SAMPLE FORMS (APPENDIX)
DOMAIN I. Planning	
Component A. The teacher plans effectively for instruction.	
IA1. Specifies learner outcomes in clear, concise objectives.	1.2, 1.7
1A2. Includes activities that develop objectives.	1.7
IA3. Identifies and plans for individual differences.	1.1, 1.2
IA4. Identifies materials, other than standard classroom materials, as needed for lesson.	1.7
IA5. States method(s) of evaluation to measure learner outcomes.	1.3, 1.7
IA6. Develops an Individualized Education Program (IEP) and/or Individualized Family Service Plan (IFSP), as needed for the lesson (special education teachers).	1.1, 1.7
DOMAIN III. Instruction	
Component A. The teacher delivers instruction effectively.	1.2, 1.7
IIIA5. The teacher integrates technology into instruction.	1.2, 1.7
Component B. The teacher integrates technology into instruction.	
IIIB1. Presents content at a developmentally appropriate level.	1.1, 1.2 (Possibly 1.7)
Component D. The teacher demonstrates ability to assess and facilitate student academic growth.	
IIID1. Consistently monitors ongoing performance of students (observation and work sample).	1.3, 1.7
IIID.2. Uses appropriate and effective assessment techniques.	1.3, 1.4
IIID.3. Provides timely feedback to students.	1.6
IIID.4. Produces evidence of student academic growth under his/her instruction.	1.3, 1.4, 1.5
DOMAIN V. School Improvement	
Component D. The teacher creates partnerships with parents/ caregivers and colleagues.	
VB1. Provides clear and timely information to parents/caregivers and colleagues regarding classroom expectations, student progress, and ways they can assist learning.	1.6
VB2. Encourages parents/caregivers to become active partners in their children's education and to become involved in the school and classroom.	1.6

types of data for all evaluatees). Based on these needs, the LaTAAP version of the work sample became the seven forms appearing in the appendixes, with the addition of a few attachments (see appendix D, The Assessment Plan, for an example).

The formatting of the work sample also lent itself to the application of computer technology. A team of faculty members from two Louisiana higher-education institutions were contracted several years ago to develop a program for use in all Louisiana institutions of higher education which could handle storage and retrieval of a range of student-developed materials, as well as other data, resources, and materials. This system is operational in all public institutes of higher education in Louisiana. The Louisiana Department of Education field-tested the application of the program to LaTAAP with success. Today, a new teacher can develop and submit his or her portfolio online. It can be scored online by all members of an assessor team, and an assessment summary report that synthesizes the observation and portfolio scores of team members can be created. Further, data, information, and products created by a teacher for potential use in the National Board for Professional Teaching Standards (NBPTS) can be stored and later retrieved for assemblage into an NBPTS portfolio.

A few comments about specific entries or information requested on several of the work sample forms provided in the appendixes are warranted. These comments follow, and the reader will want to have the appropriate form available for review when reading these comments. The comments do not cover entire contents of any form, only items where information requested of the teacher may lack clarity for readers who do not have access to the LaTAAP teacher manual.

Form 1 (appendix D): Teaching Context, Part II: Individual Differences, List of Learning Styles

While there are many ways of categorizing learning styles and a plethora of research in this area, sometimes conflicting, LaTAAP focuses teacher attention on seven well-researched perceptual modalities because these modalities are among the easiest to address in group instructional settings. It is appropriate and relatively easy for teachers, even new teachers, to identify these modalities in the classroom and accommodate them.

Form 2 (appendix D): Describing the Work Sample, Item 1

When TWSM was introduced into LaTAAP, then State Superintendent Dr. Cecil Pickard recognized the potential for using work samples to identify the instructional competence and professional development needs of K–3 teachers in language arts and mathematics, which were state targets for improvement. So he mandated that K–3 teachers develop and submit a work sample in one of those two content areas. This requirement illustrates how TWSM can inform and serve schoolwide, districtwide, or even statewide educational needs.

Form 2 (appendix D): Describing the Work Sample, Item 4

Obviously, an instructional unit can be designed to accomplish several objectives. Since the Louisiana Teacher Work Sample is being used as part of a high-stakes assessment system, essentially equal and comparable amounts and types of data are needed for each evaluatee. Therefore, the requirement that there be at least two objectives with at least one of them requiring higher-order thinking (a state instructional focus) was embedded in the system. It is clearly communicated to the new teacher that in units having more than two objectives, only the first two will be considered in the assessment process.

Form 3 (appendix D): The Assessment Plan, Items 2 and 3

Louisiana teachers developing, teaching, and submitting work samples are not required to give pre- and post-tests, as such. They are required to develop and implement pre- and post-assessments that will clearly show student knowledge/skill gains (or lack thereof) due to instruction. In reality, this means that data/information gained from formal pre- and post-assessments must be translated into gain scores. The TWS manual provides detailed information about how to do this, as well as practical examples. Mentors and assessors receive training in this area.

Form 4 (appendix D): Analyzing the Results

In Louisiana's application of TWSM, there are two primary questions regarding learning/achievement which the teacher and the assessors must address:

1. Did every student in the class accomplish the targeted objectives?
2. If a student did not actually accomplish a stated objective, did she or he make substantive gains from pre- to post-assessment?

These are actually the "bottom line" issues in all instruction. Teachers in the LaTAAP program must show the data and interpret them. Assessors score the teacher's competence in developing appropriate assessments and analyzing results. The results are also the basis for scoring the teacher's capacity to "produce evidence of student academic growth under his/her instruction." (attribute III.D.4) In LaTAAP, there is a focus on student outcomes, not just instruction and assessment processes. One reason for giving attention to student outcomes was to provide policy makers and others with evidence of learning other than annual, standardized achievement data.

Form 5 (appendix D): Reflecting on the Impact of Instruction, Items 1–4

The primary focus of the data and information requested on this form is again student outcomes. The "bottom line" issues (accomplishment of objectives, substantive gains) must be addressed by the teacher, as well as follow-up instruction/assistance for poorly performing students. Several realistic assumptions underlie the items on this form:

1. Not all students will accomplish all objectives, but most should.
2. All students should make substantive (defined in the TWS manual) gains in knowledge and skills, even if they don't fully accomplish an objective. If not, the objectives, or the instruction, or the assessments are probably not appropriate for all learners in the class.
3. There are circumstances in which a learner, not the teacher, should be held accountable for inadequate performance (e.g., extended absence, medical problems, a catastrophic event at home).
4. Students who do not achieve intended outcomes must be followed up after a unit of work is completed. Failure to do so extends the achievement gap.

Form 6 (appendix D): Communication and Follow-Up

Most of the information requested on this form was not encompassed in the original version of the TWS (Western Oregon version). The form addresses key performance components and attributes found in the Louisiana Components of Effective Teaching, components and attributes which can be assessed from information about the teacher's practices in relation to the work sample (see appendix A for a list of components and attributes covered by the TWS).

Form 7 (appendix D): Work Sample Lesson Plan Portfolio Entry Form

The focus of the Louisiana Teacher Work Sample is the unit of instruction, not individual lessons. However, the evaluatee is required to submit one illustrative lesson plan and respond to the questions on this form.

SCORING

A new teacher in Louisiana is scored/rated on his or her competence and performance in relation to the Louisiana Components of Effective Teaching. Data for this assessment are provided by (1) two classroom observations and (2) two independent ratings of the data/information provided in his or her portfolio. Observations are conducted and scored by the two members of the assessor team, and each member of the team scores the portfolio, of which one part is the Teacher Work Sample. All assessors are extensively trained and must meet reliability standards in both elements (observation, portfolio scoring) of the assessment process. Ratings from the two assessors are combined in a face-to-face assessor conference. Should there be marked disagreements between the two assessors, a third assessor enters the process, and she or he conducts and scores a third observation and scores again the teacher's portfolio. Then all three sets of scores are reviewed and final team scores are developed through assessor consensus.

When scoring the teacher's work sample, the assessor has for each attribute a rubric which focuses the information/data for each LCET attribute covered by the work sample. The scoring rubrics are quite interesting in that some scores are dependent on "if-then" relationships in the data. For example, if a teacher has identified certain individual differences (patterns of achievement, learning styles, languages, etc.) existing in the classroom (Form 1), it is expected that accommodations for at least some of those will be identified on Form 2. If that is not the case, a low score (1, 0) results. In another example, an achievement of more than 50 percent of all class members accomplishing all objectives has been established as one of the criteria for providing evidence of his or her ability to facilitate academic growth. If that outcome is not present, a low score (1, 0) results and will contribute to the ultimate score for that particular attribute.

IMPACT ON TEACHER PREPARATION

In Louisiana, unlike several other states, TWSM was introduced into the LaTAAP program before it gained a foothold in teacher preparation programs. Its use in the assistance and assessment processes and certification decisions caught the attention of those engaged in teacher preparation, and now most of Louisiana's teacher preparation programs have incorporated TWSM into their curricula. The result is a state where there is now a relatively high level of consistency among teacher preparation, new-teacher assistance, professional growth initiatives for teachers, and assessment of teacher competence for certification.

WHAT CAN BE LEARNED FROM
THE LOUISIANA APPROACH TO TWSM?

The successful application of TWSM in Louisiana's Teacher Assistance and Assessment Program provides several important "findings" about its conceptual soundness, versatility, and adaptability:

1. The components of a work sample, as originally defined by Del Schalock and his colleagues at Western Oregon University, "work" at both the preservice and in-service levels of teacher development. In Louisiana, as elsewhere, there has been understanding and acceptance of those components as the foundation of the methodology.
2. While the use of TWSM began as a tool for helping prospective teachers connect process with outcomes (i.e., teaching with learning), Louisiana's adaptation of the methodology demonstrates similar value in in-service settings as both a professional development tool and an assessment tool.
3. Teacher Work Samples can be incorporated into a high-stakes teacher evaluation program if the conditions necessary for validity and reliability of scores are present; that is, if work sample contents are aligned with state or local teacher performance standards which in turn have been validated statewide; if assessors/evaluators have been thoroughly trained and demonstrate reliability in scoring contents; and if work sample contents and format are standardized to ensure fairness and objectivity in analysis and scoring.
4. Teacher Work Sample Methodology can be used to address schoolwide, districtwide, or even statewide instructional needs and initiatives. There is no reason that work sample content (subject matter) has to be unique to each teacher.
5. In a world of standards-based education, TWSM is a valuable tool for helping prospective and in-service teachers bring their instruction and standards (student content and performance standards, teacher standards) into alignment.
6. Teacher Work Sample Methodology offers a bridge between, or a common denominator for, teacher preparation programs, the necessary assessment of in-service teacher performance, and the professional development of in-service teachers. Its utilization can be initiated at either the preservice or in-service levels. Educators at all levels understand and accept the components of a work sample as critical components of instructional design, implementation, and analysis once they receive proper orientation and training.
7. Teacher Work Samples can be easily adapted to serve a variety of educational purposes and needs, and format can be easily adapted to the

utilization of computer technology in their development, presentation, and analysis (scoring).

Louisiana's adaptation and utilization of TWSM in in-service teacher settings simply adds to the ever-growing storehouse of knowledge about and experience with this valuable educational tool.[4]

15

The Performance Assessment for California Teachers: A Policy Case Study of Teacher Work Sampling

Ray Pecheone and Ruth Chung Wei

INTRODUCTION AND THE CALIFORNIA POLICY CONTEXT

It is now widely acknowledged by policy makers and education researchers that improving teacher quality is a key component of educational reform, and that teacher quality contributes to student achievement (e.g., Aaronson, Barrow, & Sander, 2007; Greenwald, Hedges, & Laine, 1996; Rivkin, Hanushek, & Kain, 2000; Rockoff, 2004; Sanders & Horn, 1994; Sanders & Rivers, 1996; Wright, Horn, & Sanders, 1997). This connection has also filtered into public opinion. The Center for the Future of Teaching and Learning (CFTL) reported on a 2002 Harris poll which found that almost 90 percent of the 1,006 Californians polled believed that "ensuring a well-qualified teacher in every classroom" was critical to improving student achievement (CFTL, 2003). What continues to be debated, however, is what it means to be a "well-qualified" teacher (see, for example, Darling-Hammond, 2001; Darling-Hammond, Berry, and Thoreson, 2001; Walsh, 2001; Walsh and Podgursky, 2002) and how best to measure teacher competency. In recent years, the "education school establishment" has been challenged to demonstrate its relevance and contribution to teacher quality. Critics have questioned the effectiveness of traditional teacher preparation programs and have called for regulatory changes that would open the way for multiple alternate routes into the teaching profession. Meanwhile, schools of education have been engaged in research programs aimed at examining the contributions of teacher preparation to student achievement (e.g., the Carnegie-funded Teachers for a New Era initiative). State and national accreditation agencies (e.g., NCATE) have also shifted the focus of their program reviews to examine the outcomes of preparation in addition to program curriculum and design.

Moreover, the question of how teacher competency can be validly measured remains in contention. Standardized licensing tests have often been criticized as being inauthentic and reductionist, and as having little predictive value of teachers' performance in the classroom. Even tests that assess pedagogical knowledge are unable to authentically capture teachers' *application* of their content and pedagogical knowledge. While some states require that teacher candidates pass standardized tests of pedagogical knowledge and skill at the end of preservice training, California's battery of licensing tests (CBEST, a basic skills test; and CSET, a subject-matter competency test) are completed as prerequisites to program entry or clinical work, and neither measures pedagogical knowledge or skill or the impact of teacher preparation. (The exception is the reading instruction assessment for elementary teachers, RICA; however, the pass rates on this exam are so high that it has lost its discriminatory function.) Thus, teacher education programs in the state have been grappling with their capacity to measure and document the impact of their programs on beginning teachers in a valid and reliable way.

Against this backdrop, the California legislature passed Senate Bill 2042 (1998) with the goal of transforming the teacher licensing system in the state and reforming teacher preparation. One of the new requirements for the initial teaching credential introduced by SB 2042 was a teaching performance assessment (TPA) that would be completed during preservice preparation. Programs were given the option to administer the TPA developed by the state (through a contract with the Educational Testing Service) or to design and administer their own TPA, provided that it met the state's standards for psychometric quality. Beginning in 2002, a consortium of twelve universities (all of the University of California campuses, two California State University (CSU) campuses, Stanford University, and Mills College) began collaborating to develop its own TPA, the Performance Assessment for California Teachers (PACT). The consortium, which has now grown to thirty-one university and district programs,[1] has been engaged in piloting the PACT over the last seven years and has been gearing up for full implementation when the TPA requirement goes into effect. In late 2007, the PACT assessment system was reviewed and approved by the California Commission on Teacher Credentialing (CCTC, referred to hereafter as "the Commission") for use to fulfill the TPA requirement.

The PACT assessment system, like the California TPA (the state's assessment), is a high-stakes performance assessment that is also required to be used in a formative way to support teacher candidate growth. The PACT assessment requires that candidates collect evidence about their teaching practice related to a three- to five-lesson learning segment ("Teaching

Event"). In the process of documenting their Teaching Events, candidates collect in an electronic portfolio their lesson plans and instructional materials, videotaped clips of teaching, and student work samples. Candidates are also prompted to comment on the thinking behind their plans, analyze student learning, and reflect on their teaching decisions. The assessment is scored on rubrics by trained raters at each campus, and based on a passing standard, the candidate's Teaching Event is assessed as meeting or not meeting the minimum standard of competency. Thus, roughly thirty thousand new teachers credentialed each year in California will be required to complete and pass a TPA, and about a third of them will be completing the PACT assessment. This represents yet another instance of a state in which *preservice* teachers across all teacher preparation programs will be engaged in a form of Teacher Work Sampling for the purpose of gaining their preliminary teaching credentials (other states with legislated prelicensure Teacher Work Sampling requirements include Oregon, Kentucky, Louisiana, and Oklahoma).

In this chapter, we describe the policy context in which this new TPA requirement came to be mandated, provide an overview of the PACT assessment system, and describe the results of PACT implementation based on six years of field test data. Last, we discuss the place of performance assessment in state policies aimed at improving teacher quality. As a formalized instantiation of Teacher Work Sampling, the PACT assessment system and its story provide some important lessons learned about the power of assessment to drive reform in teacher education and to improve teacher quality.

CALIFORNIA'S TEACHER QUALITY
"CRISIS" AND SENATE BILL 2042

The 1990s have been characterized as a "crisis" for the teaching profession in California. That decade saw the doubling of the number of emergency-credentialed teachers in the state (from about 12,000 in 1991–1992 to about 28,500 by 1998–1999, representing 11.6 percent of certificated staff), hired in the context of massive teacher shortages. These shortages were due in part to a 24 percent growth in the student population; legislative reforms that reduced class size in elementary classrooms (1996); the high rate of new-teacher attrition in the state, with 30 percent of new teachers leaving the profession within three years; and the growing rate of teacher retirements (Shields et al., 1999).

The uneven distribution of these underprepared teachers, with most hired by schools with large proportions of minorities and poor students, has also been widely documented (e.g., Bohrnstedt & Stecher, 1999; Darling-Hammond, 2002; Oakes, 2004). For example, in 1998, a quarter of all teachers in Los Angeles were teaching without a full credential, and fully three-quarters of 3,900 new teachers hired in 1998 were teaching under emergency permits (Shields et al., 1999). Moreover, even teachers who had completed teacher preparation programs were not sanguine about their preparation experiences. In their first annual report, "The Status of the Teaching Profession," the Center for the Future of Teaching and Learning (1999) reported that in a survey of teachers across the state, new teachers did not rate their teacher preparation programs highly. Interviewed teachers expressed a need to have more clinical experiences and more experience with designing coherent instructional plans and using curriculum materials effectively, and they criticized the usefulness of preparation classes. Likewise, administrators were critical of the preparation of newly credentialed teachers to deal with the realities of full-time teaching.

These conditions in California and a public loss of faith in the quality of education in the state led state legislators, in partnership with the Commission, to propose and enact an overhaul of the state's policies with regard to the entire teacher credentialing system. The reforms, embodied in Senate Bill 2042, were to include an expansion of the pathways into the teaching profession, changes in the standards applied to preparation programs, changes in requirements for the preliminary and "clear" teaching credentials, and a scale-up to full implementation of the state's pilot induction program ("BTSA," Beginning Teacher Support and Assessment). However, these reforms were not enacted overnight. The road had been paved during the six years before SB 2042 was passed. The precursor to SB 2042 was a bill sponsored by State Senator Marian Bergeson (SB 1422, 1992) that set into motion an extensive review of the credentialing system. This review was prompted by a proposal sponsored by Senator Bergeson to scale up implementation of the popular BTSA program (formerly known as the "California New Teacher Project"), which was credited with reducing the high attrition rate among beginning teachers. The intent of the proposal was to require that all new teachers complete an induction program to gain a "professional" license. However, this proposal led policy makers to question the usefulness of layering on another licensure requirement to the current teacher licensing "system," perceived as an incoherent hodgepodge of state statutes (Sandy, 2006). At the urging of the Commission, Senator Bergeson called for a comprehensive review of credentialing. SB 1422 mandated that the Commission convene a panel to examine the entire credentialing system (including preservice preparation, induction, and requirements for credential renewal) in a comprehensive and systematic way. The advisory panel included a wide array of stakeholder groups including teachers, teacher educators, administrators, school boards, county offices, parents, and other citizens.

Between 1995 and 1997, the SB 1422 advisory panel held eighteen meetings and made its final report to the Commission in August 1997 (Bond, Tierney, & Fitch, n.d.).

The recommendations of the SB 1422 advisory panel were organized around four overarching goals:

- Improve teacher recruitment, selection, and access to the profession.
- Establish clear standards for new-teacher preparation programs.
- Increase and improve professional accountability.
- Increase and improve professional collaboration and system evaluation.

The panel made 16 general policy recommendations and 110 specific recommendations to meet these four goals (see CCTC, 1997, for the entire set of recommendations). Among the recommendations for increasing and improving professional accountability was General Policy Recommendation 13: Require broader and more rigorous assessment of teacher candidates.

> The credential system must ensure that all newly credentialed teachers meet established teaching standards. Current assessment practices in pre-service teacher preparation are disparate and inadequate for the new credential system, and must therefore be strengthened or replaced. To ensure the most effective teaching for California's children, candidates should be assessed at the culmination of both Level I and Level II preparation. (CCTC, 1997, p. 36)

This policy recommendation grew out of "a widespread acknowledgement that the way we evaluate teachers for licensure is haphazard, episodic, and very idiosyncratic, meaning that whatever a collection of faculty at any teacher preparation institution decides is the appropriate criteria to recommend a candidate for a credential, that's what they go with. . . . There was no holistic look at the candidate in any systemic way across the state for licensure" (Sandy, 2008).

The specific policy changes recommended by the panel included a proposal that preservice teachers complete a summative performance-based assessment of pedagogical skills and knowledge to qualify for the Level I credential. Secondly, for the Level II credential, the panel proposed a summative assessment of teachers that would include a portfolio as well as an observation-based assessment. The latter part of the proposal was immediately the subject of heated debate and opposition from school districts, who would be responsible for administering the assessments for the Level II credential. Districts argued that colleges and universities should be held accountable for preparing teachers and should assess their competence before they are granted a Level I credential. They also objected to the prospect of being engaged in expensive and time-consuming litigation from teachers challenging the results of the assessment (Bond, Tierney, & Fitch, n.d.). Teacher associations also objected to the Level II assessment on the grounds that it would exacerbate a critical shortage of teachers; however, the panel argued that the scale-up of the BTSA program that was also put forward in their recommendations would partially remedy this teacher shortage by stemming high teacher attrition (Sandy, 2006, 2008).

Due to objections to the high-stakes TPA proposal, among objections to other recommendations in the report, the entire set of recommendations from the SB 1422 panel was almost defeated. However, after countless meetings of representatives with key education stakeholder groups, the panel came to a compromise that would make the changes more acceptable to districts (Bond, Tierney, & Fitch, n.d.). It was agreed that a summative high-stakes assessment would be placed at the end of preservice or internship preparation (like a "bar exam") to filter out less qualified teachers before they could earn a preliminary credential, and the proposal for the Level II assessment at the end of induction was tabled until the implementation of the Level I assessment had been evaluated.

In the end, most of the recommendations of the SB 1422 panel, including a provision to include a teaching performance assessment at the preservice level, were incorporated into SB 2042. Ultimately, the State Assembly passed SB 2042 by wide margins, reacting to pressures from proponents of the K–12 accountability movement and standards-based reform, which provided the impetus for legislating reforms in teacher education.

> "We are going to have a system for teacher education that attends to the standards for students and the assessments for students, and the accountability movement in schools." That was a real driver here. The confidence level in teacher education was very low. That created a climate in the legislature that supported putting a summative bar-type assessment for teachers into play. . . . It was part of our argument back to the K–12 reform environment. "Okay, you don't like teacher education—well, we're changing the teacher education system. We've overhauled the standards and we're putting these assessments in place to increase confidence in the workforce." (Sandy, 2008)

However, the TPA provision, as well as full expansion of the BTSA induction program, was contingent on appropriations and the availability of funding in California's annual budget. Again, it appeared that the policy commitments began to unravel and that the proposal for these two programs would be defeated. However, the California legislature came through with full funding for BTSA beginning in 2003–2004, and $10 million from a Title II Teacher Quality Enhancement grant from the U.S. Department of Education was procured to begin development of a TPA prototype. Full funding for implementation of the TPA, however, has yet to be approved. While the TPA provision was to go into effect in 2003, the lack of fiscal support for the legislation has led to a moratorium on the law's enforcement up to FY 2006 (Sandy, 2006, 2008).

Subsequently the moratorium was lifted, and the TPA was required of all teacher education candidates as of July 2009. While the Commission could have easily adopted one of the performance assessments that were commercially available through test vendors such as ETS (e.g., PRAXIS III), state policy makers (at the urging of Commission staff) were motivated to develop an assessment system that was aligned with its own vision of effective and meaningful assessment. The Commission had previously conducted a pilot of the PRAXIS III. However, the Commission wanted to make sure that the assessment that was adopted reflected the state's priorities. Mary Sandy, a consultant and staff member for the SB 1422 advisory panel, recalled that the architects of the TPA idea (David Wright and Carol Bartell, Commission staff members) were drawn to the success of the formative assessment system utilized in the California New Teacher Project.

> A good deal of their perspective was informed by the work with the New Teacher Project. And what we found from that New Teacher Project (the early form of the Beginning Teacher Support and Assessment program) is that performance assessment—real examination of teaching that is reflective and that captures the teacher's thinking about, and their conscious decision making about what they're doing, and what moves they are making—was the essence of good assessment practice. And the goal was to take that essence and build it into the statewide system for assessment. . . . We really believed that we needed something that probed deeply into the domains of teaching performance that are defined by the California Standards for the Teaching Profession. . . . We wanted to make sure that whatever we were doing capitalized on the same kind of [approach] in the New Teacher Project—the "Plan, Teach, Reflect, Apply" mantra was central. That's what we were pursuing. . . . How can we make this system articulate so that the TPA and formative assessment [in BTSA] felt like they were a family of assessments? And all of that was contributing to teachers' ability to move on to the National Board [portfolio assessment]. So there was definitely an intentional articulation there. . . . California wanted to build its own, make its own mark. (Sandy, 2008)

While the recommendations of the SB 1422 panel were being considered and the language for SB 2042 was being drafted, objections were also raised regarding the Level I assessment requirement. The higher-education community was in "shock and dismay about the idea that the state would build and enforce a summative assessment that would inhabit their programs" (Sandy, 2008). Higher-education institutions resisted relinquishing their authority to select the assessments used in making the credentialing decision and objected to the state's mandate of a high-stakes TPA. Consequently, the bill was to include a provision that allowed higher-education institutions to build and implement alternative assessment models, as long as those alternatives met assessment standards adopted by the Commission. This provision "helped the medicine go down" and allowed the bill to get through the legislature (Sandy, 2008). However, the Commission's adopted Assessment Quality Standards, which incorporated the NCME standards for assessment, set a high bar for programs seeking to sponsor an alternative TPA. This would make it difficult for most teacher education programs to develop alternative TPAs due to a lack of capacity for conducting the studies necessary for documenting how their assessments met psychometric standards. On the other hand, this provision opened the door of opportunity for a group of teacher preparation programs to combine their resources to sponsor an alternative TPA, the Performance Assessment for California Teachers (PACT).

THE PERFORMANCE ASSESSMENT
FOR CALIFORNIA TEACHERS

Led by a steering committee that included Linda Darling-Hammond at Stanford, Bob Calfee at UC Riverside, P. David Pearson at UC Berkeley, Randall Souviney at UC San Diego, Harold Levine at UC Davis, Lionel "Skip" Meno at San Diego State University, and Raymond Pecheone, who was enlisted from his previous role as the director of the Connecticut BEST (Beginning Educator Support and Training) portfolio assessment, the PACT consortium began development of an alternative TPA in early 2002. The PACT consortium came together in reaction to the legislative mandate of SB 2042 but was also motivated by a collective perception that the California TPA, developed by the Commission and the Educational Testing Service, did not meet their own standards of quality for a performance assessment. They wanted to design an assessment instrument that would reflect their program missions and the high standards of teaching performance that they wanted to uphold in their programs. The California TPA, which has four distinct tasks that are scored separately by different raters on four holistic rubrics, was perceived by PACT members as not going far enough to measure teachers' ability to plan, enact instruction, and reflect on their students' learning *in an integrated way*. Consortium members also wanted to design subject-specific tasks that would measure the application of pedagogical content knowledge and devise a set of diagnostic rubrics that could provide specific feedback to candidates. Concerned about an external assessment "colonizing" their curriculum, members of the PACT consortium set out to craft an assessment that was aligned with their own program objectives.

Beginning in the spring of 2002, the PACT consortium members began to collaborate to design the performance tasks ("Teaching Events").

Kendyll Stansbury, who had worked with Raymond Pecheone in designing performance tasks for the Connecticut BEST portfolio assessment and had also worked on the formative assessments for the BTSA induction program, was hired to manage the assessment development work. Representatives from across the twelve campuses were brought together in subject-specific development teams, covering five major credential areas (elementary: literacy and math; single subjects: English-language arts, history-social science, mathematics, and science). Members of these teams were teacher educators or other university faculty with expertise in content-specific pedagogy. A separate development team for designing prompts and rubrics that specifically addressed the instruction of English learners was also convened. These cross-institutional teams met several times over the course of the year to develop specifications for the tasks and assessment criteria. By early 2003, PACT had drafted a set of six Teaching Event handbooks and subject-specific rubrics. The prompts for teacher candidates and rubrics were standardized across content areas but with variation around the instructional foci for each content area. These represented five credential areas, with the assessment of both literacy and mathematics instruction for prospective elementary teachers.[2] The instructional focus for each Teaching Event reflects a core instructional approach that is specific to the content area. The instructional foci for the first six Teaching Events are listed in textbox 15.1.

The PACT Teaching Event is similar in concept to its predecessors, the National Board portfolio assessments, the INTASC (Interstate Teacher Assessment and Support Consortium) portfolio assessment, and the Connecticut BEST portfolio assessment. The Teaching Event, a collection of teacher and student artifacts, is based on a Planning, Instruction, Assessment, Reflection, and Academic Language (PIAR-L) model in which candidates use knowledge of students' skills and abilities—as well as knowledge of content and how best to teach it—in planning, implementing, and assessing instruction. For each Teaching Event, candidates must complete several entries that are integrated around a short unit or segment of instruction. These entries include the following:

1. a description of their teaching context,
2. a set of lesson plans from an instructional unit,
3. one or two videotapes of instruction during the unit,
4. samples of student work during the unit, and
5. written reflections on instruction and its effects on student learning during the unit.

The PIAR-L model is distinctive in its placement of student learning at the center of the assessment system. While many clinical assessments of

TEXTBOX 15.1. PACT TEACHING EVENT

SUBJECT-SPECIFIC INSTRUCTIONAL FOCI

Elementary literacy
Provide opportunities to develop students' ability to comprehend and/or compose text by developing literacy skills and strategies.

Elementary mathematics
Provide opportunities to develop your students' conceptual understanding, computational/procedural fluency, and mathematical reasoning skills.

English-language arts
Provide opportunities to support students in developing an understanding and interpretation of complex text and in creating a written product responding to text.

History-social science
Provide opportunities for your students to use facts, concepts, and interpretations to make and explain judgments about a significant historical event or social science phenomenon.

Mathematics
Provide opportunities to develop students' mathematical knowledge by developing a balance of procedural fluency, conceptual understanding, and mathematical reasoning.

Science
Provide opportunities to develop students' abilities to use scientific concepts to make sense of one or more real-world phenomena by using key scientific inquiry skills.

preservice candidates focus on teacher activities and behaviors, paying little attention to evidence about student outcomes, the PACT Teaching Events place learning at the center. Specifically, the PACT assessments focus on evidence that reveals student learning of defined objectives/content standards and ask candidates to consider how these objectives can be attained for all students.

Beginning in the spring of 2003, the twelve PACT members began piloting the Teaching Events in their credential programs. Some of the smaller programs piloted Teaching Events across all candidates, while others took a more graduated approach, piloting with purposively selected cohorts of candidates or in specific credential areas based on faculty interest and initiative or available resources. Some programs administered the Teaching Event within certain courses, such as their student teaching seminars or methods courses, while others implemented the

Teaching Event across courses, providing opportunities to practice Teaching Event–like tasks along the way. In most cases, the Teaching Events are completed during the final phase of student teaching, when candidates have a solid knowledge of their students and have greater responsibility for instructing the class. In some programs organized by the quarter system, Teaching Events are submitted and scored at the end of the winter quarter to provide candidates with an opportunity to remediate failing scores during the spring quarter, which will be a requirement when the TPA provision goes into effect.

The assessment criteria for scoring the Teaching Events are currently represented in eleven guiding questions. The rubrics that accompany each of these guiding questions describe four levels of performance that were written to reflect a developmental continuum based on teacher educators' experiences with preservice teachers (1 represents a performance that is below the passing standard, 2 represents a passing performance, 3 represents a solid performance, and 4 represents an exemplary performance for a preservice teacher). The rubrics have undergone revision each year based on feedback from scorers and teacher educators and in light of the candidate performances observed. The guiding questions and rubrics are standardized across the content areas with subject-specific variations.[3]

In the first pilot year, Teaching Event "benchmarks" (representing below passing, passing, and solid performances) were selected from the work of early completers for the training of scorers. At the end of the year, centralized training and scoring sessions were conducted across four sites (one in Northern California and three in Southern California). Scorers included teacher educators and other education faculty, supervisors, cooperating teachers, National Board-certified teachers, and other teachers or administrators. (In the second pilot year and subsequent years, a decentralized training-of-trainers scoring model has been used, and all Teaching Events are scored by local scorers recruited and trained by programs. Under this model, a percentage of Teaching Events from across institutions are rescored at a central audit to check the consistency of local scores with audit scores. This scoring model will be used in subsequent years when the TPA requirement goes into effect.) In the course of development and piloting, the psychometric properties of the Teaching Event assessment were evaluated and studied. These studies of technical quality are summarized in Pecheone and Chung (2006). They demonstrate that the Teaching Event is a valid assessment of initial teaching and can be implemented reliably.

While stipulating that the TPA be used to make a summative assessment of teaching competence, SB 2042 also requires that the TPA be used to provide formative feedback to candidates to inform their learning. While the Teaching Event is primarily used in a summative way, it is one piece of the PACT assessment system which includes "embedded signature assessments" (ESAs), course assignments that are unique to particular programs but implemented across sections of a program and scored using customized rubrics. See figure 15.1 for a representation of the PACT assessment system. These ESAs are used formatively to provide candidates with feedback on their teaching knowledge and skills. In addition, the Teaching Event is designed to be implemented in such a way as to provide formative feedback to candidates as they construct their portfolio tasks. While information from the ESAs has yet to be formally integrated with the Teaching Event scores for making the licensure decision, PACT plans to undertake a study of how these multiple measures of teaching competence can be combined to inform a summative decision. This assessment system was designed from the beginning to be a multiple-measures system, recognizing that a single assessment cannot provide enough information about a candidate's competencies across all domains of teaching knowledge and skill and that a single sample of teaching performance should not be the sole determinant of a high-stakes licensure decision.

CONSEQUENCES OF PACT IMPLEMENTATION

As of this writing, the PACT Teaching Events have been piloted over the past seven academic years. During the first five pilot years, over 4,000 candidates

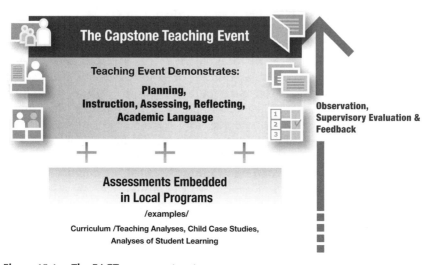

Figure 15.1.   The PACT assessment system.

at PACT institutions have completed Teaching Events (with over 1,100 in the 2006–2007 academic year), and 180 trainers have been trained to conduct the training of local scorers at their local institutions. In the University of California campuses, Stanford University, Mills College, and the San Diego City School District, programs have scaled up to full implementation of the assessment and have included completion of the Teaching Event as a major requirement for graduation, in some cases requiring passage of the assessment to qualify for the licensure recommendation. In the California State University campuses and other privates, piloting has occurred at a smaller scale and scale-up has been at an understandably slower pace, given the size of many of the CSU programs (with many graduating more than five hundred candidates a year) and a period of budget cuts for public higher-education institutions. However, these programs continue to be engaged in the development work, and many CSU programs eagerly joined PACT as the deadline for implementation of the TPA requirement approaches.

What is remarkable about the PACT consortium is that almost all of the development work has been completed without funding from the state government and with relatively modest external funding. While the PACT central office at Stanford, which provides technical support, conducts research, and coordinates the work, has been funded by private foundations (including the Flora Family Foundation and the Morgan Family Foundation), most of the development work, piloting, and scoring has been completed with donated faculty time (with no extra compensation in most cases) and other in-kind donations, with some support from the UC Office of the President. Six years of travel expenses and meetings have been covered mostly by institutional funds, and even the costs of scoring the Teaching Events locally have been absorbed by institutions and their faculty. This is not to say that the cost of developing and piloting the PACT assessment system has been negligible. In fact, if one were to add up all of the faculty time and expenses incurred by consortium members in the course of the development work and field-testing, it is likely that the total cost (including the cost of supporting the PACT central office) would surpass $500,000. Although the magnitude of resources that were used to create the PACT assessment system can only be estimated, it is a testament to the commitment of the PACT consortium members that without the financial resources that were available to the state's TPA system ($10 million), this system has been developed, field-tested, and sustained, even during the last few years of policy moratorium. It is a testament to the common vision and commitment of the PACT consortium members.

What is even more gratifying is that the work of developing the Teaching Events and other training events has led to an unprecedented level of cross-institutional collaboration among teacher education faculty and supervisors across a state with approximately one hundred teacher education programs.

Several times a year, program leaders and faculty from across the thirty-one institutions voluntarily gather to participate in program directors' meetings, training-of-trainers events, and other development events (such as selecting and scoring of Teaching Events to build a library of benchmarks for scorer training). As a consequence of this collaboration, the faculty across and within these programs have developed a common language for talking about teaching performance, a common set of performance standards for preservice teaching competency, and a common understanding of what constitutes effective teaching within each discipline and credential area. Each year at the PACT Implementation Conference, they also gather to share their program experiences with each other so that they can benefit collectively from their shared practices. The PACT consortium has contributed to the development of a professional learning community in the truest sense.

In addition, engagement with the PACT assessment has promoted learning at all levels—program learning, program faculty learning, and candidate learning. Programs have reported using the assessment results and artifacts of teacher candidate performance to develop plans for programwide improvement. Faculty members have collaborated in examining scores and candidate work samples and have used these analyses to inform changes in instruction to better support candidates to meet the needs of K–12 students and to establish closer connections between coursework and fieldwork. UC Santa Barbara, for example, involves all of its faculty and supervisors in scoring Teaching Events and conducts annual faculty retreats in which the examination of their candidates' work samples is a key component. There is evidence from programs that the PACT assessment system guides and extends quality instruction in teacher preparation programs by helping to make more clearly visible the strengths and common weaknesses of candidate performance in particular areas of teaching, such as assessment and the instruction of English learners.

> We've always gone out into the classrooms and observed and we've always assessed their work inside the classroom. Now this is asking them to write and think about, in one assessment, in an official culminating assessment process, what they're actually thinking about as they're teaching. What's important about that is that the rubrics are sufficiently detailed so that when we analyze the data, it gives us important information about the strengths of our program. And in terms of what students know, what do we think we're teaching, yet the students aren't getting? In other words, where are the holes in our program? And that has been really valuable for us. . . . One of the areas that we've found we need to work on is: What do student teachers do next? Once they've analyzed the student work in the assessment of student work [task], what do they need to do next to actually *improve* on the student learning in their classroom? And I know, because of the consortium, that's actually a weakness in many of the student teacher programs. (CSU program director)

A major change in our program has been a stronger emphasis on academic language. It's always been a goal for the program, but I think there has been historically a conception that, "Oh well, that course will handle it and the students will remember what they learned in that one course and it will carry forward." But we've been doing a lot of professional development with our supervisors, in particular around academic language, to have them think about what linguistic demands are embedded in their candidates' lessons and to help the candidates understand that they need to think about academic language development *while* they're planning, not after they've done a plan and then *modify* the plan, that it is a consideration from the very beginning of their lessons. And when they look at student work, they want to ask, "To what extent does the student performance reflect an academic language issue, in addition to a content learning issue?" (CSU faculty member and program coordinator)

Participation in PACT training and scoring events has also been appreciated by individual faculty members as an opportunity to learn. Many participants consider the trainings to be powerful professional development, stimulating new insights into their work with teacher candidates, as evident in the following quote:

I've learned more about my practice because of the Teaching Event with PACT. As a teacher of the language arts curriculum for preservice [teachers], it has taught me a lot. As I have done the scoring, I have noticed pieces that I need to go back and make more explicit within my own coursework. For example, I really felt that I needed to do more specifics about how do you actually modify a lesson and how do you know what you are teaching to, especially if we have people working within a more structured program [scripted curricula]. And so, this year I spent a lot more time focusing on struggling readers and helping them know, "This is what this is." (CSU faculty member)

Last, through research as well as unsolicited reports from teacher candidates, we have found that the process of completing the PACT Teaching Event has provided an important learning experience for candidates. During the first two pilot years (2002–2003 and 2003–2004), the PACT consortium administered a survey to all candidates completing Teaching Events across the consortium. We found that approximately 90 percent felt that the Teaching Event validly measured important elements of their teaching knowledge and skill, and two-thirds felt that they had learned important skills through their experiences with the Teaching Event. In particular, survey respondents reported that they had learned the importance of using student work analysis to guide their instructional decisions, and to reflect more carefully about their teaching. In addition, preservice teachers have reported that the experience of investigating their students' backgrounds for the Instructional Context task of the Teaching Event has prompted them to pay greater attention to their students' specific learning needs in designing instruction.

> So, you know, at the beginning the PACT lesson has you analyze: What's the context? Who are the kids? What needs do they have? Do you have English language learners? . . . What kind of English language learner are they and how much; where are they on the spectrum? Are they beginning language learners? Are they advanced language learners? And then, to take that information, take information about all the kids in your class, and then think about teaching to every single one of them—that was kind of a new experience for me. It was actually the first time in my teaching experience that everything came together from beginning to end and made sense. It made sense. (Teacher candidate at a CSU)
>
> I used to look at assessment as a way to assess kids. And this is the first time, through PACT, that I realized that in assessing, you should really primarily be assessing *yourself* as a teacher. . . . What evidence do you have that the students picked up on your scaffolding, picked up on the academic language, picked up on the advanced concepts or the medium concepts? What evidence do you have of that, and how well did you present the lesson? You know, instead of "Does this child know X?" the question is "Have I provided adequate scaffolding for this child to be able to do X, and what is the evidence showing me? How effective was my teaching?". . . It's more of a holistic thing where you're assessing you and the children, and then you can ask yourself the question of "What can I do differently the next time, to make learning accessible for these kids?" (Teacher candidate at a CSU)

How much of this reported learning translates into actual changes in teaching practice? In case studies of preservice elementary teachers (Chung, 2007, 2008), it was found that preservice teachers were able to begin enacting what they had learned from the Teaching Event in their instructional practice. Teachers showed evidence of reflecting more carefully about what students had learned and using the results of their assessments to inform their instructional decisions. Thus, including a performance assessment that places an emphasis on analyzing student learning as a component of preservice preparation could lead to improved formative classroom assessment practices. However, additional research is needed to evaluate the long-term impact of their experiences with the PACT Teaching Event on beginning teachers' classroom instruction after leaving their credential programs.

POLICY AND PRACTICES IN TEACHER ASSESSMENT

One of the few areas of consensus among education policy makers, practitioners, and the general public today is that improving teacher quality is one of the most direct and promising strategies for improving public education outcomes in the United States. Furthermore, this strategy is particularly critical for groups of children who have historically been taught by the least qualified teachers.

Interest is intensifying in how to go beyond current measures of teacher qualifications to measures that more closely evaluate teachers' effectiveness in relation to student learning. However, existing federal, state, and local policies for defining and measuring teacher quality rely, on the one hand, almost exclusively on classroom observations by principals that differentiate little among teachers and offer little useful feedback, or, on the other hand, on teachers' course-taking records plus paper-and-pencil tests of basic academic skills and disciplinary subject matter knowledge that are poor predictors of later effectiveness in the classroom. It has become clear that new strategies for evaluating teacher competence and effectiveness are needed. Any serious and systematic effort to improve the quality of teachers entering or already practicing in our nation's schools must include development of reliable and valid measures of how well they perform in the classroom, linked to multiple sources of evidence of their effectiveness in promoting learning for students.

Systematic measures of teachers' performance that evaluate teachers' classroom effectiveness have recently been developed in several states and districts. At the state level, these are being used either at the beginning of the career, as a basis for the initial licensing recommendation (California, Oregon), or in the teacher induction period, as a basis for moving from a probationary to a professional license (Connecticut). At the local level, new standards-based evaluations of practice use similar indicators to assess performance in systematic ways throughout the career. Veteran teachers can be further evaluated against high standards of accomplishment through the assessments of the National Board of Professional Teaching Standards.

Teachers' ratings on a number of these assessments have been found to predict their students' value-added achievement on state tests, as well as to help improve teachers' practices.[4] Thus, the possibility now exists for creating a continuum of performance assessments—from initial entry to the profession (Tier 1), through the granting of a professional license (Tier 2), to tenure and on to determinations of high levels of accomplishment (Tier 3)—that can evaluate and help support improvements in teachers' effectiveness (see figure 15.2).

Assessing Effective Teaching Across the Career Continuum

We are proposing an assessment system that is designed to evaluate teaching across the full range of a teacher's career, beginning with a teacher's decision to teach and culminating with National Board certification. Such an accountability system would be designed to both build teacher capac-

Three Tiers of Teacher Assessment

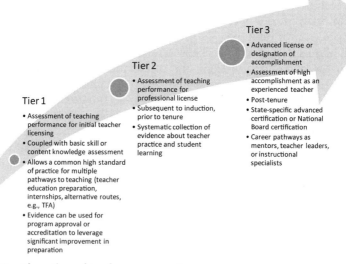

Tier 3
- Advanced license or designation of accomplishment
- Assessment of high accomplishment as an experienced teacher
- Post-tenure
- State-specific advanced certification or National Board certification
- Career pathways as mentors, teacher leaders, or instructional specialists

Tier 2
- Assessment of teaching performance for professional license
- Subsequent to induction, prior to tenure
- Systematic collection of evidence about teacher practice and student learning

Tier 1
- Assessment of teaching performance for initial teacher licensing
- Coupled with basic skill or content knowledge assessment
- Allows a common high standard of practice for multiple pathways to teaching (teacher education preparation, internships, alternative routes, e.g., TFA)
- Evidence can be used for program approval or accreditation to leverage significant improvement in preparation

Figure 15.2.   Three tiers of teacher assessment.

ity and support career advancement based on an objective assessment of teacher quality focusing on teacher licensure and teacher evaluation and its relation to student learning. The engine of this reform strategy requires the use of multiple measures of teacher quality as part of a multitiered state licensure system. The word *performance level* in place of *tier* describes a system that identifies three different performance/practice/effectiveness levels. This system transforms licensure/evaluation from a system of inputs, including an emphasis on course counting and advanced degrees, to a licensure system that is competency-based, representing what teachers should know and be able to do to advance in their career. Although space in this case study does not permit a full description of each, the following three tiers of performance are proposed:

Tier 1: assessment of teaching for granting an initial teacher license
Tier 2: assessment of teaching for granting a professional certificate
Tier 3: assessment of teacher excellence or accomplished teaching to a high level of practice

The key elements of a Tier 1 assessment are grounded in current "best practices" that use multiple measures of teaching and learning to assess preservice teacher competencies. Specifically, the design of a Tier 1 teacher assessment draws on promising practices currently in use in the California PACT assessment and the Western Oregon student work sampling methodologies. The proposed assessment system for the beginning teacher performance assessment consists of three components: (1) a standards-based, discipline-specific assessment of a learning segment (i.e., documenting three to five days of continuous instruction); (2) the systematic collection of multiple measures of teaching and learning across five dimensions of teaching: planning, instruction, assessment, reflection, and academic language (see PACT description in this chapter); and (3) the systematic collection of evidence of a teacher's impact on student learning using formative and/or summative embedded classroom assessment measures, including, if available, school/district assessments such as benchmark, interim, or end-of-course assessments. These components serve as a blueprint and starting point for the development of a nationally available teacher performance assessment that can be used to support high-stakes decisions regarding teacher licensure and national accreditation. Additionally, the assessment of teacher quality will meet high and defensible technical standards of reliability and validity (i.e., AERA, NCME, and APA test standards). Significant progress has already been achieved in initiating the development of a nationally available TPA in the formation of a national partnership and consortium that includes Stanford University, the American Association of Teacher Educators (AACTE), and the Chief State School Officers (CCSSO). As a result of a planning grant funded by the Ford Foundation, we have established a state consortium that represents twenty states, consisting of state consortia made up of representatives from state education agencies (SEAs), teacher standards boards, and over sixty teacher preparation institutions including alternate route programs (e.g., Teach for America). The Tier 1 assessment represents the first stage of a coherent system of assessment that will carry over throughout a teacher's career.

CONCLUSION

An examination of promising teacher preparation assessment practices such as PACT, BEST, Western Oregon, and NBPTS illustrates the importance of the development of a comprehensive, coherent, and educative assessment system "of and for" teaching and learning, rather than the fragmented disjointed systems that are currently in place for teacher licensure and evaluation. Educative assessment systems provide both timely and useful feedback to teachers and administrators about teacher capacity, and they can guide and shape future teacher development as well as be used to support a summative decision around teacher quality at the preservice and in-service levels.

A coherent system of teacher assessment would span a teacher's entire career, focusing on key milestones in a teacher's development from preservice training, to induction, to meaningful systems of annual evaluation, to National Board certification and beyond. These systems would be closely aligned to teacher and student standards, subject-specific performance criteria, and high-quality professional development, and would include evidence of student learning. These new systems of assessment would be designed in collaboration with teachers and administrators and would engage teachers (and higher-education faculty) in scoring to improve their professional practice and their capacity to better support student learning. Additionally, they should be designed to meet the knowledge demands of the twenty-first century by focusing on a wider range of instructional strategies that support higher-order thinking and problem solving to enable all students to be college and career ready. Finally, the new assessment systems should be designed to privilege a system that will support the strategic management of human capital throughout a teacher's career—moving from systems of mere compliance and minimum standards to assessment systems that support high and rigorous teacher standards that are linked to student learning.

REFERENCES

Aaronson, D., Barrow, L., & Sander, W. (2007). Teachers and student achievement in the Chicago public high schools. *Journal of Labor Economics, 25*(1), 95–135.

Bohrnstedt, G. W., & Stecher, B. M. (Eds.). (1999). *Class size reduction in California: Early evaluation findings*. Palo Alto, CA: CSR Research Consortium.

California Commission on Teacher Credentialing. (1997). *California's future: Highly qualified teachers for all students*. Final report of the Advisory Panel on Teacher Education, Induction and Certification for Twenty-First-Century Schools (SB 1422).

Center for the Future of Teaching and Learning. (2003). *Focus on quality: Californians' view on teachers and teaching*. Santa Cruz, CA: Author.

Chung, R. R. (2007, April). *Beyond the ZPD: When do beginning teachers learn from a high-stakes portfolio assessment?* Paper presented at the annual meeting of the American Educational Research Association (AERA), Chicago.

Chung, R. R. (2008). Beyond assessment: Performance assessments in teacher education. *Teacher Education Quarterly, 35*(1), 7–29.

CSR Research Consortium. *Early evaluation findings, 1996–1998* (year 1 evaluation report). Sacramento: California Department of Education. Retrieved from www.classize.org/summary/98-99/summary-00.pdf.

Darling-Hammond, L. (2001). *The research and rhetoric on teacher certification: A response to "Teacher Certification Reconsidered."* Retrieved from www.nctaf.org/publications/abell_response.pdf.

Darling-Hammond, L. (2002). *Access to quality teaching: An analysis of inequality in California's public schools*. Los Angeles: UCLA's Institute for Democracy, Education, and Access (IDEA). Retrieved from www.mofo.com/decentschools/expert_reports/darling-hammond_report.pdf.

Darling-Hammond, L., Berry, B., & Thoreson, A. (2001). Does teacher certification matter? Evaluating the evidence. *Educational Evaluation and Policy Analysis, 23*(1), 57–77.

Goldhaber, D., & Anthony, E. (2004). *Can teacher quality be effectively assessed?* Seattle: University of Washington and the Urban Institute.

Greenwald, R., Hedges, L. V., & Laine, R. D. (1996). The effect of school resources on student achievement. *Review of Educational Research, 66*(3), 361–396.

Oakes, J. (2004). Investigating the claims in *Williams vs. State of California*: An unconstitutional denial of education's basic tools? *Teachers College Record, 106*(10), 1889–1906.

Pecheone, R., & Chung, R. R. (2006). Evidence in teacher education: The Performance Assessment for California Teachers (PACT). *Journal of Teacher Education, 57*(1), 22–36.

Rivkin, S. G., Hanushek, E. A., & Kain, J. F. (2000). *Teachers, schools, and academic achievement.* Working paper no. 6691. Cambridge, MA: National Bureau of Economic Research.

Rockoff, J. E. (2004). The impact of individual teachers on student achievement: Evidence from panel data. *American Economic Review, 94*(2), 247–252.

Sanders, W. L., & Horn, S. (1994). The Tennessee Value-Added Assessment System (TVAAS): Mixed-model methodology in educational assessment. *Journal of Personnel Evaluation in Education, 8,* 299–311.

Sanders, W. L., & Rivers, J. C. (1996). Cumulative and residual effects of teachers on future student academic achievement. Knoxville: University of Tennessee Value-Added Research and Assessment Center.

Sandy, M. V. (2006, March 22). Timing is everything: Building state policy on teacher credentialing in an era of multiple, competing, and rapid education reforms. *Issues in Teacher Education.*

Sandy, M. V. (2008, March 19). Personal communication.

Shields, P. M., Esch, C. E., Humphrey, D. C., Young, V. M., Gaston, M., & Hunt, H. (1999). *The status of the teaching profession: Research findings and policy recommendations.* Report to the Teaching and California's Future Task Force. Santa Cruz, CA: Center for the Future of Teaching and Learning.

Walsh, K. (2001, October). Teacher certification reconsidered: Stumbling for quality. Baltimore, MD: Abell Foundation. www.abellfoundation.org.

Walsh, K., & Podgursky, M. (2001, November). Teacher certification reconsidered: Stumbling for quality, a rejoinder. Baltimore, MD: Abell Foundation. www.abellfoundation.org.

Wright, S. P., Horn, S. P., & Sanders, W. L. (1997). Teacher and classroom context effects on student achievement: Implications for teacher evaluation. *Journal of Personnel Evaluation in Education, 11,* 57–67.

V

REFLECTIONS

16

Connecting Teaching, Teacher Preparation, and Student Learning: Education's Equivalent in Theory Development and Research to Biology's Genome Agenda

Del Schalock with Mark Girod

The previous fifteen chapters cover a wide array of policy contexts and uses of Teacher Work Sampling in teacher education practices and as a context for research. In this regard, the volume accomplishes well the task of providing road maps or images of practices and procedures that can promote high-quality teacher education. However, continuous pressures from multiple stakeholders threaten the existence of university-based teacher education. Our field has openly recognized the dearth of solid, empirical support and a comprehensive theoretical framework for teacher education. It is fascinating that two prominent scholars in the field, working separately, took upon themselves as their last contributions to the field, the task of articulating how teacher education might dig itself out of this problem.

Comprehensive theory building requires linking constructs in empirically validated chains of inference, organized in a logical and comprehensive fashion. Many have lamented the complexities of this task in teacher education (Berliner, 2002; Cochran-Smith, 2005; Floden, 2001), but two have actually attempted it. Nathaniel Gage, sometimes considered the godfather of teacher education, authored *A Conception of Teaching* in 2008, and the book was released posthumously the following year. In this slim volume, Gage culls from the fields of behavioral and social sciences lessons for teacher education and assembles them as a framework for future research and development in teacher education. Similarly, Del Schalock produced hundreds of pages of text in the last few months of his life attempting to articulate a similar framework. Though both accounts are brilliant, we feature here Schalock's own words describing a framework that has at its center efforts to build empirical connections between teaching and learning using Teacher Work Sampling as the key performance assessment.

What follows has been considered by many of Schalock's colleagues as a summary or road map of what would have been his magnum opus. It describes a task he likened to biology's human genome project—the articulation and validation of a comprehensive theoretical base for teacher preparation that yields professionals able to positively influence P–12 student learning. As you read, imagine if the field of teacher education were able to organize around these tasks to achieve this goal. Arguably, we may be less likely to be buffeted by the winds of change or so easily torpedoed by our critics.

BACKGROUND

Twenty years ago, the quality of education in the United States, particularly in the upper grades, had fallen to such low regard that a National Commission on Excellence in Education declared the nation to be at risk. Dropout rates were high, SAT scores were falling, and test score comparisons with other developed nations frequently found U.S. students at the bottom.

Fueling the concern created by this picture of mediocrity getting worse was its occurrence following two decades of unprecedented investment in education by both federal and state governments, a major downturn in the national economy, and a growing challenge from other nations to the scientific and technological supremacy held by the United States since World War II. From the 1950s through the 1970s, spending on schools and colleges had increased from $11 billion to $200 billion per year, and education's percentage share of the gross national product increased from 3.4 to 6.8 percent.

In the twenty years following the release of the *Nation at Risk* report, efforts to improve the nation's schools have proceeded at a pace and level of intensity never before experienced in the history of American education. Wave after wave of blueprints for change flowed from Congress, federal and state offices, and independent study groups to state and local education agencies. Change (restructuring, choice, vouchers, takeovers, new accountabilities, new standards for learning and school personnel, and charter schools) was the order of the day.

Amidst all this, teaching and learning, as the fundamental work of schools, continued with as much stability and purpose as teachers and school administrators could provide.

Although the quality of educational performance showed improvement during these years of turmoil, levels of achievement were still sufficiently different among various groups of students, and so disappointing overall, that by the turn of the century a dramatically different approach to schooling than that practiced during most of the twentieth century was placed into law. This was formalized with passage of the No Child Left Behind Act of 2001.

This new approach to schooling did not appear ready-made, nor as a plan quickly assembled to meet the problems within an educational system that had defied resolution for nearly half a century. Educational innovation and research had progressed steadily through the 1960s and 1970s. These were accelerated in response to the *At Risk* report and took on new forms in the 1980s and 1990s. This was the case for both the organization and operation of schools, and the preparation of school personnel.

By the time Congress began work on what evolved into the No Child Left Behind legislation, prototypes of the approach to schooling called for in the legislation had already been tested and were being implemented in several states. Agreement around the approach to schooling, however, was much clearer than the approach to the enhancement of school personnel that accompanied the legislation.

At the time the legislation was being written, everyone agreed that "highly qualified" teachers would be needed to implement the model of schooling that was taking shape, particularly if *all* students were to achieve the high standards for learning it called for. Sharp divisions existed, however, as to what "a highly qualified teacher" meant, and what kind of (and how much) preparation such qualifications required.

PROBLEM ADDRESSED

The nature of and connections between teacher work and student work within the context of this new standards-based, accountability-driven approach to schooling are vastly different than they were in the norm-referenced, textbook-based, sorting-and-grading approach to schooling that most of today's practicing educators and teacher educators encountered in their school experience. It follows that the preparation of teachers to work in such schools will also need to differ from what it has been in the past.

Identifying and delineating connections that need to be drawn between teaching, teacher preparation, and K–12 learning within the context of today's standards-based, accountability-driven schools is the central problem we intend to address. For maximum impact on practice as well as research, we propose to pursue this task through the lens of theory building. Simultaneously, however, we will assemble theory-related measures and test theory-related propositions through a network of teacher preparation institutions working cooperatively to shape and test the theoretical work in progress. The demands of NCLB, NCATE 2000 standards for the accreditation of teacher preparation programs, and many state teacher-licensing policies have been crafted on the assumption that such connections do (or should, and will) exist. The work undertaken through this initiative is aimed at making these connections explicit and providing the wherewithal needed to translate them into both research and practice. It is in this respect that the task resembles the genome agenda within the biological sciences.

WHAT WE PROPOSE TO DO

Our aim is to bring as much order and understanding as current knowledge permits to the complex set of connections we aim to pursue. Our desire to do so stems from the view that many of the pressures confronting teacher education and the nation's schools, especially the enhancement of learning, can be resolved productively only if we have more useful knowledge around these connections than currently exists. Bringing order and understanding to these three interdependent dimensions of the effective schools puzzle would represent a significant step forward in this regard.

As Floden (2001) puts it in his chapter on research on the effects of teaching, "The connections between teaching and learning would be easier to demonstrate if an empirically supported theory of teaching, connected to learning, were in hand. . . . A theory of teaching is a worthy goal" (p. 14). So too, we would add, is *a theory of teacher development and licensing that connects teaching and learning within the context of a standards-orientation to schooling.*

IMPORTANCE OF THE WORK PROPOSED

After more than thirty years of work in effective schools research, it is now clear that an effective school, as defined by the learning progress of its students, depends ultimately on the effectiveness of its teachers. Academic learning occurs primarily in classrooms, and teachers manage classrooms. Without teachers who are able to help each of their students reach the high standards for learning now expected of *all* students, a school will never be successful in meeting these expectations.

This is not to say that other aspects of schooling are unimportant in helping students progress in their learning. Well-crafted curricula, adequate resources, and needed time for learning, all aligned with the outcomes (standards) desired for learning, also are essential for student success in today's schools. So are assessment systems that inform and support the work of both teachers and students, and schools that are structured and managed as contexts for high-performance learning.

All such elements that support the work of students and teachers in a standards-based school are necessary for students to succeed within such schools, but they are not sufficient. Effective teachers make them so, for it is only through the sensitive and accomplished adaptations of content, method, time, and assistance by teachers to accommodate the immediate learning needs of each student in each of their classrooms that students can be successful learners in a standards-based school.

The standards set for learning in today's schools define the successive bars to be reached by students as they progress in their learning, and standards-linked assessments indicate where students stand at a particular point in time with respect to a particular bar, *but it is each student that needs to reach each bar*, and the main job of teachers is to help each student in each classroom make steady progress toward each bar that lies immediately ahead.

Compared to schooling in the twentieth century, this is a new world for everyone involved. For schools (and students, and teachers) to be successful within this world, the connections between teaching, teacher preparation, and the kind and level of learning expected of K–12 students need to be fully understood by all who are engaged in the teaching/learning process. The business of schooling, and particularly the business of teaching and learning in schools, cannot be the same as we enter the twenty-first century as it was in the twentieth century. Nor can the business of teacher preparation and licensure, nor the business of teacher support and continued professional development. It is toward the changes needed to accommodate the demands that now exist on all these fronts that the work we propose is directed.

MAGNITUDE OF THE WORK PROPOSED

The magnitude of the task to be undertaken is as large as it is important. Connecting teaching, teacher preparation, and K–12 learning in a standards-based school environment involves a long chain of conceptual and procedural connections, and these simply are not to be found in existing literature. Pods of related knowledge and fragments of related theory exist around these connections, but the task of integrating and extending these bits and pieces into a meaningful whole is large in scope, complex in design, and demanding of conceptual and methodological connections across numerous disciplines.

The task is made harder, and probably larger, by the fact that the differences in approach to schooling in the century past and the century ahead are sufficiently great as to call into question the utility of the knowledge and theory generated around teaching and learning in twentieth-century schools for thinking about teaching and learning in the schools of today. In many respects, the model of schooling on which most of our current knowledge and theory about teaching and learning rests is antithetical to the model of schooling enshrined in the No Child Left Behind legislation, and its generalizability to the new model will need to be treated as suspect until similarities and differences between the old and the new are more fully understood. This is not to say that existing knowledge and theory are irrelevant to the task at hand, but it is to say that it cannot be accepted un-critically or expected to remain unmodified. As limited and misleading as our existing knowledge and theory base might be, however, it is necessarily the place where the work we propose must begin.

STRATEGY TO BE FOLLOWED

The strategy we have chosen to follow in pursuing our aim is *engaging in the process of theory building as this occurs within a maturing science*. A remark-able book published on theory building in the social sciences, *How to Build Social Science Theories* (Shoemaker, Tankard, & Lasorsa, 2004), can be used as a guide to our efforts.

The word *theory* comes from the Greek *theoria*, which means "a looking at." According to Shoemaker and her colleagues, theory building within a ma-turing science involves carefully prescribed ways, and a carefully prescribed sequence, of "looking at" the field(s) that one wishes to theorize about. In combination, these are designed to lead to a set of statements (a theory) that lays out "one's understanding of how something works" (p. 5).

Shoemaker et al. describe six steps that need to be followed in the theory-building process. We plan to follow these steps, but before engaging in them we think it essential to clarify the shifts in schooling that underlie the theory-building effort. We think of these as *ground-laying tasks* that clarify the paradigms governing a standards orientation to schooling, with particular at-tention given to the work of students and teachers within such schools.

Ground-Laying Tasks

At present we see four interdependent lines of paradigm clarifying as a basis for understanding the demands of a standards orientation to schooling on K–12 students, teachers, and teacher educators:

1. the essential features of a standards-based, accountability-driven approach to schooling in contrast to the norm-referenced, textbook-based, sorting-and-grading approach to schooling that dominated the twentieth century;
2. the work of students within such schools;
3. the work of teachers within such schools; and

4. the array of meaningful and defensible indicators of a teacher's impact on student learning within such schools, and accompanying measures thereof.

In essence, these paradigm shifts represent a new knowledge base for teachers, teacher educators, school administrators, and education policy makers. They need to be understood as fully as possible for related theory building to proceed on sound footing.

Sequencing Theory-Building Tasks

Once the paradigm shifts that have occurred within and among these dimensions of schooling within the past decade have been described and tentatively agreed to, the steps traditionally pursued in theory building need to be undertaken. According to Shoemaker and her colleagues these consist of

1. concept mapping;
2. defining conceptually (in sentences), and grounding theoretically (through currently available theory), all concepts included in a map;
3. defining operationally (through measures or measurement methodologies), and grounding empirically (through currently available research), all concepts defined conceptually in a map;
4. developing propositions (hypotheses), path diagrams, and related conceptual models to articulate theoretically expected linkages among variables within and across concept maps that can be defined both conceptually and operationally;
5. conducting research that tests hypotheses developed in step 4; and
6. reflecting upon, refining, and extending all of the above on the basis of findings and experience gained through step 5.

To acknowledge the dependence of theory development in teacher preparation and licensure on the nature of teaching and learning in the schools, we should attend first to theory-building tasks *at the level of schooling*. As progress is made on steps 1 through 4 in theory development around standards-based teaching and learning, we then move to theory building around the preparation and licensing of teachers to work within standards-based schools. How we anticipate this sequencing to play out in time and practice is discussed later in the proposed plan of work.

School-Level Theory Building, Steps 1 through 4

Step 1: concept mapping. This involves identifying, sorting, relating, and organizing concepts (constructs) within the various literatures pertaining to teaching and the academic learning of students in kindergarten through grade twelve as they pertain within the new paradigms underlying today's schools. As a point of departure in this process, we plan to organize existing concepts around six broad domains:

1. *learning* in a standards-based classroom,
2. *teaching* in a standards-based classroom,
3. *factors within home and family environments* that influence classroom teaching and learning,
4. *factors within classrooms and schools* that influence classroom teaching and learning,
5. *factors within school districts and communities* that influence classroom teaching and learning, and
6. *Factors at the state and national level* that influence classroom teaching and learning.

This proposed organization to school-level conceptual work is illustrated schematically in Figure 16.1.

Within each of the domains shown in Figure 16.1 concepts will be classified as *core, proximal, contextual,* or *peripheral.* Given these distinctions an illustration of the form a concept map might take is provided as Figure 16.2 on the next page.

Step 2: from concepts to definitions. As concept maps take shape, the process of firming definitions of key concepts within each map, within the context of a standards-based school environment, needs to begin. According to Shoemaker et al., this process involves

1. identifying the concepts (constructs) that represent continuous variables, or those that can be transformed into dimensions (categorical variables converted to continua);
2. defining these variables both conceptually (in sentences) and operationally (how they can be measured); and
3. articulating the linkages expected among these variables using visual as well as other forms of symbolic or mathematical models, and the rationale for these linkages.

The successful completion of these tasks within a particular domain lays the foundations needed for the methodological and empirical work that is to follow in investigating the connections across and among domains.

Step 3: from definitions to measures. Before empirical work can begin, and theoretical work tested, defensible (reliable, valid) measures for the variables of interest need to be identified. These can be measures which already exist, or measures newly established to support a particular line of

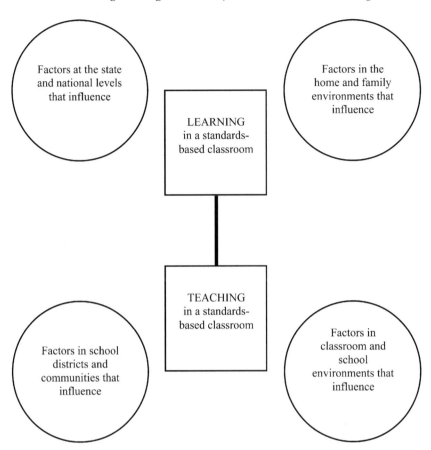

Figure 16.1. Domains to be addressed in theory development at the level of schooling. Theory development will involve identifying and connecting variables *within* each domain and across domains.

inquiry, but for work within a science to progress, strong measures must be available for each of the variables of interest.

The general lack of such measures in education and teacher education currently is a major impediment to the theory-development initiative being proposed. By contrast, reasonably strong measures exist in many of the "parent disciplines" upon which education and teacher education draw, though these measures typically are not widely known or easily accessed by educators.

To overcome these limitations, we propose that a major thrust of the initiative center on the collection and organization of defensible measures that currently exist for all of the key variables identified within each concept

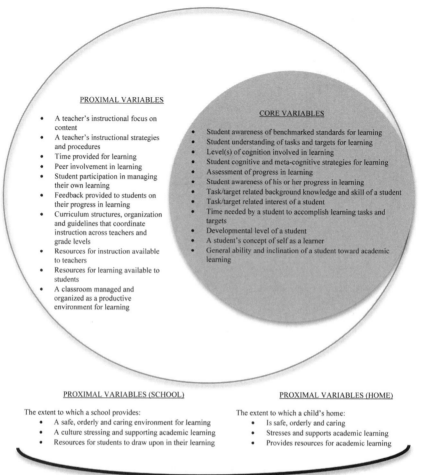

Figure 16.2.   An illustrative concept map of learning in a standards-based, accountability-driven school environment.

map developed within the initiative. To make these more easily available to both researchers and practitioners, we also propose to make these available as catalogs of promising measures that accompany each concept map.

Step 4: from concepts and measures to propositions and hypotheses. As work progresses on steps 1 through 3, attention should be given to developing hypotheses, path diagrams, and related conceptual models to articulate theoretically expected linkages among variables within and across the domains of understanding to be addressed within the initiative. Step 4 is the first that engages in what many consider to be a theory-building enterprise, that of hypothesis formulation, but, as Shoemaker and her colleagues make clear, there is much that must precede this step for it to be productive and cumulative. The work outlined in steps 1 through 3 conveys the nature and magnitude of what this entails, and suggests how critical this work is to making steps 4 through 6 in the theory-building process productive.

School-Level Theory Building, Steps V and VI

While the four steps thus far outlined stop short of the full complement of steps involved in theory building, they lay the foundations needed for the empirical, additive, and refinement/correctional steps most frequently associated with the "doing" of science. The added steps projected for the initiative, but more importantly following completion of the four steps thus far outlined, involve step 5, conducting research that tests hypotheses developed in step 4, and step 6, reflecting upon, refining, and extending all of the above.

In combination, steps 1 through 6 constitute the many and varied dimensions of a "scientific" endeavor. Reflecting upon the adequacy and appropriateness of steps 1 through 6 as a whole, recording modifications needed anywhere along the way, and reporting these "findings" in venues that permit others interested in similar lines of inquiry to build upon findings reported, are the "stuff" from which knowledge and understanding grow. Reporting venues for these various activities need to include one or more catalogs of measures, and one or more compendia of related theory development.

We presume that nearly all who are involved in helping with steps 1 through 4 will be engaged simultaneously and cooperatively, but independently, in steps 5 and 6. In so doing, many more educators and teacher educators than might otherwise be involved will contribute to the empirical testing and subsequent refinement/enhancement of the conceptual and methodological underpinnings being developed collectively by steps 1 through 4.

In combination, and in endlessly repeated cycles, these six steps represent the essence of "the scientific method." As argued by Shoemaker, Tankard, and Lasorsa (2004),

> The goal of science is to produce and test theories. As we pointed out earlier, the major difference between science and other ways of knowing is that science constantly questions itself. Science tries explicitly to state its theories, to pose them in formal ways using precise statements so that it is clear what they are saying, to test them, and to confirm, modify, or discard them. Science is the ongoing business of coming up with new ideas and finding ways to challenge them. This notion of testing and revising is what separates scientific theories from the informality that characterize informal theories. (p. 6)

Theory Building around Teacher Preparation, Licensing, and Early Career Support

Since theory building around teacher preparation, licensing, and early career support must anchor to the model of schooling in which teachers are expected to work, theory building in this arena needs to follow theory building around the six domains of theory selected for attention at the school level. This does not mean that theory building around teacher preparation and support needs to wait until theory development at the school level is complete, but some degree of lag time needs to occur between the two. In this regard, we think theory work on the teacher preparation and support side of the initiative can begin in year two.

As we currently view the task, theory building around teacher preparation and support must draw heavily upon theory development at the school level. As this has been outlined in preceding pages, this means that it will draw directly, and hierarchically, upon theory work pursued within the domains of

- *learning* in a standards-based classroom,
- *teaching* in a standards-based classroom,
- *home and family influence* on teaching and learning,
- *classroom and school influence* on teaching and learning,
- *district and community influence* on teaching and learning, and
- *state and national influence* on teaching and learning.

This is only part of the equation, however, for theory building at the level of teacher preparation and early career support also will need to draw upon what is known about adult learning, stages in the professional development of teachers, the role of colleagues and administrators in facilitating the professional development of teachers, and the like.

As a point of departure in this aspect of the initiative, we propose that we organize theory building efforts around two relatively distinct but obviously interdependent levels of preparation, licensing, and early career support:

Level 1: preservice preparation and initial licensing; and
Level 2: early career support, continued professional development, and second-stage licensing.

Each will involve the six steps reviewed previously in the theory development process, and both levels of work will proceed simultaneously.

Within this context, the central issues confronting theory development for the initial preparation and licensing of teachers are the breadth and depth of learning needed around school-level domains 1 through 6, how this knowledge and related sets of skills are best developed by prospective teachers, and the level of proficiency to be demonstrated around both understanding and application as a condition for initial licensing. The central issues to be addressed in theory development for the support and continued professional development of early career teachers are the *extended* breadth and depth of learning about school-level domains 1 through 6 needed to ensure productive job performance, how this knowledge and related sets of skills are best developed while engaged in full-time teaching, and the level of proficiency to be demonstrated around both understanding and application as a condition of continuing (or second-stage) licensing.

AN INVITATION TO THE PROFESSION

Del Schalock went so far as to even lay out envisioned timelines, tasks, and responsibilities for his colleagues at WOU as well as other teacher preparation programs and related agencies with whom he had held many informal conversations prior to his untimely death. Many of them had accepted his invitation to join this work and participated in a series of meetings. Del presided at these meetings of the Coalition for Theory Development and Testing around Connections among Teaching, Teacher Preparation, and K–12 Learning in a Standards-based School Involvement, to which almost two dozen participants traveled from all over the country at their own cost.

Indeed, his vision for the next phase of work needing to be done was amazingly on target and timely, and it is included as the closing chapter of this volume as an open invitation and challenge to any and all colleagues committed to theory building around teacher preparation and support. At a keynote address given at AACTE's 2008 annual conference, Lee Shulman, immediate past-president of the Carnegie Center for the Advancement of Teaching, referenced Del Schalock as one of the nation's most forward-thinking educators vis-à-vis his development of Teacher Work Samples. Although the work he accomplished in his lifetime provided the impetus for all of the efforts outlined in this volume, Del Schalock has also left, as part of his legacy, an invitation, a blueprint, and a challenge to the profession to carry out what is now needed to establish a solid, empirical support and a comprehensive theoretical framework for teacher education.

REFERENCES

Berliner, D.C. (2002). Educational research: The hardest science of all. *Educational Researcher, 31*(8), 18–20.

Cochran-Smith, M. (2005). Studying teacher education: What we know and need to know. *Journal of Teacher Education, 56*, 301–306.

Floden, R.E. (2001). Research on effects of teaching: A continuing model for research on teaching. In V. Richardson (Ed.). *Handbook of research on teaching* (4th ed., pp. 3–16). Washington, DC: American Educational Research Association.

Gage, N. L. (2008). *A conception of teaching.* New York: Springer.

Shoemaker, P.J., Tankard, J.W., & Lasorsa, D.L. (2004). *How to build social science theories.* Thousand Oaks, CA: Sage.

Notes

NOTE TO CHAPTER 1

1. The next several sections are taken from a draft document dated May 20, 2005, by Del Schalock titled, "Notes on the Evolution of Teacher Work Sample Methodology."

NOTE TO CHAPTER 7

1. An earlier version of this chapter was presented at the fifty-ninth annual meeting of the American Association of Colleges for Teacher Education, New York City, February 25, 2007. Correspondence concerning this paper should be addressed to Ronald A. Beghetto, College of Education, 5277 University of Oregon, Eugene, OR, 97403-5277, or via e-mail to beghetto@uoregon.edu.

NOTE TO CHAPTER 10

1. The subject matter in this paper is the result of a U.S. Department of Education Title II Teacher Quality Enhancement grant awarded to the Oklahoma State Regents for Higher Education. The views presented in this paper are those of the authors and do not necessarily represent those of the Oklahoma State Regents for Higher Education, the U.S. Department of Education, or the Oklahoma Technical Assistance Center and Child Service Demonstration Center.

NOTES TO CHAPTER 13

1. The last extended exchange that Del Schalock and I had was by telephone and hand-written and posted notes. Del responded to a paper I had drafted describing what the National Council for Accreditation of Teacher Education means by its references to "student learning" in accreditation. As always, he was complimentary and encouraging, and, also as always, he had examined my draft carefully. He thought I had the main message about right, and he concurred, but he did want to set me straight: Western Oregon University (and its predecessor, Oregon College of Education) had initiated its long study of student learning as the focus of teaching, and its development of Teacher Work Sample Methodology, in the early 1970s, years prior to their adaptation by the state of Oregon for licensing purposes.

2. NCATE, *Standards, Procedures, and Policies for the Accreditation of Professional Education Units*, February 1992.

3. NCATE, *Standards, Procedures, and Policies for the Accreditation of Professional Units*, 1995 ed.

4. NCATE, *Toward a Common National System of Teacher Education Accreditation: A Grant Proposal Submitted to the Pew Chartable Trusts*, June 25, 1991.

5. NCATE, *Standards-Based Reform of Teacher Education*, December 14, 1993.

6. John O'Neal, Kendyll Stansbury, and Anthony Rigazio DiBillo, *Toward a Vision of Elementary Teaching and Learning*, December 1, 1995.

7. Emerson Elliott, telephone interview, September 6, 2007.

8. Pauletta Brown Bracy, *Student Learning: A Limited Summary of Approaches, Initiatives, and Issues*, June 1997.

9. NCATE, *Program Standards for Elementary Teacher Preparation*, approved by the Specialty Areas Studies Board, October 1999 and February 2000.

10. NCATE, *"Student Learning" in NCATE Accreditation*, February 2005.

11. Gerald R. Girod, ed., *Connecting Teaching and Learning: A Handbook for Teacher Educators on Teacher Work Sample Methodology* (New York: AACTE, ERIC Clearinghouse on Teaching and Teacher Education, 2002).

NOTES TO CHAPTER 14

1. 1997 legislative amendments, based on a Southern Regional Education Board study of teacher evaluation systems and resultant decisions in eleven SREB states, which was conducted by Holdzkom, Kulogowski, and French, enabled out-of-state teachers moving to Louisiana to be excluded from participation in the program if they met the "appropriate evaluation results" requirements.

2. This is an important procedural inclusion because Louisiana law specifies that a new teacher who does not meet performance standards in the assessment process must leave the classroom and cannot be reemployed within the state for two years, and only then if she or he provides evidence of fulfillment of the professional growth plan developed at the conclusion of the assessment process two years (or more) earlier.

3. The *Guide for New Teachers* (both new-teacher and mentor versions) states,

"The LaTAAP has two basic functions: 1) to develop information about the new teacher's competence that can be used to structure instructional improvement activities, and 2) to develop information upon which sound decisions about the new teacher's qualifications for certification can be based" (Louisiana Department of Education, *Guide For New Teachers*, mentor version, 2006–2007, p. 6).

4. At this time, there is debate in Louisiana about continuing the Louisiana Teacher Assistance and Assessment Program in its present form. Financial conditions and administration concerns about workload may lead to a "watering down" of the present program or yet another program redesign. The future of the TWSM in this context is unclear. However, Louisiana's application of the methodology in high-stakes teacher evaluation and professional development of in-service teachers suggests that the methodology has viability in K–12 education initiatives, including the "Race to the Top," where outcomes focused on performance assessments are needed to supplement and complement student achievement data.

NOTES TO CHAPTER 15

1. PACT members currently include UC Berkeley, UC Davis, UC Irvine, UCLA, UC Riverside, UC San Diego, UC Santa Barbara, UC Santa Cruz, Cal Poly–SLO, CSU Channel Islands, CSU Chico, CSU Dominguez Hills, CSU Monterey Bay, CSU Northridge, Humboldt State, Sacramento State, San Diego State, San Francisco State, San Jose State, Sonoma State, Antioch University–Santa Barbara, Holy Names University, Mills College, Notre Dame de Namur University, Pepperdine University, St. Mary's College of California, Stanford University, University of the Pacific, University of San Diego, USC, and the San Diego City Schools Intern Program.

2. The number of subject-specific Teaching Events has increased from six to thirteen, representing the full range of multiple-subject and single-subject credentials offered by PACT institutions. Bilingual versions of the multiple-subject and core single-subject areas are available and are scored with rubrics that assess the same teaching skills as for the regular teaching credential but in the language(s) of instruction. Five Teaching Events in new subject areas were being piloted for the first time in the 2007-2008 academic year. In addition, a version of both elementary Teaching Events has been adapted for candidates earning both elementary and special education teaching credentials.

3. Handbooks and scoring rubrics for all of the PACT Teaching Events can be found online at www.pacttpa.org.

4. M. Wilson and P. J. Hallum, *Using Student Achievement Test Scores as Evidence of External Validity for Indicators of Teacher Quality: Connecticut's Beginning Educator Support and Training Program.* (Berkeley: University of California at Berkeley, 2006); A. T. Milanowski, S. M. Kimball, and B. White, *The Relationship between Standards-based Teacher Evaluation Scores and Student Achievement* (Madison: University of Wisconsin-Madison, Consortium for Policy Research in Education, 2004); D. Goldhaber and E. Anthony, *Can Teacher Quality Be Effectively Assessed?* (Seattle: University of Washington and the Urban Institute, 2005); L. G. Vandevoort, A. Amrein-Beardsley, and D. C. Berliner, "National Board Certified Teachers and Their Students' Achievement," *Education Policy Analysis Archives* 12, no. 46 (2004): 117.

Appendix A

1994 Conference Participants

OUT-OF-STATE PARTICIPANTS

Dr. Peter Airaisian, professor
School of Education
Boston College

Dr. Ted Andrews, director
Professional Education and
  Licensure
Washington Dept. of Public
  Instruction

Dr. Tom Bird, assistant professor
College of Education
Michigan State University

Dr. Elizabeth Cohen, professor
School of Education
Stanford University

Dr. Angela Covert, program officer
Atlantic Philanthropic Service Co.

Dr. Russell French, professor
College of Education
University of Tennessee

Dr. Judy Groulx, director of
  research
Professional Development Schools
  Project
Texas Christian University

Dr. Ed Iwanicki, professor
School of Education
University of Connecticut

Dr. David Mandell
V.P. for policy development
National Board for Professional
  Teaching Standards

Dr. Wayne Martin, director
Evaluation and Planning
Colorado Department of Education

Dr. Robert Mendro
Exec. director for institutional
  research
Dallas Texas Independent School
  District

Dr. Jason Millman, research
  professor
Department of Education and Life
  Sciences
Cornell University

Dr. Ray Pecheone, bureau chief
Research and Teacher Assessment
Connecticut Department of
  Education

Dr. Madelaine Ramey
Educational consultant

Dr. Michael Scriven
Education consultant

Dr. Dan Stufflebeam, director
The Evaluation Center
College of Education
Western Michigan University

IN-STATE PARTICIPANTS (NON-WOU)

Dr. Dean Arrasmith
Evaluation and Assessment
Northwest Regional Education
  Laboratory

Dr. Bill Auty, director
Assessment and Evaluation
Corvallis School District

Dr. Bob Burns
Deputy superintendent of public
  instruction
Oregon Department of Education

Dr. Shirley Clark
Vice chancellor for academic affairs
Oregon State System of Higher
  Education
(Oregon University System)

Dr. George Benson, superintendent
Centennial School District

Dr. Bob Blum, director
School Effectiveness and Evaluation
  Programs
Northwest Regional Education
  Laboratory

Dr. Joseph Cox, chancellor
Oregon State System of Higher
  Education
(Oregon University System)

Mrs. Ruth Hewett, past chair
Oregon Board of Education

Dr. Mark Gall, professor
School of Education
University of Oregon

Dr. Marcia Garrick
Director of instruction
Newberg School District

Dr. Jim Kushman
School Effectiveness and Evaluation
  Programs
Northwest Regional Education
  Laboratory

Dr. David Myton, exec. director
Oregon teacher Standards and
  Practices Commission

Karen Quigley, staff
Oregon Senate Education
  Committee

Dr. Joan Shaughnessy
Program Evaluation and
  Improvement
Northwest Regional Education
  Laboratory

Dr. Jens Robinson, dean
School of Education
Eastern Oregon State College

Craig Roessler, superintendent
Silverton School District

Appendix B

PLANNING TOOLS

CLARIFYING POTENTIAL PROJECT GOALS

GOAL	DESCRIPTION
Example: **G1. Understand impact on student learning.**	*Example:* *Develop an understanding of how teacher candidates use TWS to represent student learning and make sense of their instructional impact on students.*

ALIGNING RESEARCH QUESTIONS WITH PROJECT GOALS

GOAL	RESEARCH QUESTIONS
Example: **G1:** **Understand impact on student learning.**	*Examples:* RQ 1.1: What techniques do candidates use to assess the impact of their instruction? And how sound are those techniques?
	RQ 1.2: How do candidates disaggregate data and use that data for making inferences about learning?

EXAMPLE DATA COLLECTION AND ANALYSIS PLANNING MATRIX

GOAL	RESEARCH QUESTIONS	DATA SOURCES	DATA COLLECTION METHOD	WHEN DATA ARE COLLECTED	ANALYTIC TECHNIQUES
GOAL 1: Impact on student learning	RQ 1.1: What techniques do candidates use to assess the impact of their instruction? And how sound are those techniques?	TTWS assessment plans and assessment data w/ interpretation.	Stratified random sample of candidates' Work Samples (TTWS).	Completion of Work Sample.	Consensual assessment technique (CAT).

Notes:

Data Collection Action Plan
OCRI Planning Meeting
RECORDED BY:

Research Element:

Members in attendance:
Name:
Institution:
Contact Information:

Element (Co)leaders:
Name:
Institution:
Contact Information:

Top priority research question(s):

Data sources available and needed for each priority question:

Research Question:
Data Sources Available:
Data Sources Needed:
    1. Possible data collection methods
Possible types of analysis to be conducted

Time line for collecting and analyzing data sources:
Data source:
Collection Methods:
Dates:
Individual(s) responsible for coordinating data collection across sites:

Analytic Methods:
Dates:
Individual(s) responsible for coordinating data analysis:

Appendix C

NAEYC Standards for Early Childhood Professional Preparation

Initial Licensure Programs (2003)

STANDARD 1: PROMOTING CHILD DEVELOPMENT AND LEARNING

Candidates use their understanding of young children's characteristic and needs, and of multiple interacting influences on children's development and learning, to create environments that are healthy, respectful, supportive, and challenging for all children.

STANDARD 2: BUILDING FAMILY AND COMMUNITY RELATIONSHIPS

Candidates know about, understand, and value the importance and complex characteristics of children's families and communities. They use this understanding to create respectful, reciprocal relationships that support and empower families, and to involve all families in their children's development and learning.

STANDARD 3: OBSERVING, DOCUMENTING, AND ASSESSING TO SUPPORT YOUNG CHILDREN AND FAMILIES

Candidates know about and understand the goals, benefits, and uses of assessment. They know about and use systematic observations, documentation, and other effective assessment strategies in a responsible way, in partnership with families and other professionals, to positively influence children's development and learning.

STANDARD 4: TEACHING AND LEARNING

Candidates integrate their understanding of and relationships with children and families; their understanding of developmentally effective approaches to teaching and learning; and their knowledge of academic disciplines to design, implement, and evaluate experiences that promote positive development and learning for all children.

STANDARD 5: BECOMING A PROFESSIONAL

Candidates identify and conduct themselves as members of the early childhood profession. They know and use ethical guidelines and other professional standards related to early childhood practice. They are continuous, collaborative learners who demonstrate knowledgeable, reflective, and critical perspectives on their work, making informed decisions that integrate knowledge from a variety of sources. They are informed advocates for sound educational practices and policies.

Variable	Looking for evidence in section … of GFU Work Sample	None	Evident	Target	Description of Evidence
Understanding of Child Development	**Section 1** • Describes and references developmental stages associated with given age group; includes cognitive, social, emotional, and physical domains. • Describes individual children whose development may differ from group characteristics.				
	Section 2 • Evidence of appropriate state benchmark.				
Application of Child Development	**Section 2** • Rationale shows why unit of learning is appropriate to this group of students. • Assessments developmentally and educationally significant (may include observations, descriptive data, samples of work and student performances during authentic activities).				
	Section 3 • Lesson plans show variety of developmentally appropriate approaches, strategies, and tools; balance individual and collaborative learning, inquiry/student-instigated project work and direct instruction. • Lesson reflections discuss success/failure.				
Environment Promotes Learning	**Section 2** • Unit plans show use of/modification to environmental setup				
	Section 3 • Lesson plans show modifications to enrich the learning environment.				
Involving Families and Communities	**Section 2** • Evidence of communication with families/community. • Evidence of collaboration with families/community.				
	Section 3 • Evidence of parent/community involvement in learning experiences.				

Appendix D

Louisiana TWS Forms

FORM 1: TEACHING CONTEXT

Please complete the following information about your class.

I. Class/Classroom Information

Grade levels in class (list all that apply _____ _____)	Ages in class (list all that apply _____ _____)
# Students enrolled_____	# Typically Present_____
Time Available each day to teach entire class _____	
Place a √ beside the phrase that describes the number of teaching interruptions. _____few _____some _____many	
Place a √ beside the phrase that describes the types of help available to you. _____instructional assistant(s) _____parent volunteers _____peer (student) tutors _____resource teachers _____other (Please Specify.) _____	

II. Individual Differences

Indicate the # of students in each category below. _____ESL   _____# with IEPs or IFSPs   _____# with 504 modifications _____Title I   _____Gifted   _____Other
Indicate the # of students for each pattern of achievement. _____Low   _____Average   _____High
Enter low (L), medium (M), or high (H) to describe the level of diversity for each category below. _____Ages _____Languages _____Culture _____Achievement/Developmental Levels
Enter the Appropriate label(s) for the # of students with each learning style listed below. None (0)   Few (1-3)   Many (more than 3) _____Print _____Aural _____Interactive _____Visual _____Haptic _____Kinesthetic _____Olfactory _____Other
Describe any other classroom conditions (if any) that have caused you to adjust your instruction in some way.

FORM 2: DESCRIBING THE WORK

1.Subject Area(s) <u>Note:</u> Teachers of K-3 are required to develop Work Samples for language arts or mathematics.
2.Content
3.Length of Unit (# of days/class periods)
4.Learning Objectives/Outcomes <u>to be accomplished by students</u> (Two are required, and one must require higher-order thinking.)
5.Rationale for Objectives/Outcomes
6.Adjustments made to accommodate one or more of the categories of individual differences.
7.Adjustments made because of other classroom conditions.

FORM 3: THE ASSESSMENT PLAN

1. Describe the assessment plan for this Work Sample. (Provide an overview of the assessment points and methods. Remember to include both formal and informal measures that extend from pre-assessment through post-assessment.)

2. Describe the pre-assessment method(s) (determination of student knowledge and skills prior to instruction). <u>Note:</u> A copy of the pre-assessment must be attached. If you used an assignment or activity as a pre-assessment, attach the directions and information that were provided to students.

3. Describe your post-assessment method(s); i.e., how you determined student knowledge and skills after instruction. <u>Note:</u> A copy of the post-assessment must be attached. If you used an assignment or activity as a post-assessment, attach the directions and information provided to students.

4. How do you know that your objectives, pre-assessment, instruction, and post-assessment were aligned? Please explain.

FORM 4: ANALYZING THE RESULTS

1. How many students accomplished **all** of the objectives you established for this body of instruction? What % of students **did not** meet all objectives? What factors contributed to their success/failure?

2. Did those students who were unsuccessful in meeting all objectives demonstrate substantial gains in knowledge and skills as defined in the objectives? Were there students who demonstrated very little gain or negative gain (regression) from pre-assessment to post-assessment?

3. Describe the circumstances/conditions that contributed to the poor achievement of students who did not meet the objectives or make substantial gains.

4. Since the conclusion of the Work Sample, what have you done to help students who did not accomplish/master the objectives to improve their learning in these areas?

5. What impact will the information gained from your reflection about your students' performance have on future lessons? Describe the adjustments you will make in your instruction.

FORM 5: REFLECTING ON THE IMPACT OF INSTRUCTION

1. Describe several ways in which you introduced and provided feedback throughout the work sample. What information did you provide to the groups listed below prior to instruction, during instruction, and after the post-assessment? How did you communicate that information? Note: Several methods of providing feedback should be provided.

- Students

- Parents/Caregivers

- Colleagues

2. How did you use the information gained as a result of your communications?

3. How did you attempt to involve parents/caregivers and colleagues in the learning process?

FORM 6: COMMUNICATION AND FOLLOW-UP

1. Identify the content presented by this lesson plan.

2. How does this lesson relate to the Work Sample?

3. Why did you select the instructional activities and materials/technologies listed in the lesson plan?

4. When and how were the objective(s) of this lesson measured? Did the assessment show that this was a successful lesson? Why or why not?

FORM 7: LESSON PLAN PORTFOLIO ENTRY FORM

Work Sample Lesson Plan Portfolio Entry Form (Form 7)

1.	Identify the content presented by this lesson plan.
2.	How does this lesson relate to the Work Sample?
3.	Why did you select the instructional activities and materials/technologies listed in the lesson plan?
4.	When and how were the objective(s) of this lesson measured? Did the assessment show that this was a successful lesson? Why or why not?

Index

About the Contributors

Ronald Beghetto is an associate professor of education studies at the University of Oregon. His research and teaching focuses on teacher development, improving the use of assessment and evaluation in the classroom, and promoting creativity in teachers and students.

Meredith Brodsky served as professor, director of clinical services, dean of the College of Education at Western Oregon University, and director of Teaching Research Institute before recently retiring. She was a commissioner for the Oregon Teacher Standards and Practices Commission and was involved in state and national committees related to teacher preparation and continuous quality improvement.

Karen Buchanan serves as dean of instruction at George Fox University, formerly the undergraduate chair of teacher education and NCATE coordinator. Her research interests focus on assessment knowledge and practices of preservice and in-service teachers.

Diane Calhoun is the director of Professional Development System Partnership in the Office of Outreach Alliances at the Watson School of Education at the University of North Carolina, Wilmington. Her research interests include study groups, cooperative learning, and teaching of mathematics.

Barbara Chesler Buckner is the associate provost for assessment and accreditation at Coastal Carolina University. She has assisted numerous institutions in integrating Teacher Work Samples into the curriculum at both the undergraduate and graduate levels.

Before retiring, **Kyle Dahlem's** professional experience included forty-two years in education as a K–12 English teacher and librarian, a full-time association officer, a director for a statewide Minority Teacher Recruitment Center, and vice chancellor for administration at the Oklahoma State Regents for Higher Education.

Peter Denner is assistant dean for assessment at Idaho State University and served as the institutional and assessment coordinator for the college's participation in the Renaissance Partnership. His current scholarly interests are focused on standards-based assessments of educator quality and information systems in professional education.

Samuel Evans serves as dean of the College of Education and Behavioral Sciences at Western Kentucky University. His research interests include accountability and teacher candidate impact on student learning, and he has been actively involved on state- and national-level task forces and boards.

Tracy Fredman serves as the evaluation/research specialist for the Oklahoma Technical Assistance Center and serves as a national NCTE/NCATE reviewer and English chair for Oklahoma's Program Accreditation Review Board. She has published and presented research on teacher evaluation and Teacher Work Samples at state and national levels.

Russell French is professor emeritus and emeritus director of the Institute for Assessment and Evaluation at the University of Tennessee, Knoxville. He served as the executive director of the Tennessee Educational Certification Commission, led the development and implementation of the Tennessee Career Ladder program, and worked as consultant to many states on educational personnel evaluation systems.

Gerald R. Girod is emeritus dean and faculty at Western Oregon University where he worked extensively with Teacher Work Samples. Most recently, he served as editor for *Connecting Teaching and Learning: A Handbook for Teacher Educators on Teacher Work Sample Methodology*.

Mark Girod is chair of the Division of Teacher Education and an associate professor at Western Oregon University where he attended the university's K–8 lab school. He continues to teach, and his scholarship areas include adolescent development, science education, performance assessment, and applications of technology to teaching and learning.

John Henning is a professor and chair of the Teacher Education Department at Ohio University. He was involved in the implementation and use of Teacher Work Samples for program improvement at the University of Northern Iowa and has published in the areas of instructional decision making and semiotics in education.

David Imig, formerly the executive officer for AACTE for twenty-five years, is now a professor of practice at the University of Maryland College Park. He is leading efforts to strengthen doctoral education, working with the Carnegie Foundation for the Advancement of Teaching, and continuing efforts to strengthen policy and practice of teacher education in the United States and abroad.

Scott Imig is the interim associate dean for outreach alliances at the Watson College of Education at the University of North Carolina, Wilmington, where he also teaches courses on education policy, foundations, and supervision/evaluation. His research interests are focused on the teaching profession, teacher decision making, classroom observation and supervision, and effective teaching.

Mary Johnson is an assistant professor of education and director of the evening MAT program at George Fox University. Her content specialty and area of research is early childhood education.

Frank Kohler is professor and interim head of the Department of Special Education at the University of Northern Iowa. His research interests include preparing teachers to implement evidence-based practices and fostering team and collaboration in schools.

George Malo has recently retired from his position as associate vice chancellor for research and assessment at the Tennessee Board of Regents where he served twenty years. He also served as the associate assistant commissioner for research in the Tennessee Department of Education and has worked extensively on the development and implementation of educational personnel evaluation programs in four states.

Kathleen McKean is the director of the Oklahoma Technical Assistance Center and is an adjunct graduate faculty member at Oklahoma State University. She currently directs twenty-one evaluation projects in Oklahoma, and she provides technical assistance to all state-recognized public alternative education programs.

Jack Newsome is an associate dean at Idaho State University. He teaches undergraduate courses in motivation and management, instructional planning and delivery, assessment, and human growth and development.

Julie Newsome is an associate professor at the Idaho State University where she teaches courses on management, motivation, and educational philosophy. Her research interests include the Teacher Work Sample, performance assessments, and mentoring.

Antony Norman is the associate dean for accountability and research at Western Kentucky University. He oversees the college's assessment system, coordinates national accreditation efforts, and supervises grant and research activities within the college.

Roger Pankratz is professor of teacher education at Western Kentucky University, assistant to the dean, and consultant to Western's Teacher Education Model Program. From 1999 until 2006, he was director of the Renaissance Partnership for Improving Teacher Quality.

Ray Pecheone is the coexecutive director of the Stanford School Redesign Network at Stanford University where he is developing and researching PACT, a performance assessment for use in preservice programs in twenty states. He also was a cofounder of the Interstate Teacher Assessment and Support Consortium and developed assessments for the National Board for Professional Teacher Standards.

Victoria L. Robinson is an associate professor of educational leadership at the University of Northern Iowa. She was part of the original Renaissance Teacher Work Sample team and has presented and worked with countless universities implementing Teacher Work Samples.

Hilda Rosselli, a former middle school teacher, joined Western Oregon University as dean of the College of Education in 2002 after nineteen years in teacher preparation and administration at the University of South Florida. Her areas of scholarship include teacher preparation, performance assessment, university-school partnerships, and policy development related to both preservice and in-service teachers.

Linda Samek is the dean of the George Fox University School of Education and has served as a professor and administrator at both Corban College and George Fox University. She was the deputy director of the Oregon Teacher Standards and Practices Commission and continues to be part of many statewide task forces shaping teacher preparation.

Del Schalock passed away in 2006 after forty-five years of active involvement in education research, development, and improvement while working at the Teaching Research Institute at Western Oregon University. He is considered the creator of Teacher Work Sample Methodology and authored many articles and monographs regarding teacher effectiveness as defined by student progress in learning.

Mark Schalock is an associate research professor at the Teaching Research Institute at Western Oregon University where he has been actively engaged in educational research, development, evaluation, and technical assistance for more than twenty years at local, state, and national levels. His work has spanned issues related to both regular and special education, with significant recent emphasis on the preparation, licensure, and early career development of both regular and special education teachers.

Gary J. Skolits is the director of the Institute for Assessment and Evaluation at the University of Tennessee's College of Education, Health, and Human Sciences and a tenure-track faculty member in the Ph.D. program in Evaluation and Assessment. His research areas include evaluation methods, K–12 school improvement interventions, college access evaluation, and higher-education accountability.

Douglas Smith is an associate professor of education at Coastal Carolina University. He coordinates the M.Ed. program and has been instrumental in assisting elementary education majors in using Teacher Work Samples during internship.

Ruth Chung Wei is the director of assessment research and development at the Stanford University School Redesign Network. She was formerly a public high school teacher in New York City and has worked extensively with National Board certification, charter schools, and performance assessments for teachers.

Karen Wetherill is serving as the interim dean for the Watson School of Education at the University of North Carolina, Wilmington. She has worked extensively with university-school partnerships and has been active in writing and directing state, federal, and private grants focusing on collaborative efforts to improve education.